MW01258953

Bodies and Pleasures

Bodies and Pleasures

Foucault and the Politics of Sexual Normalization

Ladelle McWhorter

Indiana University Press

BLOOMINGTON AND INDIANAPOLIS

This book is a publication of
Indiana University Press
601 North Morton Street
Bloomington, Indiana 47404–3797 USA

www.indiana.edu/~iupress

Telephone orders 800–842–6796
Fax orders 812–855–7931
Orders by e-mail iuporder@indiana.edu

© 1999 by Ladelle McWhorter

All rights reserved

No part of this book may be reproduced or utilized in any form or by any means,
electronic or mechanical, including photocopying and recording, or by any
information storage and retrieval system, without permission in writing from the
publisher. The Association of American University Presses' Resolution on
Permissions constitutes the only exception to this prohibition.

The paper used in this publication meets the minimum requirements of
American National Standard for Information Sciences—Permanence of
Paper for Printed Library Materials, ANSI Z39.48–1984.

MANUFACTURED IN THE UNITED STATES OF AMERICA

Library of Congress Cataloging-in-Publication Data

McWhorter, Ladelle, date
      Bodies and Pleasures : Foucault and the politics of sexual normalization / Ladelle
McWhorter.
        p. cm.
        ISBN 0-253-33558-2 (cloth : alk. paper).— ISBN 0-253-21325-8 (pbk. : alk. paper)
        1. Sex role.   2. Gender identity.   3. Body, Human—Social aspects.   4. Body,
Human—Political aspects.   5. Foucault, Michel—Political and social views. I. Title.
HQ23.M369 1999
305.3—dc21   98-49787

    1 2 3 4 5 04 03 02 01 00 99

CONTENTS

ACKNOWLEDGMENTS

I am indebted to Elizabeth Grosz, Todd May, Jana Sawicki, and Dee Mortensen for their careful readings and helpful suggestions for revisions of this book. I am especially indebted to Pamela Parent and Ellen Armour for their support and encouragement as well as their rigorous textual criticism throughout the writing process.

I gratefully acknowledge permission to use all or portions of the following publications:

"Foucault's Genealogy of Homosexuality," *Bulletin de la Société Américaine de Philosophie de Langue Française*, Vol. 6, Nos. 1–2 (Spring, 1994): 44–58. Reprinted with permission of *Bulletin de la Société Américaine de Philosophie de Langue Française*.

"Foucault's Attack on Sex-Desire," *Philosophy Today*, Vol. 41, No. 1 (Spring, 1997): 160–65. Reprinted with permission of *Philosophy Today*.

"Natural Bodies/Unnatural Pleasures," *Symplokē*, Vol. 3, No. 2 (Summer, 1995): 201–10. Reprinted with permission of *Symplokē*.

ABBREVIATIONS
FOR WORKS BY FOUCAULT

WORKS IN ENGLISH

BC   "The Battle for Chastity," in *Michel Foucault: Politics, Philosophy, Culture: Interviews and Other Writings, 1977–1984*, ed. Lawrence D. Kritzman. New York: Routledge, 1988: 227–41.

CF   "The Confession of the Flesh," in *Power/Knowledge: Selected Interviews and Other Writings, 1972–1977*, ed. Colin Gordon. New York: Pantheon, 1980: 194–228.

CQP   "Clarifications on the Question of Power," in *Foucault Live*, trans. John Johnston, ed. Sylvere Lotringer. New York: Semiotext(e), 1989: 179–92.

CT   "The Concern for Truth," in *Foucault Live: Interviews, 1966–1984*, trans. John Johnston, ed. Sylvere Lotringer. New York: Semiotext(e), 1989: 293–308.

DP   *Discipline and Punish: The Birth of the Prison*, trans. Alan Sheridan. New York: Random House, 1977.

ECS   "The Ethics of the Concern for Self as a Practice of Freedom," in *Ethics: Subjectivity and Truth*, Vol. 1 of *The Essential Works of Foucault, 1954–1984*, ed. Paul Rabinow. New York: New Press, 1997: 281–301.

FL   "Friendship as a Lifestyle: An Interview with Michel Foucault," *Gay Information*, Vol. 7 (Spring, 1981): 4–6.

FWL   "Friendship as a Way of Life," in *Foucault Live*, trans. John Johnston, ed. Sylvere Lotringer. New York: Semiotext(e), 1989: 203–9.

HB   *Herculine Barbin: Being the Recently Discovered Memoirs of a Nineteenth Century French Hermaphrodite*, trans. Richard McDougall. New York: Pantheon, 1980; this work was originally published, without the introduction to the English edition, in 1978.

HS1   *The History of Sexuality, Volume 1: An Introduction*, trans. Robert Hurley. New York: Random House, 1978.

HS2   *The Use of Pleasure*, trans. Robert Hurley. New York: Random House, 1984.

HS3   *The Care of the Self*, trans. Robert Hurley. New York: Pantheon, 1985.

NGH   "Nietzsche, Genealogy, History," in *Language, Counter-memory, Practice*, ed. Donald Bouchard. Ithaca: Cornell University Press, 1977: 139–64.

OGE   "On the Genealogy of Ethics," in *Michel Foucault: Beyond Structuralism and Hermeneutics*, ed. Hubert L. Dreyfus and Paul Rabinow, 2nd ed. Chicago: University of Chicago Press, 1983: 229–52.

OT   *The Order of Things: An Archeology of the Human Sciences.* New York: Vintage, 1970.

P&S   "Power and Sex," in *Philosophy, Politics, Culture: Interviews and Other Writings, 1977–1984*, ed. Lawrence D. Kritzman. New York: Routledge, 1988: 110–24.

SC   "Sexual Choice, Sexual Act," in *Ethics, Subjectivity and Truth*, Vol. 1 of *The Essential Works of Foucault, 1954–1984*, ed. Paul Rabinow. New York: New Press, 1997: 141–56.

SPPI   "An Interview: Sex, Power and the Politics of Identity," *The Advocate* (Aug. 7, 1984): 26–30, 58.

SR   "An Interview by Stephen Riggins," in *Ethics: Subjectivity and Truth*, Vol. 1 of *The Essential Works of Foucault, 1954–1984*, ed. Paul Rabinow. New York: New Press, 1997: 121–33.

TL   "Two Lectures," in *Power/Knowledge: Selected Interviews and Other Writings 1972–1977*, ed. Colin Gordon. New York: Pantheon, 1980: 78–108.

TP   "Truth and Power," in *Power/Knowledge: Selected Interviews and Other Writings 1972–1977*, ed. Colin Gordon. New York: Pantheon, 1980: 109–33.

TS   "Technologies of the Self," in *Technologies of the Self: A Seminar with Michel Foucault*, ed. Luther H. Martin, Huck Gutman, and Patrick H. Hutton. Amherst: University of Massachusetts Press, 1988: 16–49.

WE   "What Is Enlightenment?" in *Ethics: Subjectivity and Truth*, Vol. 1 of *The Essential Works of Foucault, 1954–1984*, ed. Paul Rabinow. New York: New Press, 1997: 303–19.

WORKS IN FRENCH

AMV   "De l'amité comme mode de vie," *Gai Pied*, No. 25 (April, 1981): 38–39; reprinted in Vol. 4 of Michel Foucault, *Dits et écrits*, ed. Daniel Defert and François Ewald. Paris: Gallimard, 1994: 163–67. Notes in this volume refer to the latter edition.

CC   "Le combat de la chasteté," *Communications*, No. 35 (May, 1982): 15–25: reprinted in Vol. 4 of Michel Foucault, *Dits et écrits*, ed. Daniel Defert and François Ewald. Paris: Gallimard, 1994: 295–308. Notes in this volume refer to the latter edition.

MC   *Les mots et les choses.* Paris: Gallimard, 1966.

SP   *Surveiller et punir: Naissance de la prison.* Paris: Gallimard, 1975.

SS   *Le souci de soi.* Paris: Gallimard, 1984.

UP   *L'usage des plaisirs.* Paris: Gallimard, 1984.

VS   *La volonté de savoir.* Paris: Gallimard, 1976.

INTRODUCTION
FOUCAULT'S IMPACT: CHALLENGES AND TRANSFORMATIONS

Michel Foucault's work gripped me from the very first encounter I had with it as a first-year graduate student back in 1982. Though at the time I could not explain why, I knew immediately that that work embodied a philosophical promise nothing else I had studied before had ever held out to me. Where the work of other philosophers of history and other social critics and theorists had seemed to falter or stall, Foucault's work pushed on, and both pushed and lured me on. I wasn't always (or even usually) sure where I was going, but I was sure from the beginning that this undertaking—reading and thinking with and coming to understand the work of Michel Foucault—would be rewarding in itself, no matter where the path might end. Fifteen years of intense effort later, I'm more convinced than ever of that endeavor's worth.

Not all of Foucault's readers share my enthusiasm. In fact, a great many are positively condemnatory. A lot is at stake, for Foucault does violence to many of our most cherished philosophical traditions and places in question or de-centers a number of our most basic epistemological, moral, and politico-theoretical assumptions. That violence scares some people, excites others, and challenges us all. It's no surprise, then, that Foucault's methods and claims have always been and still are extremely controversial. What is surprising is how long it has taken for most North American scholars to make any real effort to come to grips with Foucault and grapple with the challenges that his writings put forth. In the early 1980s, despite the fact that Foucault had already made several trips to the U.S. to lecture, most of his major works were available in English, and several commentaries were already on the market, North Americans tended to ignore him or dismiss or denounce his ideas without much thought. Serious scholars reserved their energy for study of other issues and texts.[1] A few renegades read and liked the work, and some scholarly attention did come to focus on it. But those first few friendly forays didn't win Foucault many allies; in fact, they won him enemies, because some very serious scholars then felt compelled to persuade the still silent majority not to take Foucault any more seriously than they already did. Often, when even well-known and highly respected intellectuals wrote on Foucault's work, their tone was hostile and their scholarship less than exemplary. Commentary that proclaimed itself to be thoughtful evaluation often amounted to little more than Francophobic invective, or just plain derision. As late as 1994, Alan Hunt and Gary Wickham noted in the opening paragraphs of their book *Foucault and Law,* "The work of Michel Foucault continues to excite controversy. Passions often run high; his name still produces more partisanship than dispassionate evaluation."[2] The truth is that Foucault's fairly radical philosophical assertions and his innovative interpretations of the histories of social and governmental institutions just were not taken very seriously (except as an irrational threat) by intellectuals in the U.S. and Canada, even by those—like critics Charles Taylor, Peter Dews, and Michael Walzer—who might be characterized as leftists.

By the time of Foucault's death in June of 1984, there had emerged a rather large contingent of well-credentialed left-leaning thinkers—philosophers, sociologists, historians—who expressed suspicion of and even contempt for his work and who expended no small amount of energy to warn the less wary away from it. Most—but by no means all—were grounded in Marxist theory (which Foucault critiques and in many respects attempts to undermine[3]) and some, like Charles Taylor and Nancy Fraser, had intellectual ties to the Frankfurt School. Their message was, roughly, this: Don't let Foucault fool you; beneath his radical pronouncements and provocative exposés there lies only a gnawing nihilism, a dissipating quietism, a throwing up of hands. Feminists couched the risks in more explicitly carnal terms: Foucault's work may look sexy, girls, but don't let yourself be seduced.[4] In the vocal majority's appraisals, feminist and non-feminist alike, the note of caution sounded was much the same. Foucault is insidious, a glamorous con artist, a human wolf in sheep's clothing, a sort of Franco-Trojan horse designed and thrust among us by a neoconservative backlash—in sum, he is a dissembler who threatens to corrupt. Pull away the rousing rhetoric, the high-fashioned Gallic glitz, and what you will find first of all is . . . nothing, nothing new, nothing useful, nothing very interesting. There is no theory, no program, and no basis for the creation of any such thing. But second, and far worse, what little substance Foucault *does* offer is downright dangerous; he launches a vicious attack on everything that might serve as a foundation for progressive politics, justice, liberation, or any kind of social reform. Feminist theorist Toril Moi's warning is not atypical; she asserts, "If we capitulate to Foucault's analysis, we will find ourselves caught up in a sado-masochistic spiral of power and resistance which, circling endlessly in heterogeneous movement, creates a space in which it will be quite impossible convincingly to argue that women under patriarchy constitute an oppressed group, let alone develop a theory of their liberation."[5] So, it was widely asserted, Foucault's work is not merely a waste of time; it is actually political poison. Not only will it not help us to do the political and social work we need to do, but it will actually prevent us from doing what we need to do. In fact, given its mesmerizing scintillations, it may even prevent us from *seeing* what we need to do. Michel Foucault's work is dangerous indeed, and all the more so for its superficial radical appeal—for what Michael Walzer terms its "infantile leftism" and Richard Rorty once called its "self-indulgent radical chic."[6]

By mid-decade there were a few articles in print defending Foucault against some of the standard criticisms or at least suggesting that some of his work had its positive political uses.[7] But not one of those essays ever matched in passion and intensity the denunciations of a Michael Walzer or a Toril Moi. Defenses and sympathetic appraisals of Foucault at the time were almost always provisional and qualified. Most focused on his work's value for limited critical projects within particular political movements, usually emphasizing its character as a "tool-box" rather than its power to generate or incite political or social movements or its value for existing movements as they define their long-range goals. And virtually none of those essays simply explored the work for its own sake as philosophical experimentation. Hence, it appeared, Foucault's alleged attempt at seduction had failed. Despite fearful predictions, no newly deflowered, Foucault-inseminated zealots of nihilism appeared on the political horizon. It seemed that the warnings had worked.

And yet, while Rorty, Walzer, Moi, Dews, Taylor, Fraser,[8] and countless others offered warnings to activists not to waste their time getting sidetracked by theories that in the end would be useless to them, not to get seduced, not to get mired in Foucault's nihilistic muck, scores of gay bookstores quietly stocked and sold Foucault's books. While relatively mainstream philosophers, historians, and political theorists insisted that Foucault's work could never form the basis for or even aid any successful political movement, queer readers were making Foucault a part of their intellectual lives. And, given the extremely politically ramified conditions under which non-heterosexual people live, making Foucault a part of their intellectual lives usually meant making him a part of their political lives. David Halperin goes so far as to claim that Foucault "is to contemporary AIDS activists as Norman O. Brown or Herbert Marcuse was to student radicals of the New Left."[9] Most of those readers never thought to seek out a professional political theorist to help them decide whether Foucault had something valuable to say. They just read Foucault. Later, when some of them stumbled upon the debate of the early 1980s with its reiterated cautionary message, rather than try to respond and explain to the debaters why they held the work in relatively high esteem, they just kept reading Foucault.

From late 1982 on, I was one of those diligent but relatively reticent readers. For at least a couple of years I devoured Foucault's books, essays, and interviews with a sense of excitement that far outstripped my ability to describe or explain, while blissfully unaware that anyone was seriously critiquing the works or attacking Foucault for his alleged implicit or explicit political theories. Later, even after I ascended into the rarified atmosphere of professional philosophy in 1986[10] and began producing work that took its heading from Foucault, I tried to avoid engaging with professional colleagues in theoretical debate about his works' political value, positive or negative. I didn't feel deeply compelled to make a case for Foucault over and against any of the standard Anglo and Germanic political criticisms or to justify my interest in and use of his work to people who took those criticisms seriously. In fact, I don't think I could have justified it to them or anyone else, since the process of reading it was changing me in some fundamental ways such that my own standards for evaluating texts and my own conceptions of philosophical significance and truth were undergoing massive and almost constant revision. I saw little to gain from engaging with my professional elders in debate over the merits of works I had not mastered but that were, in effect, slowly mastering me.

I was young then and suffered from the restlessness of youth, which may account for why I found all those technical philosophical evaluations of Foucault's work so very tedious. But there was more to it than my own intellectual impatience. It seemed to me that most of the people who condemned Foucault did not really want to hear about his works' merits, their strengths, the possibilities that they opened up. It sometimes even seemed that none of Foucault's critics had ever picked up any of the books that I had read. Their perspectives on the work and on the issues the work raises were almost totally alien to me. What could they possibly have to say that would interest me, then? The liberal theorists with their delusions of autonomy bored me; the self-satisfaction of both the British and North American socialists tended to get on my nerves; most boring, irritating, and seemingly irrelevant of all were Habermas' tortured and contorted critiques of Foucault, which became only marginally more intelligible when reiterated by his American followers.[11] The Foucault those people were generating so much heat talking about was almost unrecognizable to me. To enter the debate as it was then unfolding would have required that I bend the trajectory of my own thinking and postpone reaching my own goals in order to take into account the categories and terminologies of people who seemed to share virtually none of my political, social, or philosophical concerns and who, I thought, did not evince any understanding of the political acts that Foucault's writings enable and in fact constitute. On the few occasions when I did venture to assert the political value or defend some strategic use of Foucault's analyses, my writing always seemed stiff, flattened, tremendously awkward, as if a Foucaultian *apologia* were a mutant literary life-form whose survival was, as physicians say, contraindicated. I should have known better than to try.

It is 1998. I am older and wiser, more patient and sedate.[12] Now, though I have come to have much more respect for Foucault's critics than I did in earlier years, I do know better than to try to offer an *apologia*. What follows is not a defense of Foucault. Although along the way I'll offer arguments against the standard criticisms of his work, my primary purpose is not to prove to anyone that Foucault's philosophical positions are the true and right ones. Rather than questions about the logic of his argumentation or the accuracy of his reportage or even of the works' political utility or danger, what I am interested in here is the question of what has kept someone like me reading Foucault's work for the last fifteen years, the question of how it has been able to push me in the directions I have gone both philosophically and politically, the question of how that work has been able to excite, stimulate, enliven, and empower me for the greater part of my adult life. I am not so interested, then, in what his works have to say, although what they have to say is crucial to my study; instead, I am most interested in what they tend to do.

This "doing" of the texts, the manifestations of their potency, occurs at two analytically distinguishable levels: the level of the thinking, feeling individual and the level of the political situation. At the level of the individual, I'm interested in how the works—especially the last five books: *Discipline and Punish, The History of Sexuality* (volumes 1, 2, and 3), and *Herculine Barbin*—operate as a discipline, as an *askesis,* an exercise of thinking that transforms its reader. (Since the reader I'm best acquainted with is me, the processes of transformation that I have undergone during that fifteen years will serve as a sixth primary "text" here.) At the level of the political situation, I'm interested in how those works operate to open possibilities, how they transform the reader's world, how they interfere with heterosexist business as usual. Clearly these two levels are only analytically, not ontologically, distinct; reader and world are not really separable. If one changes, they both do. It might be better, then, to state my central interest this way: I'm interested in how Foucault's works operate to transform various politically charged sites, not the least of which is the site of the act of reading itself, the politically complicated, multiply valenced site that is the reader. I'm interested, then, in what one might call, after Nietzsche, the *undergoing* of Foucault's texts and in particular the undergoing that occurs when the reader in question is—as I am—a non-heterosexual person formed by and living within a world that defines her in her being, in her very truth, as deviant and criminal and sick; that daily undermines, through both formal and informal means, her well-being; and that with a banal but unremitting regularity openly opposes her very existence. The undergoing that is occurring and is simultaneously under examination here is, then, in an important sense *my* undergoing, even though from the outset the possibility of the "my"—of ownership, of property, of the proper, of the strictly identifiable—is in question. How I read Foucault—or, how reading of Foucault occurs with, for, or through me—cannot be definitive or normative for any other event or act of reading. But I'm convinced that it can be interesting, beneficial, and useful for many—both for philosophers and other intellectuals who study Foucault and for non-academic readers who care about the political struggles of queer people. For, after all, what the present book amounts to is a local political study, a study of the impact of Foucault's texts at a site of political oppression, at a site that serves as an anchor point for power and that constitutes itself as a locus of resistance and transformation.

In some senses—and I'll be the first to acknowledge it—this enterprise is a little bizarre, especially for someone steeped in and favorably disposed toward the analyses Foucault offers of society and many of the positions he takes regarding it. Foucault was well-known for his desire not to be known. He kept his private life out of his writing, claiming at one point that he wrote his books precisely "in order to have no face," to be unidentifiable. He was suspicious of any discourse that smacked of confession, and he believed that whereas in the past biography might have been aggrandizing, nowadays it is belittling, because it turns its subject into nothing more than a collection of specific deviations from the norm or, to use his words, into "a case." It is possible, therefore, that Foucault would have urged me not to publish this book. At the very least he would have pointed out that my extensive use of autobiographical material throughout is dangerous, that my writing runs some terrible risks as it parallels and mimics again and again the confessional, therapeutic, and liberal individualistic and humanistic discourses that it critiques. It risks being read as exactly the kind of discourse that it attempts to displace. It risks being taken as confession. And, since it is to a great extent my own personal experiences that serve as the text for this undertaking, it risks turning my life, my *self*, into a "case." Why do it then? Why run these risks?

I have two reasons. One has to do with what I will call for lack of a better word my "vocation." As I understand and practice it, philosophy is not primarily a body of knowledge or a collection of skills; it is a way of living. Foucault called it an art of life, a practice of freedom. Because of that, it is impossible not to be passionately involved in the philosophical reading one does and in the philosophical writings one produces. To imagine otherwise is to delude oneself into a belief in something like pure Cartesian thought divorced from histories and bodies. I am implicated in what I write, so I may as well make myself part of the writing in a conscious and obvious way. That inclusion of myself in the text, however, need not function as an act of self-identification in contrast to Foucault's attempt to "have no face." On the contrary, my self-examination here is the reverse of self-identification. As Foucault's analyses so often show, there are many ways in which our socially and historically produced identities endanger us, make us vulnerable, and close us off from possibilities. Identities often stand opposed to freedom. Insofar as they do, examination of them and of the processes that generate and maintain them is philosophically urgent. Because I am identified in particular ways and because I can't simply "disidentify," I must acknowledge my identities and work to understand them if I hope for a future that they do not dictate entirely, a future that remains open to the practice of philosophy. The other reason to run these risks has to do with the more mundane though much more frequently discussed question of whether Foucault's work really does function as a help or a hindrance to political activity by and on behalf of non-heterosexual people, as so many theorists over the years have said or at least implied. Does his work really promote a kind of apathy or quietism, or does it stimulate, as he claimed, a pessimistic but potent and "hyper-" political activism (OGE, 232)? Instead of asking what kind of political stands Foucault takes and whether he is justified in taking them, I'm interested in asking what kind of political effects Foucault's texts have. I believe that question can only be answered if we examine the practices of those who read the work carefully and take it seriously as nourishment for their political lives. I offer this book as just that sort of examination.

To the best of my knowledge, a study of this kind—one that takes an experience of reading Foucault's works as its point of analysis—has not been done before. Instead, most of the commentary on and critique of Foucault's work focuses on its logical argumentation, its reasoning and evidential warrant, rather than on its power/knowledge effects upon those who undergo the texts. Consequently, critics who assert that

Foucault's work has little or no positive value for political struggle necessarily base their negative assessments upon abstractions and theoretical projections, many of which may have nothing to do with the ways that the works operate in sites of concrete oppression and resistance. No genuine assessment of Foucault's work is possible, I would argue, until the kind of careful reading that I undertake here has been done, that is, until studies of his works' effects are not artificially and arbitrarily limited to the level of the purely theoretical. And perhaps, once that task is completed, the question of assessment will have settled itself . . . or quietly disappeared.

Bodies and Pleasures

1

Views from the Site of Political Oppression
Or, How I Served as an Anchor Point for Power and Emerged as a Locus of Resistance

I was not a well-adjusted child. I know that because I remember hearing it from lots of people lots of times: "not well-adjusted." From early on there were doctors, social workers, and later (when my father earned a union wage) psychiatrists and their therapies, a decade-long series of technicians all intent upon adjusting me. (A word of warning: The fact that I am writing this book is ample evidence that they did not have, as the sports announcers like to say, "good success.") Midway through that long decade, at the age of twelve, I stumbled upon a word for at least one aspect of my maladjustment in the *Ladies' Home Journal*. I carried the magazine to the kitchen and asked my mother to define the word, a request I had made many times and many words before. But this time and word were different. The word was *homosexual*. A look of utter revulsion crossed her face. She spat out her one-sentence answer with a finality that put an end to discussion of that topic for all time. I was stunned. Not that what she said was so terrible—just: "It's a kind of person that falls in love with a person of their own sex." It was the force she put behind her words that stunned me, as if with such an effort she could eject them—both the words and the people to whom they might attach—from her presence.

I had been erotically and romantically involved with another girl for some time already, but it had never occurred to me that this fact made me into any "kind of person." And, though I knew my mother would disapprove of every kind of sex (I had carefully hidden *that*), it had never occurred to me that she would disapprove of any kind of love. After all, God is love, right? I hadn't known God was only heterosexual love. I had trouble grasping why my loving and taking my pleasure with another girl made me into a "kind of person," especially a kind of person my mother thought it right to hate.

I didn't ask any more questions about homosexuality. But I did begin to watch and listen very carefully all the time in order to gather as much information as possible about what most people believe about homosexuals, expect from homosexuals, and do to homosexuals when they find one. In the next months and years I learned a lot. For example, I learned that homosexuals are sick people whose brain chemistry drives them to their unnatural and repulsive acts but who may be controlled with hormone injections. I learned that homosexuals are child-molesters who should be executed—extralegally if need be. I learned that homosexuals are ridiculous people—weak, manipulable, pathetic, worthless—who deserve whatever bad things happen to them. Finally, I learned that homosexuals are only homosexuals, never neighbors or Presbyterians or dentists or secretaries or citizens or mothers or people whose hobbies include anything beyond the consumption of pornographic material. Queers are nobody, just queer, one-dimensional. When somebody finds out you're queer, they forget everything they ever knew about you; or, if they remember anything about you at all, the things they remember just get reinterpreted as nothing more than symptoms of your disease.

I worried: What if everybody finds out you're queer and forgets everything else they ever knew about you? What happens? I was afraid I would just erode away. I would stop being a bright student, a competent athlete, a creative writer. All those diverse qualities would fuse together into one identity—queer—only to disappear. "Of course she plays ball and makes top grades in science; she's masculinized." "Of course she likes fiction and theatre; it's their nature to dissimulate." All my abilities, interests, quirks would become nothing more than signs of the hated thing I was, until I was only that thing. Nothing more. Nothing really.

I did not want to be a homosexual. It wasn't that I wanted to be a heterosexual. I just wanted to be left alone to do the things I liked to do—including playing ball, studying biology, admiring the bodies of other adolescent girls. But being queer precluded that. Being queer precluded doing anything besides being queer, which as far as I could tell from what I heard lacked any subjective dimension, any interiority whatsoever. Being queer even precluded loving and making love to my girlfriend, since the love I felt for her and tried to show her, being queer, was only a symptom of disease or depravity rather than a sweet, tender, significant reality in itself. It wasn't real love; it wasn't real sex; it wasn't real, only a sign, a symptom, a thing that had no meaning in itself.

I did not want to be a homosexual. If I had to be something, why couldn't I be my religion, my ethnicity, my standardized test scores? Why did it have to be this one thing, this one despised and dangerous thing? But over and over again it was made clear to me that homosexuals are never judged by any criterion other than their sexuality, and the judgment is always negative. Over and over again when that fact was reiterated—in classrooms, at family gatherings, in church—I literally shook with fear and rage. I wanted to demand some justification, to force the world either to account for what it was trying to do to me or to stop trying to do it. But that demand could never be made, because I dared not openly acknowledge that what was happening was happening; I dared not accuse anyone of hurting me for fear they would only hurt me more. And they would have.

I did not want to be a homosexual. But gradually they—peers, teachers, ministers, therapists—made me. Not that they wanted me to be queer, of course; God help us, nobody wanted that. There certainly was no intentional conspiracy to make me anything at all. It's just that in our culture people who engage consistently in homosexual relationships and in some other forms of gender transgressive behavior are taken to be categorically and fundamentally different from everybody else, so if you fall into that fundamentally different category, it is imperative that you *stay* there and *be* that or else you threaten the very order of things. I couldn't do what I did and escape being what those actions implied to most people that I was. Eventually, then, I was made to understand that queer was what I had to be. Socially, culturally, my homosexual behavior was definitive of me; compared to that, nothing else about me really mattered. It would be my lot in life to be reduced forever to nothing more than my sexuality, collapsed into it like a neutron star, cold and dense and silent. My homosexuality was what I was, most essentially.

For awhile, although I persisted in my homosexual behavior, I refused to assume an identity that would consume me and erase all I took myself to be. I resisted the imperative to be a homosexual. But I failed. The very project of resisting this essentializing and totalizing categorization of me propelled me into it. In order to protect myself from a serious harm—from losing my sense of myself by being reduced to my sexuality—I had to make my sexuality into a central category, a central issue in my life; I had to allow my sexuality and the epistemic demands surrounding it to pervade (as a rigidly policed silence) everything I said and did. I don't know if it was ever necessary to destroy a village in order to save it, but it was necessary thoroughly and completely to sexualize myself in order to save myself from being thoroughly and completely sexualized.

I am queer—really, fundamentally, and unchangeably. But, regardless of any as yet unproven physiological causes of homosexuality,[1] my being queer is not natural; it is an historical, social accomplishment. And it is not my accomplishment alone. It is an effect of vast networks of discursive and institutional powers. My identity—call it what you like, "homosexual" or "lesbian" or "gay"—was steadily and progressively constituted and enforced at both micro- and macro-political levels for over a dozen years before I "willingly"—whatever that can possibly mean here—affirmed it. I am a cultural creation.

Eventually, of course, this creature surrendered itself to sexual knowledge. I admitted the truth. I *am* queer. They were right about me from the beginning. I am a lesbian. That is my identity. It grounds my feelings, desires, thoughts, actions, and physical appearance. *There.* Mission accomplished. I've confessed.

But then what? Once I conceded the struggle and acknowledged (to myself at least) "what I am," the issue that confronted me was how to be it.[2] According to everybody around me, homosexuals didn't have an inner life, didn't think or feel anything. Queers were surfaces merely, across which gender transgressions were written. It was as though to "be queer" was to be some sort of puppet whose strings were pulled by sexuality alone. Queers did nothing but perform—gaily, of course. Real feelings, thoughts, analyses, assessments, decisions, dreams, hopes, and ideas were only for straight people; only straight people actually had a point of view. Homosexuals could be seen, but their eyes just stared blankly back. There was no real person in there. So, once I'd acknowledged that I was a homosexual, what then? How could I *be* that? How could *that* have an *I*?

My foremost problem in those early years was physical survival, which mostly amounted to information control. I could not risk my parents finding out that I was one of those people they hated, because economically I was helpless. I was afraid they would send me away or lock me up. I didn't think they would beat me, but I was sure other people would. I was especially afraid of the high school boys who intimated that they knew how to "set those lezzies straight." But even when I felt physically safe, I was confronted with issues of another kind of survival. How could I possibly *be* a homosexual on a daily basis, how could I possibly *be* this brute, blank thing and yet make choices and think thoughts, how could I possibly inhabit a homosexual point of view? From the outside, I guess, "being homosexual" must look simple; you just *are*. "Being homosexual" is what we queers do best; it's our essential nature, our constant state. Everything we do bespeaks it. But from the inside, it isn't simple at all; it's amazingly difficult—*because there isn't supposed to be any inside,* because there isn't supposed to be any potential, any power, any freedom to become. Yet there is.

It becomes necessary to invent oneself.

Which is amazingly difficult. Many, many of us never manage. We die too young. We are beaten, stabbed, shot, or burned to death by people who say our presence on the planet is a threat to their way of life, or we are harassed to the point of hopelessness and suicide in a world where even our own parents see no value in our existence.[3] A 1996 Canadian study shows that gay and bisexual male youth are "nearly 14 times more at risk than their heterosexual contemporaries of making a serious attempt on their own lives," and a Massachusetts study released in 1998 found that more than a third of self-identified gay, lesbian, or bisexual teenagers reported having attempted suicide in the preceding year.[4] As many as twenty-five percent of all children and adolescents living on the streets are queer kids who are unwelcome in their parents' homes.[5] When you look at these statistics, together with the rising rate of violent crimes against transgendered and homosexual people,[6] you wonder how any of us ever manages to live to middle age. Imagine what the percentage of non-heterosexual men and women in the general population would be if all queer kids survived into adulthood. The proverbial ten percent might be far too low.

Some of us, in order to survive, try to minimize our homosexuality, try to limit its ability to define and absorb our lives, try to preserve ourselves from our society's radical reductivity by exclaiming, "Yes, I am what you say I am; I'm gay, but otherwise I'm just like you." These are the lesbians and gay men who exhort all queers to come out in order to show straight people that we pose no threat, that we are *ordinary.* "See, we're everywhere; we're your neighbors, your classmates, your dentist, your secretary, the guy sitting next to you in the pew. We're queer, but we're not *strange.*" But to most people, if you're not strange, you're not queer. A homosexual is a dense, silent object without an interior, without any connection to anything human. Insofar as I am not an object, insofar as I engage with most straight people, I am not queer to them; I am an honorary heterosexual. Just as they "forget" anything else they knew about you when they discover you're queer, so they "forget" you're queer when they have to deal with you as a neighbor or co-worker. Putting the concepts "homosexual" and "person" together is like putting together the concepts "round" and "square"; you get an oxymoron. Yet I was both, simultaneously; I was that round square. And I realized I had to be, every day of my life. I had to do the impossible if I intended to go on living at all.

For the next several years, I didn't have much "good success." I made no headway in my attempts to defy logic and affirm my oxymoronic existence, and I didn't encounter anyone else who succeeded at being simultaneously gay and human either. In 1981, Michel Foucault asked: "Is it possible to create a homosexual mode of life?" (FWL, 206–7; AMV, 165). For a European intellectual in 1981, this was still a *question*. So how could any teenaged grain elevator employee in Decatur, Alabama, in the 1970s have possibly answered affirmatively? I couldn't. I just couldn't see how to reconcile being a homosexual and being a human being. I just couldn't see how I could assume an adult position in the world, how I could possibly live a life. I struggled with it; I worked on it; I explored every cultural avenue open to me (though this was pretty much limited to the public library and prayer). But as I approached my eighteenth birthday I came to the conclusion that all of life's doors were firmly closed. I would always be alone in the world, since all honest connections with other people would be precluded by their prejudice; I would always be useless to the world, since my gifts and contributions were unwelcome in every arena an eighteen-year-old Alabama girl could imagine entering; I would be a burden for the world, since I would consume resources that others who had a rightful place and real contributions to make could better use. Absolutely the only role I could imagine being open to me was that of the spinster librarian growing senile in a one-room apartment lit by a single sixty-watt bulb. At best I was an embarrassment to my family and a liability to my community. At worst I was a monster who would be tracked down, tortured, humiliated, and killed. Like so many queer teenagers, I arrived at the only conclusion my society's premises supported: It would be better for everyone if I should die.

"I should die." It was a logical conclusion. Everything I saw around me confirmed it. Homosexuals are not real living human beings, so they should stop pretending to be. Homosexuals should die. I had been told that again and again and *again*, until finally I believed it. A lot of queer kids believe it. We are taught it at our mothers' knees.

But what physically healthy eighteen-year-old human body really *wants* to die? I didn't. What I really wanted above all else was a chance to *live*. I just didn't see how, and the day finally came when I couldn't think of any more excuses. It was time to grow up and face the fact that killing myself was the only responsible, decent thing to do.

On the morning of that day I lay in bed for a very long time. Carefully I thought out how to dispatch myself with as little drama, pain, and gore as possible. At the same time I hoped some miracle would occur and I wouldn't have to. My mother tried to get me out of bed for school. I ignored her. She persisted. I just lay there, unresponsive to her exhortations, stone-faced, silent. Since I was usually an obedient child, this resolute indifference frightened her. She kept leaving and then coming back into the room, pleading with me to talk to her, to get up. She grew more and more distraught. She brought food to tempt me, but it sat spoiling on the nightstand. She made frantic phone calls to innumerable helping professionals from the adjoining room. I felt very removed from her distress and confusion. Calmly I pondered how I might get past her to the car keys, to the river bridge, to the water that would fill my lungs quietly and without too much mess. But her presence was an obstacle; she was in the way.

I didn't want to die. I just couldn't see any honorable way to live. There was no reason to live, nothing to live for. Yet I wanted to, somehow. So when she came in after one of her calls and asked if I would consider going into a hospital for a couple of days, just to get some rest, I agreed. Why not? I couldn't get past her to the car keys today anyway. And what difference did it make whether I died today or two days from now? Nothing mattered anymore, not even that. I felt very calm. I felt nothing at all. I felt like inside I was mostly dead already.

Things didn't happen exactly like she said they would. The hospital officials had no intention of letting me out after "a couple of days." In fact I soon realized they had no intention of letting me out at all. Days stretched into weeks, then months. My botched life was worth something, after all, at least to the corporate officers who could measure it in terms of insurance dollars and cents. Because of that, I had become their prisoner.

And so I found myself, late one evening in the summer of 1978, sitting dumbly in the garish glare of fluorescent lights while a young psychiatric technician named Russell, who was taking college courses by day, offered me this unsolicited advice: "Whatever you do, don't ever study philosophy. It'll screw you up." He looked at me, waiting to hear what I'd say, but I just smiled politely and said nothing. I liked Russell, and no doubt he was totally sincere; he genuinely wanted to protect me from psychic harm. Still, I knew that at the end of his shift he would enter my response in an aluminum-bound dossier so that the next day a dozen other technicians could read it too and evaluate it in relation to their diagnosis and long-term treatment plan. Between two aluminum sheets the technicians were accumulating bits of my mind for the purpose of changing it. I smiled at him, but I knew: Silence, not Russell, was my best protection then.

I was silent for a long, long time. Long after the insurance money ran out and I was released into the big wide world, I kept silent. I had learned a lesson: If you are powerless enough, even your own words can belong to your enemies.

With my release, the decade of technicians drew to a close. Free from therapeutic restrictions, I did exactly what Russell had warned me against: I began to study philosophy. The reason was simple: I was still looking for an answer to that question; I still needed to figure out some way to reconcile my humanity and my sexuality, some way to be a homosexual and live a good life, some way to be a round square. My entrance into academia, my exposure to new ideas, gave me hope. I thought philosophers, people who spent their lives trying to determine what really mattered and what a good life would consist in, might give me a clue.

Well, the nonviability of round squares is about the only thing philosophers have generally agreed on, but fortunately, as I explored, my interests broadened. It seemed as if philosophers had tackled almost every question imaginable, and their proposed solutions seemed to cover the entire spectrum of what it was possible to think. Nothing has ever mattered to me more, in fact, than my philosophical education. An education like mine is not something somebody like me can take for granted as a bourgeois destiny. I worked hard to get it. Never was a student more proud of a diploma; never has an initiate felt more grateful for the right to wear a Phi Beta Kappa key; never has a doctoral candidate bowed for conferral of the hood with a greater sense of dignity and accomplishment. These things were, and are, symbols of the best aspects of my life, the aspects I then believed might redeem and remake the rest. Nevertheless, invaluable though it was to learn to see the world from so many different perspectives, to consider the aspects of the world those various perspectives revealed, and to learn to analyze and theorize and critique, something was still missing for me. It was as if no one ever saw quite the world I saw. My perspective, which of course was never acknowledged or even acknowledgeable in my subculture of origin, was equally unrepresented there. Even in that colorful academic world bazaar of foreign tongues and strange ideas, I could not scrape together the vocabulary to articulate what my daily existence told me repeatedly was real.

Not that I expected to. That no one said what I thought, that no one described what I so plainly perceived, that no one even raised the questions much less offered answers to the puzzles that at times so tortured me—this was all quite predictable, quite in keeping with what I'd learned as a child: My (round square) perspective on the world was in the end a logically inarticulable one. After all, one cannot think or speak as a homosexual; a homosexual is something one can only be. I didn't even try to speak from that place. Instead I adopted European "high culture" as my second home. I learned the language of philosophical dialectic—the foreign language that people like Leo Strauss and Dinesh D'Sousa and others ignorant of the semirural South so arrogantly insist is my own cultural legacy. To what they call "mine," I assimilated as best I could. I tried not to think about the silences that legacy perpetuates.[7]

Then, on January 7, 1983, I read Foucault's *The History of Sexuality* in its entirety, and for the first time in my life I heard something I believed it was impossible to hear: the articulation of a homosexual point of view. I had believed it was impossible to speak as a homosexual, from a homosexual perspective, because I had believed there was no way to *be* a homosexual except to be totally objectified. But Foucault's book proved me wrong. I was astonished. I was excited. I was overjoyed. Never have I been so happy with a book between my hands.

There are many things to be said about *The History of Sexuality*. In this chapter, I will not say most of them. I only want to show here why I experienced Foucault's book as homosexual—that is, what about its angle of vision seems queer to me and how it manages to overcome the tendency for homosexuality to solidify into an inert identity without a voice. In other words, I want to show how Foucault's book defies the political odds and emerges as a queer voice—an event that is in itself politically powerful and that had a tremendously empowering impact on me. The rest of this chapter is divided into two sections. In the first I'll describe the sexual world that unfolds through the first forty-five pages of *The History of Sexuality* and show how those pages can be read as emanating from a queer perspective.[8] In the next I'll explore the ways in which the book as a whole manages not to stumble into the trap of homosexual identity and thus manages not to reify its own voice and cancel itself out.

THE ANGLE OF VISION

As I've already said, a question that I often asked in those days—though in silence, because it was dangerous to ask it aloud—was: Why do I have to be judged as a sexual being at all? Why does *that* have to be the most important thing about me? Why can't I be defined by something else, some other aspect of my personality or my daily life? This question isn't likely to enter the mind of a well-adjusted heterosexual person, not because well-adjusted heterosexual people are not judged by their sexuality (they most certainly are) but because the judgment is positive. They are rewarded in every conceivable way all the time, and they get used to that and consider their privileges to be a part of the natural course of things rather than a set of benefits they get for being straight.[9] Those of us who are judged less positively are far more apt to recognize that judgment for what it is—a socially generated mechanism of discrimination. And we know quite well that as long as somebody is being discriminated *against*, somebody else is being discriminated *for*. (If I get fired from my job because I'm gay, and a straight person then gets my job, that straight person has been discriminated *for*.) We queers tend to see very clearly that sexuality is central to the disposition of everybody's life, not just to homosexuals'. So we are apt to ask, "Why does it have to be *this* way? Why do we all have to be judged by our sexuality rather than something else?" This question is queer in the sense that being situated in the world as a queer person is what is most likely to motivate someone to ask it and look for an answer. And it is this question that motivates Foucault's whole book, provides its energy and direction throughout.

Near the beginning of *The History of Sexuality*, Foucault makes three interrelated descriptive claims. First, he asserts that in the West at least since the third quarter of the nineteenth century, sexuality as a concept has functioned as something like an essence, as that without which human being would be unthinkable. It is the name for what supposedly lies at the root of each and every human life and each and every society.[10] It is the foundation of our subjectivity; it is the matrix from which our very humanity draws its sustenance. As such, sexuality must be seen as our most fundamental truth, and this in turn means that sexuality, as truth, both marks and occupies an epistemic field—that is, a field of potential and/or actual knowledge. It is possible, theoretically at least, to know the truth that is our sexuality, to take it as an epistemic object and interrogate it.

Second, however, Foucault reminds us, this power that pervades us, this essence that identifies and grounds us singly and socially, this founding and governing truth of our subjectivity is not under our control. We do not choose our sexuality; on the contrary, it may well be said to choose us. For it shapes us, makes us who we are, and yet it remains profoundly other to our rationality and our civility. Our sexuality thus poses a perpetual danger. We must protect and nurture it, but we must also beware of it as a force capable of destroying what it enables us to create. Because of this, sexuality is necessarily "an object of great suspicion; the general and disquieting meaning that pervades our conduct and our existence, in spite of ourselves; the point of weakness where evil portents reach through to us; the fragment of darkness that we each carry within us: a general signification, a universal secret, an omnipresent cause, a fear that never ends" (HS1, 69; VS, 93). As the ground of meaning and even of our very existence as human beings, sexuality is to be respected, but it is also to be feared.

Third, given that sexuality is our truth and that it endangers as surely as it enables, sexuality not only *can* be taken as an object of epistemic investigation; it *must* be taken as such. Like nature itself, which both engenders and destroys, sexuality must be understood. By whatever means necessary, we must ensure that our sexuality becomes known, that it steps into the light of reason and, given that it is a great danger as well as a great gift, submits itself to managerial judgment. Sexuality, in the person of the sexual subject, must be made to confess, its confession must be heard, and account be taken.

In sum, Foucault asserts, in the Western world today, we understand sexuality to be the name of who we are. Simultaneously, we understand it to be the name of what most threatens us and what we most urgently need to know. Of course this is a set of beliefs that Foucault wants to question, but he starts by merely describing them.

All three of these beliefs are founded upon the assumption that sexuality is a universally present aspect of human being, the assumption that each person, everywhere and always throughout all of human history, has had something called a sexuality, has been a sexual being. Foucault is suspicious of this assumption, as we might well be. There is evidence against it. We know, for example, that many people have lived completely celibate lives and have considered themselves happy and even blessed despite their alleged repression. We also know that sexual expression varies geographically and historically. Anthropologists and social workers tell us there are people who require their young boys to perform fellatio on their elders,[11] people who insist that a priest deflower a bride before her husband touches her,[12] people who believe that vaginal intercourse before marriage is immoral but that heterosexual sodomy is an acceptable alternative.[13] Historians and legal theorists tell us our own society's laws bear the traces of extreme variations in what sorts of sexual expressions have been recognized, protected, and disallowed through time.[14] If sexual expression has varied so much through time and space, what justifies anyone's assertion that sexuality is just one, universally present phenomenon? Nevertheless, despite a dearth of justification, hardly anyone doubts that what underlies all these different expressions is one single thing, namely, some fundamental drive that brings the sexes together, some natural desire for procreation and genital pleasure. This thing, however we may characterize or display it or however we may disguise or deny it, is taken by most Westerners nowadays to be an immutable part of us; more, it is the very essence of what we are.

Given that assumption of universality, how unfortunate it seems that in the recent past our European and Euro-American foreparents were unable to acknowledge and enjoy the natural goodness of sexuality! It is sad and even shameful that they became so ashamed of something so basic to their very being. We look back at them moreover with anger and dismay when we contemplate the legacy of repression they have left us. An injustice has been committed against sexuality, and we have to set things right; an injury has been done us at the site of our most intimate being, and we have to heal it. Our principal means of doing these things is to talk about sex and sexuality as much as possible, to bring our sexuality "out into the open," to name and affirm it. Thus the demand to come to know and to make known one's sexuality, the demand that we all confess the truth that each one of us harbors at the core of our being, at the source of our very selfhood, is quite simply a kind of therapy that we all must undergo.

This is the story of sexuality that Foucault recounts in the first part of *The History of Sexuality*, where he lays it out only in order to discredit it. His suspicion pleased me enormously, because I shared it. This tale of a natural (hetero)sexuality that needed to be rescued from Victorian bondage was a story I knew well. By the time I reached puberty in the 1970s, even Alabamians were aware that we were supposed to liberate ourselves by exploring our sexual feelings rather than repressing them, supposed to affirm our sexuality, supposed to manage its more dangerous potentials through the transformative power of confessional speech. We'd had it drummed into our heads that silence is dangerous. We believed that repressed sexuality is destructive, debilitating, and unhealthy and that confession is healthy, liberating, and self-affirmative. Even in church we learned that we had to affirm our bodies and our sex and that that meant we had to talk about them; our ministers conducted and oversaw courses on sexuality for parishioners of all ages. All progressive people understood this truth and the social and therapeutic benefits adherence to its demands would bring. So I knew all about the dangers of sexual repression when I read Foucault's book in 1983. But I was also intimately acquainted with the grim realities consequent upon sexual confession. I knew only too well that my best interests were not served by labeling myself queer and making that label's attachment to me a matter of public knowledge. By 1983 this was painfully obvious to me: Unless you're straight-**straight**-*straight*, if you're honest about your sexuality, liberation is not what follows; lockup is. The truth does not make deviants free. For any sexual deviant, confession, whatever its benefits, comes at an extremely high price. To name oneself queer in our society is to put one's job, one's family, one's freedom, and even one's life on the line.[15]

From my queer perspective, Foucault's choice to begin a study of sexuality's political status with a series of questions about the meaning and function of confessional practice was irreproachably logical. In order to judge a person on the basis of his or her sexuality, society has to know what the nature of that sexuality is. Knowledge is the first step toward discrimination. What we're always told, of course, is that knowledge is the first step toward health, happiness, and freedom, because the opposite of knowledge is repression. But Foucault questions that. He begins by questioning the reality of the repression that confession is supposed to offset. Is it true, he asks, that Victorian society silenced sexuality? Did it "subjugate it at the level of language, control its free circulation in speech, expunge it from the things that were said, and extinguish the words that rendered it too visibly present" (HS1, 17; VS, 25)? A look at the historical evidence, Foucault says, tells us no; the evidence does not support the hypothesis of a general repression of sexual discourse in the nineteenth century but, on the contrary, indicates an expansion of discourses and a proliferation of discursive centers. Instead of less being said about sex in the eighteenth and nineteenth centuries, a great deal more was said than had ever been said before. Of course there were changes in the "authorized vocabulary," and certainly there were new standards of propriety; "where and when it was not possible to talk about such things became much more strictly defined" (HS1, 18; VS, 26). Silence surely was enforced in some areas at some times, but these scattered repressions were nothing compared to the surrounding explosions of speech. More was said about sex, said in more places, and said in a great many more ways than ever before. And it wasn't just that more people happened to be talking about sex. There was "an institutional incitement to speak about it, and to do so more and more; a determination on the part of agencies of power to hear it spoken about and to cause *it* to speak through explicit articulation and endlessly accumulated detail" (HS1, 18; VS, 27). The powers and institutions we often credit with repression actually enjoined people to talk about their sexual practices, fantasies, and desires. Agencies of power—government officials, medical specialists, priests, educators, criminologists, and legal theorists were requiring and thus producing discourse on sexuality far more than any of them were prohibiting and silencing it. General repression, Foucault concludes, is not an historical fact. Therefore, confession simply cannot be the gesture that liberates a sexuality that powerful authorities and institutions have silenced, distorted, and suppressed.

But what is confession, then? Where does this drive to know our sexualities and to tell others about them come from? If people didn't start confessing their sexual natures because sexuality was generally repressed, what did prompt them to do so? This is an empirical question, and it can only be answered if we look at the history of confessional practices. Hence, Foucault asks: How did confession come to occupy the place in our society that it occupies? What is confession's history as a practice in the West?

An obvious starting point is the Roman Catholic Church, where confession has been a sacred practice for many centuries. In very early church history, confession was most important to those with clerical vocations. Monks, for example, confessed their wicked deeds and even their wicked thoughts to their superiors, in order both to purify themselves and to receive instruction and advice about how to avoid such temptations and stirrings in the future; confession was necessary for self-transformation. Foucault points out that the role of confession in Catholic religious practice was changed by the Council of Trent (1545–1563). Because of the widely acknowledged immorality of the clergy and the outrage that it had caused among the laity, the Council voted to put more restrictions on the conduct of those in the Church's employ. One result was an increase in the annual number of confessions for each member of the clergy. Subsequently, new guidelines for confessions emphasized both the importance of confessing sins of the flesh and the delicacy with which one must handle their confession. Confessees were to avoid detailed descriptions of the acts—"respective positions of the partners, the postures assumed, gestures, places touched, caresses, the precise moment of pleasure" (HS1, 19; VS, 27), facts that had been commonly requested before; however, the scope of what was considered appropriate matter for confession was increased—to include, for example, "thoughts, desires, voluptuous imaginings, delectations, combined movements of the body and the soul" (HS1, 19; VS, 28). As the scope of confession of the sins of the flesh increased, so did the scope of confessional practice itself. Guidelines that were first simply to be imposed on the clergy came to be imposed on the laity as well. The ideal, even if it was never actually achieved, was the frequent and full confession of every Catholic on the face of the globe, and that ideal full confession would include, in a suitably refined vocabulary, the slightest stirring of voluptuous desire. Church officials also instituted detailed rules for self-examination, which many Catholics probably followed.

Voluptuous stirrings were not sought out in order to be enhanced or liberated—quite the reverse. The point was to minimize and if possible eradicate them. Sexual desires were not seen as signs of the true nature of the individual. If they were signs at all, they were signs of our fallen state, a state that could and should be abandoned as soon as possible. Although for the time being we might be essentially fleshly creatures, we were not essentially sexual beings, and our destiny lay in our relation with our creator, not in our relation with our libido. The purpose of Catholic confession was not to find the truth at the center of a sick or injured self and make it healthy again; on the contrary, the purpose was to mortify the self, to renounce it as a fleshly, willful creature in order to live in complete obedience to God. Therefore, the Catholic practice of confession at the end of the seventeenth century was still at a far remove from the practices of "healthful" confession ubiquitous in our society today.

Mortification is not especially pleasant in the absence of any larger end in view, so confession might have remained a religious practice only—"tied to the destiny of Christian spirituality" (HS1, 23; VS, 33)— if another set of events had not occurred. "Toward the beginning of the eighteenth century," writes Foucault, "there emerged a political, economic, and technical incitement to talk about sex" (HS1, 23; VS, 33). This was not because some great theory of sexuality had emerged; rather, it was because statesmen saw a need for "analysis, stocktaking, classification, and specification" (HS1, 24; VS, 33–4). With their ever-increasing civil concerns (and in some cases their budding nationalism), statesmen became administrators who came to see themselves as managers of populations. They had to manage standing armies, large groups of armed men with, at times, nothing much to do; they had to develop and manage production, which now included factories housing valuable tools that might be broken or stolen; they had to train and manage laborers, some of whom had to be skilled. To do all this, they needed theories of group and individual discipline and ways to insure that the numbers of healthy youths would stay high enough to keep their armies and workforces strong. These concerns—though initially somewhat disparate—eventually coalesced into a concern with "population," with public hygiene, maternal health, infant mortality, and the spread of venereal disease. Thus, "[a]t the heart of this economic and political problem of population was sex: it was necessary to analyze the birth-rate, the age of marriage, the legitimate and illegitimate births, the precocity and frequency of sexual relations, the ways of making them fertile or sterile, the effects of unmarried life or of the prohibitions, the impact of contraceptive practices . . ." (HS1, 25–6; VS, 36). It was necessary, then, to know how "each individual made use of his sex" (HS1, 26; VS, 37). How were civil officials to obtain that knowledge? Haphazardly at first, but as the value of systematic and complete information became evident, officials developed more careful techniques for acquiring it. Depending on the population in question, information could be extracted through either direct observation or voluntary admissions. Observation worked well if the group to be studied was schoolboys or soldiers, people already under the watchful eyes of superiors, but for some groups it was impractical. For example, if the issue at hand was the contraceptive practices of peasants, individuals had to be persuaded to provide information. Some techniques for convincing people to talk were less gentle than others; some involved blatant coercion. Foucault cites the example of a "somewhat simple-minded" farmhand in Lapcourt in 1867 (HS1, 31; VS, 43). This man paid a little girl to do him sexual favors, was denounced to the authorities by the girl's parents, and was arrested. Though found not guilty of any crime, he was held in custody until his death and put through numerous physical and verbal examinations. Deprived of virtually all civil rights, he was forced to reveal every detail of his activities and his desires.[16] But most information was gathered by less violent means. Nonviolent techniques for sexual confession—such as the demographic questionnaire—multiplied throughout the eighteenth century. "Incitements to speak were orchestrated from all quarters" (HS1, 32; VS, 45). No doubt officials also interrogated the children of Lapcourt about their sexual activities in order to educate and protect them; physicians and administrators used such events to impress upon parents the need to monitor children's behavior very carefully and to report any irregularities to the authorities. Some people, like the simple-minded farmhand in Foucault's story, began to speak about their sexuality because they were compelled to—more or less at gunpoint. But most began to speak about their sexuality—and the sexuality of those around them and in their charge—without obvious compulsion, perhaps because they were afraid of unregulated sexual expression or because they desired the benefits promised them by those who wanted to hear what they had to say, or perhaps just because they liked feeling important.

Types and centers of sexual discourses proliferated through the eighteenth and nineteenth centuries. These discourses operated virtually independently of one another for a long time; there was no unifying theory of sexuality before the development of psychoanalysis (if then).

Each social institution developed its own theoretical framework and techniques for data collection; different mechanisms operated in different places in different ways. Foucault writes,

> Rather than the uniform concern to hide sex, rather than a general prudishness of language, what distinguishes these last three centuries is the variety, the wide dispersion of devices that were invented for speaking about it, for having it be spoken about, for inducing it to speak of itself, for listening, recording, transcribing, and redistributing what is said about it: around sex, a whole network of varying, specific, and coercive transpositions into discourse. Rather than a massive censorship, beginning with the verbal proprieties imposed by the Age of Reason, what was involved was a regulated and polymorphous incitement to discourse. (HS1, 34; VS, 47)

Sex was not silenced. It was reported, so that the authorities could figure out how to manage populations and administer resources. The age of secular confession began, then, not because anybody was particularly phobic or vengeful but just because there were decisions that had to be made and work that had to done. Concern for the individual as well as for the general welfare demanded that information be gathered. There was nothing fundamentally malicious here.

Things start to look malicious when the questioners turn their attention toward what heretofore had been considered immoral or illegal practices. If the point simply was to gather information about birth rates, sterility and fertility, contraception, infant mortality, and maternal health, we might expect that epistemological focus would remain primarily on those people most likely to procreate. But in the discursive explosions of the eighteenth and nineteenth centuries epistemological attention shifted away from such people. "The legitimate couple, with its regular sexuality, had a right to more discretion" (HS1, 38; VS, 53). Officials became much more interested in "the sexuality of children, mad men and women, and criminals; the sensuality of those who did not like the opposite sex; reveries, obsessions, petty manias, or great transports of rage" (HS1, 38–9; VS, 53). Of course, the people who were thus scrutinized "were condemned all the same; but they were listened to; and if regular sexuality happened to be questioned once again, it was through a reflux movement, originating in these peripheral sexualities" (HS1, 39; VS, 54). Gathering information about what might be called normal heterosexuality was of only secondary importance from the late eighteenth century onward; the Victorians were interested in perversion.

It wasn't that the Victorians just had it in for deviants. Promotion of the general welfare made the relentlessly careful study of "peripheral sexualities" imperative. In the nineteenth century, as the category of development became fundamental in biological and human sciences, the study of deviance was institutionalized and statistical techniques invented to take account of it. Deviance—be it deviance in the sexual characteristics of human beings or in the morphological characteristics of pigeons—can help scientists understand how a given type of organism will develop under favorable conditions. This is because deviance, at least of many kinds, is presumed to occur because of some unfavorable conditions obtaining in the developmental environment. Deviance tells us a lot about normality, much more than normality tells us about deviance. As sexuality came to be an epistemic object—a gradual occurrence through the first part of the nineteenth century—deviant sexualities came under close scrutiny. But deviant sexual practitioners can't usually be observed committing their deviant acts, so official attention focused on identifying sexual deviants and getting them to confess.

One of the chief reasons for this nineteenth-century undertaking— that of delineating the normal development of sexuality—was to find ways for controlling populations, in the sense both of influencing the number of births and deaths and of regulating large groups of people engaging in various activities (like material production or national defense). Marxists might claim that the aim was simply "to reproduce labor capacity, to perpetuate the form of social relations: in short, to constitute a sexuality that is economically useful and politically conservative" (HS1, 37; VS, 51). Foucault is not sure "whether this was the ultimate objective" or not (HS1, 37; VS, 51). But he is sure that, even if it was, the means used in attempts to achieve that goal for the most part did not attempt to eliminate sexualities that did not adhere to what we might call the norm or at least to what then might have been seen as the Church's version of acceptable expressions of carnality. Repression is not a primary phenomenon in the history of sexuality, and confession is not its remedy. Rather, confession is simply an administrative imperative.

As I absorbed Foucault's account of sexual confession, disparate pieces of my own experience began to fall into place. For years I had wondered why categorization of people on the basis of their sexuality was so prevalent a practice. Why was sexuality so important? I could see no logical or ontological reason for its significance, and yet there was tremendous pressure on everyone to take on some sexual identity, to submit to sexual classification, to confess their sexual desires. Why? According to Foucault, there was a reason, but I was right to observe that it wasn't logical or ontological; it was historical: Things are as they are just because that's how our culture's recent history has unfolded.

Thousands of people helped to make that history. Some undoubtedly had malicious intentions, just as nowadays there are local conspiracies designed to isolate and injure if not annihilate certain sexual groups. But most of the people who helped to make that history had no intention of doing any such thing. Administrative imperatives tend to take on a life of their own, fed by innumerable and often conflicting individual aims and augmented by all kinds of other movements and events. The current configurations of forces that compel us to confess and submit are in no way inevitable; it is historical accident that dictates the importance of sexuality in the structure and course of our lives.

I liked this answer to my question. I liked it because I know that whatever emerges in history can disappear in it as well. I liked it, too, because it fit so well with what I saw and gave me a framework for understanding the particular and sometimes really weird forms that both confession and discrimination take. It gave me a way of understanding some parts of the world that didn't make sense. Foucault's narrative breaks off at the end of the nineteenth century, but the world he describes as coming into existence then exists still, in outline at least, as my own. I'll continue my attempt to show why I read Foucault's book as originating from a gay perspective by looking closely at the ways he describes the administrative strategies that form what he calls "the *dispositif de sexualité.*"[17]

Foucault studies the means employed by individuals and institutions in the late nineteenth century in their attempts to understand, influence, and use specific populations' sexualities. He points to four widespread operations or strategies that emerged during the period:

1. the disposition of lines of penetration (HS1, 41–2; VS, 57–8);
2. the incorporation of perversions (HS1, 42–4; VS, 58–60);
3. the institution of constant, proximate observation (HS1, 44–5: VS, 60–2); and
4. the development of devices of sexual saturation (HS1, 45–6; VS, 62–4).

I'll describe these in detail. Then I'll conclude this section with a discussion of the ways in which Foucault's description of the *dispositif de sexualité,* in particular these four strategies, accords with the world as I perceived it in 1983.

Once various administrative projects began to coalesce into larger social projects and movements, certain broad strategies for gathering information and maintaining and even extending control began to repeat themselves. Thus there arose vast networks of interrelated mechanisms of power. Foucault sets out to show how these mechanisms of power operated in the nineteenth and into the twentieth centuries, and what these operations indicate about the purposes at work in their deployment. First and most obviously, he says, these mechanisms operated not to stamp out their targets but, apparently, to expose them and cause them to proliferate.

His first example is the war on masturbation, which he contrasts with prohibitions on incest and adultery. "On the surface," he writes, "what appears in both cases is an effort at elimination . . ." (HS1, 41; VS, 57). The appearance is probably reality in the case of incest and adultery; officials were probably doing their best to reduce the incidence of these violations of law. But adultery and incest are different from masturbation in some crucial ways. The former were known quantities; that is, the average person not only pretty much knew which acts constituted them, but he or she probably also already believed such acts were wrong and dangerous. The supposed evils of masturbation were less well publicized, however. It's likely that prior to the "war on masturbation" a lot of people didn't know what acts counted as masturbation, had no idea how widespread its practice might be, and did not associate it with sterility or monstrous births. Officials had to educate, which was especially important since masturbation, unlike adultery and incest, was not against the law; officials would have to convince people not to masturbate in the absence of any legal penalty. People had to be talked to about masturbation and they had to be encouraged to talk about it among themselves in order to control the behavior of children and others in their care. Thus, while officials at first no doubt were attempting to eradicate masturbation, the techniques they used not only failed to do that but may have had the opposite effect—they may have increased the incidence of masturbation, because they taught people about the practice.

If we assume that people are not completely stupid, then we must also assume that if a practice fails to yield desirable results, it will be discontinued and another put in its place. That is not to say, however, that desirable results are always identical to intended results. Sometimes it happens that we initiate a practice because we project Result A, but then, when we actually get Result B, we keep engaging in the practice anyway, because we like Result B. Our desires can change in the course of trying to satisfy them. Something like that may have happened in the midst of the war on masturbation. Because the law was not the locus of the prohibitions on "self-abuse," these prohibitions could not operate punitively in the usual ways. And because the target population was bourgeois children, special care had to be taken in administering these prohibitions; it was important not to damage the future citizens and mothers of the realm. The methods used, then, were different from legal interdiction. Children had to be convinced not to masturbate; parents and teachers had to be taught to prevent it in younger children and to inculcate the prohibition in older children. A lot of talk was necessary, and that talk had to be regulated carefully, despite the fact that most of it had to occur in very private and intimate settings. But why did these efforts continue despite their failure and, in fact, redouble and spread in succeeding decades? Foucault suggests that, even though officials failed to get their intended result, Result A, they did get another result, Result B, and they liked what they got. The war on masturbation continued not because it helped prevent masturbation, but because it enabled something else, namely, the infiltration of the family by the medical profession (among others) and, generally, the extension of extralegal mechanisms of control through some of the heretofore most private corners of human existence.

> Wherever there was the chance [masturbatory pleasures] might appear, devices of surveillance were installed; traps were laid for compelling admissions; inexhaustible and corrective discourses were imposed; parents and teachers were alerted, and left with the suspicion that all children were guilty, and with the fear of being themselves at fault if their suspicions were not sufficiently strong; they were kept in readiness in the face of this recurrent danger; their conduct was prescribed and their pedagogy recodified; an entire medico-sexual regime took hold of the family milieu. (HS1, 42; VS, 58)

Again, this infiltration of the family was not the intended goal, nor was it one single event. It consisted of lots of little extensions of individuals' power or influence and lots of little changes in how people interacted with one another. Each little change that served someone's interests was then perhaps intentionally perpetuated and reinforced whenever possible, but no one ever intended to effect the huge rearrangement of society that followed from all those minute shifts.

Nevertheless, regardless of the original intentions of those who initiated this attack on masturbatory practices, the result obtained was the spread of knowledge about masturbation, which probably increased its incidence, and the spread of mechanisms and effects of regulatory and eventually therapeutic power. It may appear that we are dealing with a full-scale attempt at eradication, with a "barrier system," as Foucault puts it, but that is not how this network of relays and effects actually operates. "[I]n fact, all around the child, indefinite *lines of penetration* were disposed" (HS1, 42; VS, 58). The solitary pleasures of childhood—whatever they might have been—were now objects of medico-scientific study subject to careful regulation according to theo-ries and norms constructed by people most of those children would never even meet. And those lines of penetration would remain in place, long after childhood ended and even long after masturbation was no longer considered an abnormality or vice. The systematic regulation of childhood is a fixture in our own day, and now its uses far exceed any purposes for which it may have originally been set up. We've all been subjected to and shaped by it, while officials still maintain that their only interest is in the welfare of children and the future of the nation. When I was a child, many of those same "lines of penetration" and the mechanisms built to maintain and exploit them were used to monitor drug use, prevent teenaged pregnancy (out of wedlock, that is), and, of course, track down little queers.[18] It was in great part this vast surveil-lance system, rooted in the war on masturbation, that made my life so very miserable through adolescence. I recognized Foucault's descrip-tions immediately. That was my world, all right.

Interlocked with this regulation of childhood, Foucault goes on to claim, was the incorporation of perversions, the steady effort, through the latter half of the nineteenth century, to identify types of perverts, to classify them according to body type as much as behavior, and to trace their personal and biological histories so as to be able to locate the point at which their lives had deviated from the moral or healthful norm. Before this time, sodomy was believed to be an act that anyone might commit; but in the nineteenth century sodomy came to be seen as a symptom of something other than itself, something at once both more and less concrete than an isolated act. "[T]he psychological, psychiatric, medical category of homosexuality was constituted from the moment it was characterized . . . less by a type of sexual relations than by a certain quality of sexual sensibility, a certain way of inverting the masculine and the feminine in oneself. Homosexuality appeared as one of the forms of sexuality when it was transposed from the practice of sodomy onto a kind of interior androgyny, a hermaphrodism of the soul" (HS1, 43; VS 59). Sodomy became a sign, and only one of many possible signs, of a particular sort of personhood. As a result of this transposition, a human type was born, incarnated, incorporated; thus a new kind of body was produced, a signifying body, the body of the invert.

This incorporative move was repeated dozens of times in psychiat-ric practice as new forms of perversion were identified and described: "Krafft-Ebing's zoophiles and zooerasts, Rohleder's auto-monosex-ualists; and later, mixoscopophiles, gynecomasts, presbyophiles, sexo-esthetic inverts, and dyspareunist women" (HS1, 43; VS 60).[19] These newly embodied subjectivities were not simply offenders against the law or against good taste or even against nature. They were, quite specifically, deviants, their life courses turned aside from the paths of normality or stuck indefinitely in what should have been a passing phase of development. What was the purpose of this classificatory system and these repeated attempts to localize practices and freeze them into the countenances of their practitioners? Foucault suggests that this "machinery of power that focused on this whole alien strain did not aim to suppress it, but rather to give it an analytical, visible, and permanent reality" (HS1, 44; VS 60). Again, like the war on masturbation, this attempt to reify behavior into personality types seems aimed not at eradicating sodomy or other despised practices so much as at giving those practices a new kind of stability, a new home in the world, a home that justified therapeutic interventions in personal and family life on a scale not seen in previous centuries. If the homosexual or the presbyophile is a deviant from the path of normal development, it makes sense to inquire after the causes of his or her deviation and to seek answers by examining the person's whole life course, family relationships, and physiology. The most obvious result of this incorporation of perversions was not the control or eradication of them but the extension of power throughout the populations that harbored them.

The forms of power relations that emerge in the nineteenth century, then, Foucault argues, are not legalistic; they do not function as interdicts, and they do not confine themselves to punishing the deviant behaviors they identify. These forms of power are not intermittent as legal power is; they are not activated only when an infraction has been detected. Rather, they are constantly in play, constantly alert to the potential for deviance, constantly striving to uncover its etiology and its own peculiar developmental course, constantly seeking to correct deviance before it becomes incorporated as a way of life. Therefore, these forms of power relations "implied a physical proximity and an interplay of intense sensations"; they "demanded constant, attentive, and curious presences" (HS1, 44; VS 60). Observation is required and made as permanent a part of daily existence as possible. But observation does not remain detached; it does not merely await the moment when it must alert those with authority to act; instead, observation relentlessly solicits that which it allegedly desires to correct. These mechanisms of power summon forth the behaviors upon which they seek to act, invite them to show themselves; they might almost be said to seduce their targets into displaying the behaviors the observers work to detect. Often the work of observation itself affords pleasure both to those who observe and to those who are solicited. Foucault writes, "Power operated as a mechanism of attraction; it drew out those peculiarities over which it kept watch. Pleasure spread to the power that harried it; power anchored the pleasure it uncovered" (HS1, 45; VS, 61).

These seducing, incorporative, penetrating powers did not, as should be clear, banish all sexuality to the parents' bedroom. They spread sexuality throughout the social fabric, fixing it in complicated relationships between teachers and students, doctors and patients, psychiatrists and clients, as well as between parents and children and other family members. Sexuality became a dimension, more or less visible, in all significant relationships in any person's life. Thanks to the devices of sexual saturation invented in the nineteenth century and developed ever since, it is now possible to analyze absolutely any human interaction in sexual terms. Sexuality, its discourses and mechanisms, saturates our society and each of our lives completely. We drip with it.

Here, in these five pages (41–45; VS, 57–64) of Foucault's little book, I saw described, for the first time, the world in which I struggled to survive. My world was saturated with sexuality; sexuality was the preoccupation of virtually everyone I knew. Concern over sexual truth and sexual knowledge dictated everything from clothing styles to library collections. Sex was visible everywhere as the all-pervasive secret. Though he was describing the late nineteenth century, I was intimately acquainted with the mechanisms of surveillance and control that he detailed, and I often saw through the pretexts for intervention that made extension of those mechanisms possible. For most of my life I had been watched almost constantly for any signs of sexual deviance—which might include acts or expressions of desire but might also include almost anything else from the length of my stride to the pitch of my voice. This watching went on everywhere, all the time, and was performed by everyone, even strangers—many of whom did not hesitate to offer unsolicited comments. My peers were as conscientious in their observations as our superiors, who coached and encouraged them. At the same time, however, I knew that this ubiquitous network of surveillance was not the product of a conspiracy, nor was it aimed particularly at me. We were all being scanned constantly for information regarding our sexuality; we were all constantly scanning ourselves. And nobody in particular was in charge of the whole enterprise. But under the right conditions, the sex authorities would be notified, and there could be dire consequences for those subject to their investigations. I also knew that one of the reasons the system kept running even without a central command or master engineer was that many people, regardless of whether they actually believed that deviants were dangerous, enjoyed the game of hide and seek it allowed them to play and wanted to extend the reach of their personal or institutional influence. Foucault's description of the world accorded perfectly with what I could see.

Based on this description of the sexually saturated society that he claims constituted itself during the end of the last century, Foucault makes several observations, two of which resonated especially strongly with my experience. The first is that "[m]odern society is perverse, not in spite of its puritanism or as if from a backlash provoked by its hypocrisy; it is in actual fact, and directly, perverse" (HS1, 47; VS, 65). The second is "that sex was not only a matter of sensation and pleasure, law and taboo, but also of truth and falsehood, that the truth of sex became something fundamental, useful, or dangerous, precious or formidable: in short, that sex was constituted as a problem of truth" (HS1, 56; VS, 76). These two observations, it seemed to me, could also be made about the mid-twentieth-century society into which I was born, the American heir of European Victorianism.

Foucault did not have to do much to convince me that the society out of which I came was directly, blatantly, and persistently perverse. "At issue," Foucault writes, "is the type of power [society] brought to bear on the body and on sex," a type of power that "had neither the form of law nor the effects of taboo" (HS1, 47; VS, 64). In other words, it did not prohibit sexuality of any sort; it did not limit sexual expression to one approved type. "On the contrary, it acted by multiplication of singular sexualities. It did not set boundaries for sexuality; it extended the various forms of sexuality, pursuing them according to lines of indefinite penetration" (HS1, 47; VS, 64). This power encouraged the expression of what it defined as deviance so that it could extend itself more deeply into the lives of individuals and specified populations, and, by claiming that sexual expressions of certain sorts were signs of the existence of certain sorts of (perhaps dangerous or unhealthy) individuals, it justified incursions into domains where the law had never before had any footing. This power did not seek to eradicate sexuality; "it attracted its varieties by means of spirals in which pleasure and power reinforced one another" (HS1, 47; VS, 65).

To illustrate the accord between my experience and this picture, I offer an example from high school. (This example is by no means an isolated one. I have others, and every person I know who was sexually deviant in adolescence can tell at least one similar story.) I had a ninth-grade teacher who spent many hours of class time telling us what were to me chilling tales about sexually deviant teenagers she had known. In these stories, which she told with great gusto, she was always the heroine. A new student would come into her class. He or she would seem slightly, but only slightly, unusual in some way. No one else would notice. Only she had the clear-sightedness to recognize the situation for what it was; only she had the courage to face the facts. Finally, it was she who had to summon the medical, legal, or moral authorities. Though initially there might be some resistance, eventually everyone involved was grateful to her. She taught us, her pupils, how to recognize the signs of sexual abnormality so that we could carry on her good work—so that we, too, could ferret out abnormality when it threatened to pass as normality and could force it into the open and into submission to the authorities.

The woman was supposed to teach basic biology, but her enjoyment of that subject was very much exceeded by her enjoyment of human anatomy, which absolutely fascinated her, at least in its less common forms. More than telling self-aggrandizing stories and teaching important identificational skills, however, this woman enjoyed the work of observation and detection itself. She was a practicing scientist, not a mere transmitter of scientific fact. Often the signs of sexual abnormality she discussed were physical or medical characteristics that she knew I possessed—for example, a history of epileptic seizures—and usually by the end of the lesson her gaze would come to rest on me. She always looked hard into my eyes and smiled, as if she were my opponent in some kind of game in which she had the upper hand.

I was well aware that I was not singled out as the only pupil under her surveillance. She watched everyone for "signs." The difference was only that in me her efforts were rewarded. She told her stories in our class partly because she enjoyed watching me sweat in my seat out of fear, humiliation, and rage. And she smiled at me because she knew she had me in a position that I would have to be very crafty indeed to find any way out of—for either I would remain silent, and she could have the pleasure of tormenting me with her thinly disguised threats the entire school year, or I would eventually acknowledge the truth by trying to defend myself, and she could have the pleasure of intervening and could add my story to her collection for her pupils the following year. But she watched us all. Nobody escaped her gaze.[20]

Foucault's assertion that mechanisms and functionaries of surveillance drive sexuality into hiding so that they can penetrate ever further into people's lives struck a deep chord in me. My biology teacher wasn't content with identifying me and having me carted off. If she had been, she wouldn't have revealed her identificational techniques. She was looking for an excuse to interrogate me more closely, to call my parents and question them, to discuss me with a doctor or psychologist or social worker. ("She wants to get me," I used to think—to have me, to possess me. The sexual dimensions of her pleasure—its perversity—were not lost on me, even at fourteen.) But further extension of her investigation would have had to be prompted by something, by my emitting some sign of abnormality not quite obvious to everybody else. Her classroom discourse was teaching me, in fact, how to be cunning, how to hide. From her I learned exactly what not to do or say, because she blatantly told me which acts, gestures, or words would result in "intervention." She taught me the rules of the closet. Did she do that because she wanted me to efface my perversion totally so she would never have to think about it again? Hardly. She would have felt awfully impoverished without any signs of perversion to identify. No, she wanted me to challenge her, to complicate the play, to hide myself a little better next time so she would have cause to delve deeper into my life and so she could feel smarter when she caught me. It was a sickening game. It was nerve-wracking and debilitating. She enjoyed it thoroughly. I enjoyed it not at all. Nevertheless, the game itself did hold out a promise of pleasure for me, too, the pleasure of surrender. I could end the torture if only I would confess—go to her, let her "intervene." No doubt she would have welcomed me, probably with great kindness, even love; she would have "helped" me as she had helped others, tenderly and with Christian charity. She would have led me to others who would have taken a deep interest in hearing my secrets, who would have regarded me as "special," who—as scientific experts—would have subordinated their intellects to my truth.

I didn't surrender to her. I didn't confess. But after a few years of unremitting surveillance and subtle and not-so-subtle threats, you get tired. The thing you fight, the thing you fear, gradually stops seeming so frightful after all. You can't go on alone. You really do need help. What's the difference, either way? So eventually you find yourself in somebody's badly furnished office, huddled on a chair, saying the words they want you to say. And they listen. And they are interested. And that's a relief; it feels good. They ask questions. At times you hesitate. Some questions seem irrelevant; some embarrass you. They insist, gently. You refuse. They suggest that you are resisting therapy, don't really want help, want to persist in your illness. If you still won't answer they take your clothes, lock you in a cubicle with nothing but a mattress, watch you through a two-way mirror, and write down all the nasty words you say. They ask more questions, make you draw pictures, administer drugs. They acquire your medical records, look in your mouth, take samples of blood, give you intelligence tests and plug you into electroencephalographs. They watch you interact with peers, listen to your phone calls, withhold your mail because unmonitored interactions will impede therapy. They bring in your family, videotape you together while they question them, and study your facial expressions while you listen to their answers. Then they tell you whether you're really gay or not. (They told me I wasn't, but then they put me through three months of Gender Identification Therapy so I'd stop acting like I was.) They want truth all right, but not exactly the truth you think you possess. They want the truth that possesses you, that you contain, the secret that makes you what you are. They don't think that you know the secret; they just think that you *are* it or that your body is the medium through which it expresses itself. Confession is not the end of the game. You'll go on confessing for the rest of your life. That's what your sexuality becomes, or maybe always was: a thing to be known, an epistemic object. And that is what you are, are desired as, and desire as.

Foucault, in less personal terms, makes this same point. The sexual subject is constituted, in its very essence, as a confessing subject. Sexual subjectivity is pervaded by epistemological concerns; every aspect of its being is ordered by issues of truth and falsehood, knowledge and ignorance. Its constant engagement with the dynamics of the known and the unknown, the revealed and the concealed is its defining feature. For straight people, this kind of existence is not horrifically painful, but there is always the possibility that it could become so if something goes awry and "intervention" occurs. Straight people's existence, too, is defined by their sexual truth. They are driven to confess that they are indeed straight, and many of them spend much energy discussing and analyzing their heterosexuality in all its splendidly superior detail. Thus, Foucault's analysis situates sexual subjectivity—*all sexual subjectivity*—in relation to what has come to be known as the "closet." No matter what its individual nature, sexuality's initial locus is always a "closet"; otherwise confession would have no meaning. Sexual subjectivity is, essentially, an epistemological phenomenon. To be the subject of a sexuality is, essentially, to be an entity whose true identity must be made known.

Reading Foucault's text was not a cognitive act so much as it was a re-cognitive act. The text changed the way I saw the world, but it changed the way I *saw* first of all. It showed me precisely what I saw. No book had ever done that for me, or to me, before. Whether Michel Foucault, the man who sat down one day and wrote those words, was queer or not, the voice I heard was queer. It bespoke an angle of vision that I recognized, an angle of vision more or less forced on me because of the social position I as a particular kind of sexual subjectivity was forced to occupy, an angle of vision I had thought could never come to speech.

ON UNDERMINING HOMOSEXUAL ESSENCE

One reason for my many years of silent protest against sexuality's privileged status over other characteristics a person might have was that, as I said at the beginning of this chapter, once I was identified as a homosexual my lived interiority, my subjectivity and potential for creativity and change, ceased to matter to anyone. It seemed I was capable of decision, action, growth, and responsibility only on some basis other than my sexuality, yet the narrow confine of my sexuality was where most people wanted to keep me most of the time. I could not act or communicate as a homosexual; I did not know how. Homosexuality was merely a mute thing in the world I inhabited. The word "homosexual" had little meaning beyond "object of ridicule and scorn." If I wanted to connect with another person, I had to speak from some position other than my queerness. I had to speak as a student, a neighbor, or a teammate. Of course it was possible for me to do that, because I was also those other things; I occupied multiple positions in the social world. But often if my "true nature" was discovered, the person with whom I had connected on some other basis would accuse me of betrayal or deceit. Eventually I came to *feel* deceitful whenever I didn't "warn" anyone that I was gay before befriending them. I began to feel dishonest whenever I didn't make my sexuality into an object for other people to know, whenever I didn't give them the opportunity to decide whether they would accept me or reject me on that basis at the outset. Yet I knew rejection, and worse, was what I risked. If I gave in to that feeling and made my sexuality available as an epistemic object, I would simply be identified with, or as, that object and be treated as something other and less than a human being.

Of course, that was Alabama twenty years ago. It's the nineties and I live in Virginia now, and things are oh so different. There are so many liberated, tolerant heterosexuals around who emphatically assert that a person's sexual orientation makes absolutely no difference to them. They won't reduce me to or identify me with my homosexuality. They will go on treating me as an intellectual or a neighbor or a teammate. I run no risks with them, they proudly assure me, apparently without the least inkling of the implication of what they've said—that they would never be so crass and uncivilized as to treat anyone as a homosexual.

Though sexually tolerant yuppies are less dangerous than small-town boys who rape lesbians as a means of "converting" them, in a sense this "liberal" position is more insulting. I'm glad, on the one hand, that these paragons of tolerance don't want to make my sexuality and me with it into an object; but, on the other hand, I abhor the fact that along with refusing to do that they also refuse to take any account of it at all and thereby exclude it from our interactions altogether. Once again, homosexuality is outcast; once again the "homosexual human being" is declared oxymoronic; once again the homosexual person is silenced. I can't speak as a homosexual from my lived homosexual experience if the smiling, nodding faces all around me keep telling me that it's none of their business whom I love or what I do in bed. I can't speak as a homosexual from out of my homosexual experience if homosexuality is a sexual orientation merely rather than a social location that I inhabit and a collection of culturally meaningful practices that inform every aspect of my life. When tolerant acquaintances insist that my homosexuality doesn't matter to them, they say in effect that homosexuality is not a social or cultural phenomenon at all but rather some sort of brute quality inherent in me and totally disconnected from them; they say in effect that my homosexuality is a kind of object that is obviously there but (like a mole or wart) has nothing to do with me as a person. Thus this "tolerance" in the final analysis amounts basically to the same stance as that taken by reductivistic homophobes. To both groups homosexuality is a known quantity, an epistemic object rather than a subject position or social location intimately related to other subject positions or social locations from which self-aware human beings perceive the world and speak. To both groups, to identify with the object "homosexuality" is to cease to be a human agent.

This conception of homosexuality as an essence or reified type must be dismantled or at least undermined if we who are queer are ever to come to speech at all. And that was exactly what Foucault's book managed to do. It is precisely because he undermines objectified sexual identities that his very queer perspective on the world is intelligible at all. Thus, in January of 1983 Foucault's book showed me not only *that* it is possible to do the impossible—to speak as a homosexual, to articulate a view of the world from a homosexual perspective—it also showed me *how* to do the impossible. It showed me how to occupy a homosexual position while resisting the demand that I thereby *be* an object. It showed me how I could be a homosexual fully and completely while at the same time I could refuse to be a homosexual essentially. It showed me how to begin to think of homosexuality as something other than a given, reified object. The reductive categorization could be undermined even while the social position and identity could be acknowledged and affirmed.

The key was Foucault's genealogical approach. Genealogy affirms the existence of something while at the same time acknowledging its historicity, its inessentiality. Foucault's genealogy of sexuality affirmed the existence of various forms of sexual subjectivity while at the same time acknowledging—in fact, demonstrating—that the phenomenon of sexual subjectivity arose within a particular historical context out of disparate administrative projects, institutional and individual preoccupations, scientific disciplines, and social and economic conflicts. Sexual subjectivity is quite real, but it isn't timeless or unchanging. It took shape through the action of historical and political forces, and it remains a creature of such forces; without them it would cease to exist, and some other way of organizing the social and procreative world would take its place.

There is no question that I am a lesbian. I fit all the descriptions exceedingly well. On the Kinsey Scale I'm about a five. In the state of Virginia I can be labeled an incorrigible felon. I wear my hair short, I garden, and I listen to k.d. lang. I don't yet own a motorcycle, and I got rid of my truck, but these aberrations are merely technical; the essential thing is: I like girls, and I know how to line dance. I'm a deviant. It's who I am. It's my identity. But it's not my nature. It's a position I occupy in a historically formed classification scheme. My adolescent longing for an alternative classification scheme—if I have to be something, why can't I be my religion, my ethnicity, or my standardized test scores?—made perfectly good sense. In another place and time, as Foucault shows, somebody like me (somebody who liked girls, gardening, and country dancing) might very well be classified quite differently and conceivably might not be punished for her position in that other classification scheme. I can acknowledge that, given the classification system our society insists upon, I am homosexual, and I can and do inhabit that position openly. But I will not stop reminding everyone around me that that position is the result of a nineteenth-century production of these categories and the subjects to fill them. Foucault's genealogy gives me the tools to undermine other people's assertions that the way I am appropriately classified in the sexualized Western world today is inevitable, politically neutral, and at least potentially benign. Our classification system—both its requirement that people be their sexualities and the division of sexualities into hetero and homo—is a social construct used to manipulate and manage people and to distribute or withhold goods; it is a political tool, and its employment is never disinterested.

There have been other types of sexual subjectivities besides homosexuals and heterosexuals: zoophiles and zooerasts, automonosexualists, mixoscopophiles, gynecomasts, presbyophiles, sexoesthetic inverts, and so on. But these deviant types have passed away, whereas the homosexual has remained and helped give shape to its "normal" counterpart, the heterosexual. Normalizing disciplines require deviance, but not all kinds of deviance serve disciplinary purposes equally well. Deviance to which few people are prone, for example, is of little use, because it cannot serve as justification for regulating most people's behavior. Only deviance that is relatively widespread and to which almost everyone at some stage in life or under some conditions is believed to be susceptible can justify widespread regulation of private behavior. Prior to the characterization of the homosexual as a subject-type, sodomy as an act was considered to be a carnal sin of which all people were thought capable, just as all people were thought capable of adultery. One of the things the homosexual inherited from the sodomite was his ubiquity. Homosexuality, far more than other sexual deviations that were reified in the nineteenth century, implicated huge sectors of the population and thus enabled (partly by creating popular demand for) general observation, regulation, and control.[21]

Eve Sedgwick writes of the tension that exists in our society between what she calls the "minoritizing view" of homosexuality and the "universalizing view."[22] On the one hand, homosexuality affects a minority of the population, because it is held to be the condition (or nature) of a small group of people—between two and ten percent of us. On the other hand, homosexuality affects everyone, because it is that which most people seek not to be defined as, that against which most people define themselves, but at the same time that which their sexuality always threatens to become (for example, in prisons, in boarding schools, in the military, following sexual abuse, following gay-positive sex education classes). On the one hand, only a few deviants are homosexual; on the other, anyone may turn out to be homosexual at any time. Thus, in one way or another homosexuality affects virtually everyone and so can be used to regulate virtually everyone's behavior. Those who are homosexual can be compelled to confess and endure punishment or spend their lives in silence and emotional exile from their families, neighbors, and colleagues. Those who are not homosexual can be compelled to confess that they are not (and often to show that they are not) or endure the punishments inflicted upon those who are. One must prove oneself sexually normal or be branded a queer. One must flaunt one's heterosexuality, measure up to all the standards the parents, the teachers, the coaches, the fraternities and sororities, the sergeants, the advertising executives, the bosses, the therapists, and the talk-show hosts set forth—or be subject to the punishment that is usually reserved for those who are queer. And that is precisely the reason that homosexual deviance is so valuable to our society and why it remains when all its perverted kinspeople have died away: It is effective in disciplining entire populations, whereas other, less binary-prone categories do not afford that possibility to as great an extent. The classification of some people as homosexual deviants is a tool for disciplining not just the people so classified; it is a tool for disciplining absolutely everyone.

Through years of personal experience I already knew that Foucault's descriptions of how sexuality and sexuality subjectivity and classification actually worked were accurate, but his genealogy gave or at least suggested answers to the questions that that knowledge had generated, such as: *Why* does it work that way, and how did this all come about? I was able to let go of that still lingering belief that, after all, heterosexuality was superior in some organic or natural way to homosexuality. Heterosexuality, like homosexuality, I was able to maintain, is a social construct; its power and prestige rest solely on its embeddedness within the classification system that invents it. With the advent of those new abilities, the grip of a crushing form of power was gradually loosening around me.

2

Genealogical Diversions

Wherein the Ascetic Priestess Loses Her Way and Begins to
Wander Aimlessly through Dem Ole Cotton Fields Back Home

Long before I ever read Foucault's work, I harbored suspicions about the high value placed on sexuality and on obtaining sexual knowledge. I emphasize that these were *suspicions*, though, not conclusions. As such, they didn't serve me especially well; they may have prevented me sometimes from yielding to authority, but they never gave me the grounds to challenge it or the strength to throw it off. Since suspicions lack the epistemological status of knowledge, they also lack the power to fortify a person the way that knowledge can.

Most out-of-the-closet participants in established queer communities like to look back at the past and remember how hard we fought, how valiantly we resisted, how heroically we stood alone against the world. I like to remember such times—times when I fought hard, times when I was strong and wily and brave. But that's not the whole story. I was no hero. I lacked the single-minded stubbornness that in heroic epics goes by the name "purity of heart." I also remember times when I wasn't tough, times when I wasn't smart, times when I condemned myself with all the virulence society had ever brought to bear. And I remember times when I was so damned tired I just didn't care enough to fight, and I stopped believing anything at all and just let them do with me what they pleased. I suspected they were wrong. But I didn't *know* they were wrong. I also suspected myself.

When I picked up Foucault's book, I was barely twenty-three years old. For over eleven of those twenty-three years, I had been despised, victimized, tormented, caged, and blamed for my own pain. Rarely did anyone even acknowledge what I was going through, much less support or stand by me. By the end of those eleven years I was, for all practical purposes, utterly alone. I knew if I intended to survive, I had to find something to fortify me. If only I could *know*, I thought; maybe this awful state of suspicion, self-doubt, and oscillation would end if I knew the truth about sexuality and sexual identity. I wanted an account that squared with the facts, including my facts, not just with the facts the televangelists and the technicians saw fit to consider. I wanted the *real* truth. Truth, I thought, would empower me to act. If I had truth, I would know whether I should give myself over to them and let them do their best to make me normal or stand firm and resist them with full assurance that they were wrong and I was not a monster after all. If only I knew the truth, I could commit myself to believing and doing something, some one thing and not another; I could become single-minded; I could achieve purity of heart.

Foucault's book spoke to precisely that tangle of epistemic and strategic desires. It engaged me first of all at an epistemic level by addressing questions about the facts, by trying to determine what we do and do not know. The truth of my sexuality, my homosexuality, Foucault seemed to be telling me, was that it was constructed and instituted by sexologists in the nineteenth century on the basis of a loose collection of observed and reported behaviors, practices, tastes, desires, fantasies, and embodiments. Prior to 1867, Foucault asserts, homosexual identity didn't exist, even though practices and people we would now call homosexual did. If he was right, and as far as I could tell his evidence supported his claims, then my homosexuality was not a manifestation of my essential nature any more than my language or religion was. If homosexuality was an invention with a particular history, it wasn't the sort of thing that *could* be the manifestation of an essence. Thus, Foucault gave me reasons to disbelieve the people who wanted to reduce me to my alleged essential identity as a homosexual. But he gave me more than that. He also gave me an account of why people try to reduce me to my homosexuality and why they lie about its allegedly essential nature and cover over its past. Homosexual identity makes me visible and therefore targetable, Foucault pointed out.[1] Furthermore, he claims, authorities use homosexuals as an excuse for controlling everybody's behavior and for gathering information about everybody's private life, so they perpetuate the category and even revamp it now and then to serve their purposes. My experience confirmed Foucault's assertions, and in turn, his arguments substantiated my suspicion that sexual categorization was not a politically neutral scientific practice; it was a practice that was profoundly politically *interested*.

My newfound knowledge made me feel good. At last I had the truth, and I could commit myself to it single-mindedly. I could purge myself of all the fears I'd had that those people were right about me. I could define my oppressors not only as my personal enemies but also as enemies of the truth, because I knew that the assertions they used to justify the insults, injuries, deprivations, and threats of worse were nothing but lies. With truth on my side, I could stand against them unwaveringly. But the book offered more than fortification merely. Not only did it reinforce a number of beliefs I already held, but it also gave me new insights and ideas. Through it I could begin to see the shape of a possible counterattack. With work, I could imagine going on a kind of intellectual offensive. For, not only did I know the real truth about homosexuality, but now I knew the real truth about heterosexuality too. Now I knew that, contrary to what the teachers and the televangelists said, heterosexual identity was not the projection of some inherent sexual essence either; it, too, was a construct, which meant that heterosexual people were totally unjustified in their claims to be natural or normal. Drawing on Foucault's research, over time I thought I could prove it to other people. Thus I could begin to undermine the power that heterosexuals have in our society.

My ideas about how exactly to launch my counterattack were fairly vague then, but what I could only dimly imagine in the mid-1980s had taken shape by 1990 in the work of historian Jonathan Ned Katz. In his 1990 article entitled "The Invention of Heterosexuality," Katz underscores the power of studying the history of heterosexuality as a way of undermining heterosexism:

> By not studying the heterosexual idea in history, analysts of sex, gay and straight, have continued to privilege the "normal" and "natural" at the expense of the "abnormal" and "unnatural." Such privileging of the norm accedes to its domination, protecting it from questions. By making the normal the object of a thoroughgoing historical study we simultaneously pursue truth and a sex-radical and subversive goal: we upset basic preconceptions. We discover that the heterosexual, the normal, and the natural have a history of changing definitions. Studying the history of the term challenges its power.[2]

Katz's strategy in this article (and later in his book, also entitled *The Invention of Heterosexuality*[3]) rests on the conviction that the power of heterosexuality comes from its unchallenged claim to be natural— meaning ahistorical, not produced in history—from its claim that it exists prior to and independently of any social institutions and is in essence unaffected by social struggles. If we could show the opposite, that in fact heterosexuality has not always existed or existed in the same form, then its power as norm would be diminished.

The facts Katz marshals amply support his contention that heterosexuality was invented. First of all, he notes, the word *heterosexual* did not appear in English until 1892, and then it named not "normal" sexual orientation but rather an allegedly pathological condition that many would now recognize as bisexuality.[4] Only decades later did the word acquire its current meaning. *Heterosexuality*, meaning a normal desire for sexual union with members of the "opposite" sex, made its debut in *The New York Times* no earlier than 1930.[5] One might still argue that the absence of the word itself does not warrant any claim about the presence or absence of the fact, either the fact of what we now call heterosexual desire or the fact of a heterosexual social position that might have been differently named; however, Katz argues, neither the specific desire nor the social space of anything very much like heterosexuality existed before 1860.

To make this point, Katz examines what he calls the period of "Early Victorian True Love, 1820–1860," which is, he argues, a time before the invention of heterosexuality. He presents four types of evidence to support this claim. First, he asserts that what we now call gender, not what we now call sexual orientation, was the organizing principle of early Victorian sexual arrangements. A healthy, normal, good person strove to achieve the ideals of his or her gender type—the True Man or the True Woman. True Manhood and True Womanhood, though complementary in some ways, were not defined in opposition to one another. Fulfillment of either ideal involved, for example, cultivation of freedom from uncontrolled sensuality. Thus, second, what drew men and women together was not heterogenital lust (which was conceived as wanton and even random in its fixations) but rather a natural desire for motherhood or fatherhood; one desired intercourse because one had a natural, inborn drive to procreate, from which the pleasure of the act itself (should there be any) was merely derivative. Wantonly sensual people—like masturbators and prostitutes, "archetypal Victorian erotic monster[s]"[6]—were unnatural or immoral because they eschewed the satisfaction of natural desire in favor of the pleasure that should only have been a by-product of the means to satisfaction, much like misers whose love for gold coins may prevent their purchasing adequate shelter or food. Thus, third, natural manhood and womanhood were not defined in opposition to same-sex lust but rather in opposition to lust itself. Although the concept of lust has lost most of its force in modern society, most people probably would equate it with desire for genital pleasure, of which heterosexual desire is one variety. Clearly, then, the Early Victorian ideal did not celebrate heterosexual desire as natural or normal. Finally, according to Katz, the categories for conceptualizing people who experienced and acted upon same-sex genital desire, those most closely related to the modern homosexual, were the sodomite and the sapphist, "terms with no antonyms"[7] whose bearers appear to be conceptually singular, definitionally unrelated to bearers of other erotic labels. The natural early Victorian state of erotic well-being, then, occupied none or very little of the social and conceptual space that modern heterosexuality occupies. Therefore, Katz concludes, heterosexuals simply did not exist before 1860; heterosexual identity and the concept of heterosexuality as a norm and a kind of natural desire were invented in the succeeding decades by medical doctors, legal theorists, poets, and social reformers.

To the degree that readers find Katz's arguments persuasive, the power of heterosexuality to assert itself as a norm rooted in nature and to shield itself from political critique will be lessened. As Katz writes, "a new sense of the historical making of the heterosexual and homosexual suggests that these are ways of feeling, acting, and being with each other that we can together unmake and radically remake according to our present desire, power, and our vision of a future political-economy of pleasure."[8] If heterosexuals want to maintain their claim to normality and rightful hegemony, they are cast by Katz's analysis into a rhetorical position much like the one in which they have tried to keep homosexuals: They must justify the civil and cultural positions they wish to occupy vis-à-vis the rest of us. The burden of proof has shifted.

When I first read Foucault's *The History of Sexuality*, I couldn't foresee the exact direction that a history of heterosexuality would take. The work of a careful historian like Jonathan Katz was necessary for that. But Foucault's book did give me some confidence that such a history was possible, because it showed that sexuality itself had a politically charged history. At an epistemic level, the truths Foucault's work offered me were deeply satisfying. The work was also satisfying at a strategic level; I was very excited and gratified by the prospect of proving that heterosexuality was not a natural phenomenon.

But some part of me was also deeply troubled, and that sense of uneasiness only intensified through 1984 as I read Foucault's essays in *Language, Counter-memory, Practice* and Nietzsche's genealogical writings for the first time. I found such passages as the following (wherein Foucault discusses Nietzsche's essay "On the Uses and Disadvantages of History for Life") acutely troublesome:

> The third use of history is the sacrifice of the subject of knowledge. In appearance, or rather, according to the mask it bears, historical consciousness is neutral, devoid of passions, and committed solely to the truth. But if

it examines itself and if, more generally, it interrogates the various forms of scientific consciousness in history, it finds that all these forms and transformations are aspects of the will to knowledge: instinct, passion, the inquisitor's devotion, cruel subtlety, and malice. (NGH, 162)

It was becoming clear that genealogy was not what it had first appeared to be. Whether the genealogy in question was of morals or of sexuality, eventually what was at stake was the knower or knowledge-seeker him or herself. In *The History of Sexuality*, Foucault suggests that all knowledge about sexuality is politically charged and that the desire for that knowledge is itself historically constructed in networks of power. What did that say about my newfound social constructionist knowledge? What did that say about my motives for acquiring such knowledge and, worse still, about the knower I now took myself to be? According to Foucault, genealogy "disturbs what was previously considered immobile; it fragments what was thought unified; it shows the heterogeneity of what was imagined consistent with itself. What convictions and, far more decisively, what knowledge can resist it?" (NGH, 139). The answer, I began to fear, was no knowledge, not even the social constructionist knowledge I thought Foucault's own genealogy put forth. The stability Foucault's historical evidence at first had given me from my doubts and suspicions had now given way to yet another stretch of unstable epistemological ground. What genealogy disturbed most profoundly was me—the would-be knower. I wanted Foucault's story about sexuality to be the final word on the matter; I wanted to be able to rest with this constructionist account of sexual identities. But if genealogy "refuses the certainty of absolutes" (NGH, 153), then social constructionist knowledge was no more absolute than anything else. I hadn't gotten hold of the truth about sexuality after all. I wasn't quite sure what I had gotten hold of in fact. What exactly was the epistemological status of Foucault's story of sexuality supposed to be anyway? If it wasn't a triumph of truth over ignorance or ideology, then what was it?

Reading Foucault's book was certainly a different experience from reading, for example, Jonathan Katz's history of heterosexuality, although it may look on the surface like the two pieces of work are very similar. With Katz, I was on very familiar epistemological territory. I started out with a clear idea of what would count as good evidence for his thesis and as a sound and valid argument. Nothing Katz says in the course of his study disturbed these clear ideas. Because he doesn't raise epistemological issues, Katz is able to mount a political intervention on behalf of non-heterosexual people erected upon his refusal "to privilege

the 'normal' and 'natural' at the expense of the 'abnormal' and 'unnatural.'"⁹ In the analytic space opened by this refusal, it is possible to make
the normal, the heterosexual, "the object of a thoroughgoing historical
study" and thus to "pursue truth."¹⁰ The truth the historian then brings
to light is, of course, that heterosexuality's power to order our social,
political, economic, and moral worlds—rooted as it is in a claim to be
utterly natural and apolitical—is illegitimate; historical events shaped
by human decisions and acts, not God or ahistorical nature, are the
sources of heterosexuality, the matrix in which it was formed. Katz's
conclusion is asserted with assurance; he knows what he is talking
about, and his article and book are intended to help the reader come to
know likewise.

But what is the status of this new truth, and of the thinker who
knows it, and of the politically engaged agent who deploys it? The truth
that Katz offers us purports not to be socially constructed. That truth
and the thinker who knows it are exempted from constructionist critique. Katz's narrative voice, telling us the story of heterosexuality's
birth, bespeaks no awareness of its own history, or of the history of
historical investigation itself. Historical truth remains curiously
unsusceptible to historicization in this work of Katz's, enabling him (as
knower, if not as homosexual) to transcend the shifting power relations
that structure and de-structure and re-structure his language and society. Foucault's work, by contrast, cannot escape the same kind of
critique to which it subjects its targets, because it undermines not only
sexuality and sexual identity but also the epistemic ground upon which
critique usually stands. Our sexual identities are socially constructed—
fabricated in networks of power—but, more importantly, so are our
epistemic identities. Like the sexual subject, the knowing subject has a
genealogy, Foucault argues; it, too, came into existence in and through
networks of power. If we believe Foucault on this crucial point, then in
the very same moment that we hear his claim as truth we must also hear
it as self-undermining or self-overcoming. That is what makes Foucault's work so disturbing and so very different from the work of a
traditional historian like Jonathan Katz.

Non-heterosexual people's lives unfold in a region staked out by
two extremes: On the one hand, we can dissemble; on the other, we can
confess. On the one hand, we can be closeted; on the other, we can be
out. Not that these extremes are really so simple, but our choices are
usually very limited, and sometimes we have no choice at all. Still, most
of us manage to take some control over various information flows and
to negotiate a very complicated passage between these two extremes for
most of our lives. Neither of these extremes, however, nor the field they

demarcate is directly related to what most straight people think of when they think of homosexuality: Neither is directly related to desire or physical pleasure. Rather than an erotic space, the space in which most of us queers live most of our lives and perform these incredibly difficult daily maneuvers is primarily an epistemological space, a space structured by truth and falsity, a space wherein very often what is most important is not who has what kind of pleasure but, rather, who has control over who knows and what is known. Thus, this space is also a political space, a space where our power, our well-being, our future, and our very selves are always at risk.

Foucault's text, unlike Katz's, is about this space in which we live; it is about the emergence of sexuality as an epistemological field. That's why Foucault investigates confessional practices—by doing so, he places at the center of his analysis the issue of what it is to know one's, or anyone's, sexuality at all. The aim of his book, Foucault says, is not "to determine whether these discursive productions and these effects of power lead one to formulate the truth about sex, or on the contrary falsehoods designed to conceal the truth, but rather to bring out the 'will to knowledge' that serves as both their support and their instrument" (HS1, 12; VS, 20). Foucault brings into question much more than a couple of historically emergent sexual identities; he places in question the subject of sexual knowledge him- or herself. And that, in turn, calls into question Foucault's own discourse and, therefore, my knowing appropriation of it.

I had been very glad to learn that homosexuality was socially constructed, because homosexual identity was oppressive to me, but this further step was more difficult. I had not wanted to learn that my self, especially myself the knower, was socially constructed. I had, in a sense, wanted to save my identity from identification. I had wanted to use Foucault's genealogy as a weapon to defend myself against the attacks of social identification that would have reduced me to silence. But there was a self that I wanted to defend and preserve, the autonomous self that chose and freely committed its acts, the reasoning self that could legitimately claim to know. That self wanted to be in charge of its sexuality; it did not want to be annihilated or consumed. That self wanted to be in charge of its knowledge; it did not want its power to assert and claim and prove to be undermined.

Genealogy, however, doesn't exempt anything from historical critique; it never rests content with any stable identity. "Where the soul pretends unification or the self fabricates a coherent identity, the genealogist sets out to study the beginning—numberless beginnings whose faint traces and hints of color are readily seen by an historical eye. The analysis of descent permits the dissociation of the self, its recognition and displacement as an empty synthesis, in liberating a profusion of lost events" (NGH, 145–46). One could write a genealogy of various kinds of knower-selves. "If a genealogical analysis of a scholar were made," Foucault suggests, "of one who collects facts and carefully accounts for them—his *Herkunft* [his ancestry and lineage, his descent] would quickly divulge the official papers of the scribe and the pleadings of the lawyer . . ." (NGH, 147). Allegedly objective scholarship grows out of something very different from what it takes itself to be.[11]

The implications of this genealogical historicization of the knower are pretty staggering. If the knower is an event in the history of human being, if it is formed out of disparate drives, interests, conflicts, and the random play of forces, the knower him- or herself cannot be pure and disinterested. Objectivity, then, is either an illusion altogether or very limited in scope. The knower is not just sometimes limited by non-epistemic factors; the knower is *completely conditioned* by non-epistemic factors. Knowing always takes place as an effect of non-epistemic forces.

Our knowledge is always partial, then, in both of two senses. It is partial in the sense that it is never complete and in principle can never be complete. And it is partial in the sense that it is interested in, invested in, some and not other epistemic possibilities. Some students of Nietzsche and Foucault assert from time to time that genealogy works simply by pointing out the incompleteness of dominant theories or histories, by offering equally plausible alternative accounts that highlight the partial (or the undecidable) nature of the "truths" we hold. This maneuver, they contend, destabilizes hegemonic discourses. I would argue, however, that if that were all genealogy did, it would hardly be empowering or effective as political critique. In fact, genealogy is not like describing some aspect of the world from some discounted or ignored angle. Genealogy works, when it works, not by claiming to describe a view or a set of events different from the one the dominant discourse describes but rather by redescribing the *same* set of events that the dominant discourse describes and, more importantly, *in a way that undercuts the dominant description of them*. This happens either because it does a better job of describing those events in accordance with the justificatory standards the dominant discourse employs or because it demonstrates that the dominant discourse somehow violates its own standards in its description. Usually a genealogy does both these things. Foucault's genealogy of sexuality reveals both that the historical data, treated historically, do not square with the claim that during the last three hundred years sex was repressed and that the dominant discourse's thesis of sexual repression, despite its claims to scientific neutrality, serves non-epistemic, political purposes. A genealogy functions as a critique of the dominant view, not merely as a supplement or a thought-provoking alternative.

Genealogy is a critical redescription of a dominant description. But then what is its epistemic force? Why should anyone believe the redescription over the description? Naive empiricists would say that the only reason to believe in either the description or the redescription is that one or the other is truer, meaning that one or the other corresponds better to the world. But that view commits one to the further view that there is a stable, real world behind the descriptions and to a theory of truth as correspondence between propositions and non-propositional, extralinguistic facts. Foucault refuses these commitments, as have a number of analytic epistemologists over the last three decades.[12] He asserts, with Nietzsche, that history is a series of interpretations and that interpretations are not "the slow exposure of the meaning hidden in an origin" but rather "the violent or surreptitious appropriation of a system of rules" (NGH, 151). Descriptions, or interpretations, are always redescriptions or reinterpretations.[13] There is nothing behind or beneath them that is not itself an interpretation; there is no nonlinguistic origin to which we could return to check the accuracy of our accounts.

But, if we are blocked from returning to some common but extralinguistic origin to check our interpretations against, how will we ever settle the matter of which description to believe? Aren't the two descriptions equally good, or bad, since they are equally ungrounded? Doesn't it just come down to a matter of personal opinion? Doesn't Foucault's work just degenerate into sophomoric relativism? These questions and their implied affirmative answers are frequently put forth in critiques of Foucault. But it is important to realize that Foucault's position does not necessarily lead to either relativism or nihilism. A story may help illustrate this point.

My second cousin Rory decided to close out his checking account and buy his family a new refrigerator. He reckoned that he had $500.32 in the bank, which he went down to the bank to request. When the teller, who happened to be his next-door neighbor Clara McMurtrie, informed him that he only had $487.18, he exclaimed "You're wrong, Clara, and I'll prove it to you. Let's go in the vault and count my money."

Unfortunately for Rory, bank accounts are not like safe deposit boxes. Since there is no physical money in a physical space, there was no fact of the matter that Rory and Clara could check. Still, no one would claim that the absence of any physical fact of the matter means that the dispute between Rory and the bank couldn't be settled or that any description of the amount of money to which Rory was entitled was equally good or bad as any other. How much money Rory should have gotten is not just a matter of personal opinion, and the international banking system is in no danger of degenerating into sophomoric relativism.

Traditionally, philosophers have defined knowledge as justified, true belief. Any proposition that is to count as knowledge must meet all three criteria. Many commentators in effect contend that Foucault operates with a set of epistemological principles that together amount to a system in which knowledge, so defined, is ultimately impossible. If he is right to assert that everything is just a redescription of a previous description rather than a description of, and founded upon, direct access to an extralinguistic world, some epistemologists would hold, then there's no way to tell the difference between descriptions that are true—that accurately describe how things are in themselves apart from the conditions of the events of (purported) knowing (which on Foucault's view include the politically interested perspectives that are the very conditions of possibility for the knowers)—and descriptions that are not true. Therefore Foucault undercuts any claim to knowledge, including his own. We knowledge-seekers are in no better position, then, than the man who has a disagreement with the bank. The facts of the matter are irrelevant, so what it comes down to is who can play the game of justification better, the man or the bank. If Rory couldn't find a mathematical error in the bank's record of his account and hadn't saved his deposit receipts so he could prove that there was a deposit that the bank failed to record, then the bank would win the game of justification, and Rory would get only $487.18. But the fact that the bank would have been able to produce more justification for its claim than Rory could produce for his surely doesn't *make* the bank's claim true. Justification, most people would hold, *indicates* truth; it doesn't *create* it. But, if every proposition is, as Foucault claims, just an interpretation of an interpretation, if we don't actually make claims about an extralinguistic world, then the truth-value of any given proposition must come not from its correspondence with such a world but rather from the place it occupies in relation to other propositions. So it would seem that Foucault might very well hold that winning the game of justification actually amounts to creating the truth of the proposition that justification was designed to support. Further, since standards for justification are set by the powerful (banks, not customers), it isn't a stretch to read Foucault as asserting that, in the final analysis, might makes right—not only in ethics but even in disciplines like accounting, mathematics, or physics.

Some people would probably contend that right made solely by might is no right at all—or, more to the point, that truths created by the very propositions designed to justify belief in them are no truths at all. Such people might feel inclined to say Foucault just doesn't believe in truth. Foucault himself says otherwise, however; shortly before his death he went so far as to assert, "All those who say that for me the truth doesn't exist are simple-minded" (CT, 295). We seem to be left, then, with the view that truth is relative, that a proposition is true if and only if it arises in a discursive context in which it can be justified according to the justificatory rules embedded in that context, the view that truth is relative to the justificatory rules (or procedures or practices) of a given context and can therefore vary with context.

Relativism of this sort is often dismissed as self-refuting. Indeed, it does appear to lead to some odd consequences. First, it leads to the possibility that a given proposition could be true in one context and not true or even false in another. It all depends on which justificatory procedures are in use, on what counts as evidence and reasonable argument, things that have in fact varied in our own cultural history. If we accept the theory that truth is relative, we are forced to hold that contradictory propositions, if justified, are true, which means that we inhabit a world where everything, even the laws of nature, may vary depending on what religious or scientific beliefs arise in a given culture. Second, defining truth as relative leads to the possibility that a true proposition could become a false one (or vice versa) in the same context if the standards for justification shift slightly. For example, there are some geneticists who say that the statistical standards used to determine whether a significant correlation exists between a strip of DNA and a complex behavioral trait need to be raised.[14] If truth is relative to justificatory standards and if they succeed in changing professional standards for justification of a claim of significant correlation, then some propositions in genetics that were true last month will be untrue or even false next month. Normally we would simply say that what we thought we knew we discovered we didn't actually know, not that the truth of the matter had changed; but if a proposition's truth is simply a matter of its justificatory status, then truth will change with changes in standards of justification. Finally, defining truth as relative to justificatory standards leads to the question of how to set the justificatory standards in the first place. If truth just amounts to whatever is justified under a given set of standards, we could get a lot more truth just by lowering our standards. But of course no one actually thinks we should do that.

Now, these three strange consequences are the sorts of things that epistemologists worry about and that other people will worry about if epistemologists get hold of them and start posing questions. My cousin Rory didn't, though, because he knew that truth wasn't really the issue in disputes like the one he had with the bank. The issue was how much money the bank was going to give him, or, in other words, the issue was what someone was going to do next, not what really and truly happened in the past. Clara might have believed—she might even have remembered—that Rory came in and made a deposit that the bank didn't record, but as an employee of the bank she has to follow the rules of procedure when she determines what amount of money to hand a customer. Rory, having no deposit receipt, insisted that he was in possession of a truth that the bank was denying because that was the only strategy available to him for getting the money he thought he deserved. And in fact it's a strategy that could work, because everybody down at the bank knows Rory and his reputation for honesty. In other words, Rory was simply appealing to a larger justificatory context, one that all the bank employees share with him, one that allows consideration of other kinds of evidence such as memories. And he was doing that in order to get Clara to behave differently than it first appeared she was going to behave.

Putting aside reality momentarily, however, let's assume the issue is determination of truth rather than determination of behavior. How should one decide which justificatory standards ought to apply in such a case? Are all standards equally good? Certainly not—at all kinds of non-epistemic levels. Edna wants the new refrigerator to be equipped with an ice maker, so Rory wants the standards from the larger community context to apply; that is, he wants to be able to include his memory, his known habits, and his good word in the justificatory mix. Those standards would work better for him. Clara is Rory's and Edna's neighbor and has an interest in their welfare, so she wants the standards and practices of the larger community to apply. Clara's boss Harry McNash wants to make as much money as possible and has other, less honest, customers to worry about, but he goes to the same church as Clara and Rory and Edna, and he knows that between them Rory and Edna count half the county as kin, so it may be in his interest, too, to let the larger community standards rule. But what about epistemic differences between the two sets of justificatory standards? Epistemically speaking, are the two sets of standards (one of which includes reported memories of habitually honest people as valid evidence and the other of which does not) equally good? If there is no fact of the matter outside of the context of justification, then this question seems to be unanswerable.[15] There is no purely epistemic reason to choose one set of standards over another if truth is generated within justificatory contexts. Thus, it seems, there is no way for propositions to be justified; hence, there can be no knowledge. If we imagine a contextless adjudicator who has no connection to Rory, Clara, or the international banking system, he/she/it will need a set of justificatory standards in order to choose a set of justificatory standards. We imagine that such a being would want to choose a set of standards that somehow accorded with truth, but if we say truth is generated within justificatory contexts at least in part by the justificatory standards themselves, that avenue is blocked. So we imagine our contextless adjudicator getting very frustrated. It doesn't matter which set of standards he/she/it chooses; all are equally good, because none is ultimately justified by reference to anything outside itself. *Voilà*, seriously ugly relativism, pointing to radical skepticism.

Fortunately, there is no such thing as a contextless adjudicator. Instead, there is Harry McNash. He lives in Rory's community. His beliefs and epistemic commitments have been shaped by that community just as Rory's and Clara's have. He is not faced with all possible sets of justificatory standards; he is faced with Rory and the bottom line. He will make a choice about whether to give Rory that extra $20.14. But he will not actually make a choice about which justificatory standards form his conception of the truth. His conception of the truth will simply be formed in accordance with the history of the community in which he was raised. He'll find himself holding a belief about that twenty dollars and that belief will stand as part of the context in which he decides how to act. Regardless of whether he lets Clara issue the money or not, he will go home that night and say to his wife Hilda that he is sure the bank owed Rory that extra cash. And Hilda—who is not from these parts because Harry met her when he went off to the University to study accounting—will ask why in the world he believes some crazy old coot who works swing shift at the GE plant. And Harry will answer, "Because I know Rory, and that's the end of it."

And that is the end of it for Harry. Justification goes no further. He simply does not doubt Rory's word. But it is not the end of it for foundationalist epistemologists. Harry's belief cannot be justified if the standards he uses to justify it are not themselves justified, and those standards cannot be justified if there is no truth independent of justificatory practices. Either there is a truth independent of contexts and practices, or justificatory chains are endless or circular (both of which will render them impotent). If Harry's standards for justification are not grounded in something epistemically viable, then his beliefs are not justified and he is bereft of knowledge altogether.

In *Between Genealogy and Epistemology*, Todd May reminds us that Ludwig Wittgenstein has a lot to say about justificatory practices and about radical skepticism. According to Wittgenstein, May points out, wholesale doubt of the sort foundationalists assume Harry ought to engage in as long as his standards go unjustified is just not possible. We have to hold some things exempt from doubt in order not only to proceed with our lives but also even in order to doubt anything. To doubt everything all at once, as foundationalists would have Harry do, "would remove any possibility of removing the doubt."[16] The whole epistemological enterprise would just end in nonsense.

This point is easier to see if we look at it from Rory's position. In the absence of a deposit receipt, Rory insists that he clearly and distinctly remembers visiting the bank, depositing a certain amount, and taking a certain amount in cash. While we know that memory is fallible, for Rory to doubt this particular memory is tantamount to opting out of the epistemic language-game altogether. For, if Rory incorrectly remembered depositing the usual amount from his paycheck, he would also have to have forgotten or to remember incorrectly a lot else besides: Clara would have noticed he didn't come to the bank on Friday as usual and would have leaned over the back fence to ask Edna if Rory was sick; Edna would have pitched a fit if Rory hadn't brought her her household expense money, and there wouldn't have been any groceries in the house for the next week. But Rory would have had to remember all that otherwise. Alternatively, maybe he did go to the bank but cashed the whole check instead of depositing any. But in that case he either would have the twenty dollars and fourteen cents on him now, or he would have spent it doing something unusual, which he would remember (or at least he would remember the hangover). For Rory to doubt that he deposited part of his paycheck on that Friday is for Rory to doubt his memory entirely, which is to doubt his sanity and the credibility of all those around him. If Rory does this, he ceases to be able to affirm or deny any proposition; he can't be sure of anything at all. The justification for Rory's belief that he deposited the money, then, is his memory of having done so. But that is not because memory serves as an indubitable epistemic foundation and perfect representation of a context-independent truth; it is because justification comes to an end where doubt ceases to make any sense. If there is no basis for doubt in a given context or if doubting would usher in total nonsense, we say we know. That is just how we do in fact use the words *to know*. Therefore May, following Wittgenstein, asserts that even if knowledge is justified, true belief, it is justification that matters rather than truth.

According to May, then, Foucault's critics are wrong. Even if they undermine all purported absolutes, Foucault's genealogies do not eliminate the possibility of knowledge and in fact can legitimately claim to correct our knowledge and to present new knowledge. What counts as real may indeed be relative to contexts and produced in networks of power, but propositions within contexts can still have truth-values relative to that context (in fact they can't have truth-values outside of contexts) and can still be justifiable. In short, knowledge is still possible. Foucault is not a nihilist; he is simply an anti-foundationalist. And that is all he needs to be for his genealogies to do the political work that he wants them to do. Genealogies simply undermine particular know-ledges or knowledge systems by casting doubt on claims that assert themselves as fully justified. By marshaling overlooked evidence, a genealogy shows a community of believers that those claims are not fully justified according to their own standards of justification. The choice then is either to give up those discourses or claims or to give up the standards of justification that ground both those claims themselves and the counterclaims that genealogy makes. Timeless, universal truth does not enter into the picture at all on this construal. Foucault can avoid saying anything about the true meaning of *truth*, because univer-sal truth at the genealogical level is simply irrelevant. Foucault doesn't need to attend to the foundationalist question of truth at all. He only has to show that his genealogical stories are better justified than those histories. And he typically does that very well.

Foucault's genealogies, then, do not undercut themselves. They do not throw us into an irrational tailspin where any belief is just as good as any other belief and where the only arbiter of right judgment is power. We can still legitimately claim to know various propositions—including the ones the genealogies put forth—and to place in doubt claims to know various others. In the context in which the reader and Foucault find themselves, Foucault's genealogical account of, for ex-ample, sexuality is epistemologically superior to what it attempts to displace. And the mere fact that Foucault's account also grows out of a particular perspective and particular interests does not invalidate it, since the problem with the dominant discourses on sexuality is not that they aren't objective and neutral (which is impossible) but rather that they have the particular values and interests and historical investments that they have.[17] In other words, not only is the genealogy epistemologi-cally superior, but it is politically superior as well if you happen to hold certain fairly basic and common political precepts.

Why, then, don't I—the sexual knower—feel completely safe yet? Why can I not rest assured and commit myself to this knowledge single-mindedly, with purity of heart? Why do I feel that discontinuity has been introduced into my very being? C. G. Prado contends that, though it is possible to make out a reasonable, epistemologically viable account of Foucault's genealogical work, nevertheless the threat of nihilism in his writing remains quite real.[18] I think Prado is right. The threat operates, right along with genealogy's knowledge-effects, to produce an experience of reading that is very different from that of reading a traditional historiographical text such as Katz's work. One undergoes a genealogical text as a knower, and one does not emerge the same.

Like Jonathan Katz's text, Foucault's text drew me in precisely because I wanted to know the final and total truth of sexuality. By reading it I hoped to learn what sexuality truly was. But because Foucault starts by examining society's demand (or individuals' drives) to confess our sexuality—whatever that sexuality may be—his book's effect was to turn the very energy of my desire or will to know back upon itself. In other words, the text operates by drawing in the desire to know the truth, but instead of telling us the truth, it offers us a genealogy of that very desire itself and a plausible account of how that desire to know, itself an effect of power, produces sexual identities, the objects of the knowledge that we crave. I wanted to know the truth about my sexuality, but what Foucault gave me was a genealogy of my wanting to know the truth about my sexuality. What Katz's text knows about sexuality is that there is a truth that heterosexist society has suppressed in order to maintain its hegemony. But what Foucault's text knows about sexuality is that knowing, including the text's own knowing, is an effect of power and is thus contingent upon a certain arrangement of force relations. And though that knowledge was repugnant to the precepts about knowledge that I happened already to hold, I found it impossible to resist.

A lot of energy had already gone into my pursuit of sexual truth. A lot of energy goes into any search for truth. But in a genealogical text, the energy of that desire for truth gets turned back on itself and works against itself again and again. With regard to any given historical object, the truth seems to be that there is no stable truth but only more and yet more social constructs and changing forms. There is no absolute origin and thus no epistemic stopping point. Though genealogy certainly produces knowledge-effects—for example, it may provide a ground for doubt of something that previously seemed indubitable—it does not aim to tell us the final truth about how things were, nor does it aim to isolate the laws of history in order to predict the future. Instead of taming the flux of time by drawing it together into one all-encompassing perspective and showing how, in fact, everything has really always at some level been "the same . . . Same . . . Always the same,"[19] genealogy will deprive us "of the reassuring stability of life and nature, and it will not permit itself to be transported by a voiceless obstinacy toward a millennial ending. It will uproot [history's] traditional foundations and relentlessly disrupt its pretended continuity" (NGH, 154). Genealogy is not about capturing and representing the world in language so that we can know it once and for all. For genealogical thinking, there is simply no conclusive judgment to draw. Therefore the will to truth, the desire to exercise final judgment, can never be satisfied.

Dissatisfaction, frustration of a desire, can have two different kinds of consequences. One is a loss of intensity, of energy. A desire may simply dissipate, become relatively unimportant, lose its power to configure a network of meaning or to command other desires. Another possible consequence, however, is that a desire's energy will turn back upon itself, return toward itself and thus intensify itself, although with a diverted aim. This is something that is especially apt to happen with a desire for truth. Turning inward, this desire may question itself, seek its own truth, ask about its own nature and value. Whence this drive for truth? Why truth? Why not rather untruth?

This kind of return (what Charles Scott calls a recoiling movement[20]) may well provide the motive force of Friedrich Nietzsche's work—from which Foucault takes the term *genealogy*. Nietzschean genealogy is born when the desire for truth begins to question itself or the value of its own object. In Nietzsche's writings new questions begin to take prominence; the desire for truth begins to ask after its own truth and its own value, which leads it to ask after its own history, its origins, its heritage. In *Toward a Genealogy of Morals*, Nietzsche puts forth the possibility that the modern, truth-hungry self—a complex, multifaceted, pluri-enfolded entity bearing with it memory, conscience, and the capacity for making promises—takes shape within the coalescences and tensions of a certain collection of drives, prominent among them being a kind of finicky concern with cleanliness. He tells the story this way:

Once upon a time there were great warriors, doers of deeds. If we were to look back at their world, we would see decisive, single-minded action performed by people with nerves of steel. But before we admire their self-control, we must look again. These men and women have no deep sense of themselves; they act without reflection. They are never hampered by self-doubt simply because they lack the interiority such questioning requires. They *cannot* reflect. They are hardly different from any other animals; in fact, Bataille's description of animals fits them quite well: They are "in the world like water in water."[21] And that would be the end of the story, except, Nietzsche continues, among these ancient nobles there are some whose impulses are frequently frustrated, who cannot succeed in combative displays of force, who cannot simply take whatever they want. Some of these physically inferior ones gradually settle down to a more routine life and, in the process, take account of their bodies in new ways. They begin to take care of themselves—for example, they bathe now and then; they refuse to eat raw meat; they cease to copulate randomly and may even insist that their partners wash. Over time, the more contemplative of these people make rules—rules governing diet and sex acts, menstruation, the disposal of corpses—by which they organize their lives and those over whom they have influence. In making these rules, this group of people—whom Nietzsche begins to call the priestly caste—empowers itself. It feels powerful in the act of creating rules, and if it can successfully impose those rules on itself and then on others, that sense of power is intensified. Perhaps some members of the group actually become more powerful physically by following some of the rules. They may be sick less often; they may live longer. Or they may not. Either way, by formulating rules and then abiding by them, this group of people produces for itself a sense of time, a sense of a future that could be at least partially governed by decisions made and acts performed in the present. And that sense, that sense of a now and a not-now, a presence *and an absence* that might be shaped, produces the kind of double consciousness that is the forerunner of all the powerful complexity of human mentality in the present day. Gradually this new kind of power, mental power, begins to compete successfully against brute strength.

Priests are dangerous animals, Nietzsche maintains. Unlike their more active, impulsive aristocratic counterparts, they can plan ahead, control their impulses—which means that, among other things, they can *lie*. Thus does evil come into the world. With the priests there can be deception, manipulation, ulterior motives, premeditated and concealed crime. It is here, "on the soil of this *essentially dangerous* form of human existence," as Nietzsche puts it, ". . . that man first became *an interesting animal*, . . . only here did the human soul in a higher sense acquire *depth* and become *evil*—and these are the two basic respects in which man has hitherto been superior to other beasts!"[22] Eventually the priestly caste—those men and women whose physical weakness had forced within them the development of a new kind of power—triumphed over the old aristocracy.

Nietzsche says this new kind of power came about more or less by accident out of nothing more significant than physical weakness coupled with a kind of simple-minded fastidiousness, a prissy repugnance in the face of dirt and disease. But gradually out of these preoccupations there emerged an unthinking dedication to purity itself, which in time took on a life of its own, becoming what Nietzsche calls a kind of instinct. Nietzsche names this new instinct or drive *asceticism,* and he suggests that it is the principal characteristic of the modern soul.

When we hear the word *asceticism* we tend to think of self-denial. But, according to Nietzsche, asceticism is not so much about self-denial as it is about the acquisition of some form of control, strength, power, and, interlocked with that, the intensification of the pleasures most closely associated with that process of acquisition. However, no drive becomes dominant, Nietzsche tells us, unless it is able to achieve (near) singularity. Whatever opposes the dominating motive or force must either be redirected to supplement it instead, or neutralized, or split off and renounced. (However, it would be a mistake to attribute agency to a drive in the early stages of its formation. Perhaps we might think instead of the spinning out of heavy gases from a star as it is born, and the forces of attraction and repulsion that gradually form planets, moons, asteroids, and comets—bodies in motion in relation to one another. Dominating drives would be those with the greatest force of attraction; they influence and give order to the rest.) Empowerment is a process of unification, then. It is also a process of sorting and separating out. Like "circling the wagons," the process of empowering produces a unified interior space over against a heterogenous exterior space. Sometimes in such a process, there comes to exist something we call an identity. Sometimes there constructs itself a unity that is "it," and a difference that is "not it." (The awkward grammar is deliberate; the unity does not precede the constructing.) When such a unity becomes self-conscious, the "it" becomes an "I" and the "not it" becomes "you," "world," "them," etc. Asceticism proper begins at the point at which the I seeks to further its own power by purifying itself of all that is not I.

Our culture is a result of the force of what Nietzsche calls the Ascetic Ideal. We are all formed in its shadow. We engage in ascetic practices of one or another sort almost all the time, but we are especially apt to engage in them when we feel weak and threatened, because through them we aim to fortify ourselves. For example, it is out of weakness that we pay careful attention to our bodies. Sick people and old people pay more attention to their bodies than anyone else, not because a sick body or an old body is intrinsically more fascinating than a strong, healthy body, but because sick people want to be as well as possible and old people want to preserve as much of their strength as possible. They take care of themselves in order to guard against more loss of energy and capacity, in order not to injure themselves or weaken themselves further. One must keep oneself away from whatever might dissipate one's energy, disrupt one's digestion, corrupt one's blood. (Younger people do this in anticipation of getting old, and healthy people out of fear of falling sick.) Weakness, therefore, gives rise to various sorting-out processes, to a desire to know what's what, what is good for me and what is bad for me, what is properly assimilated to my body and what is properly ejected, prohibited, and placed under taboo. The weaker we grow, the more fastidious we become. Like a weak body—and along with it, as another aspect of it—a weak will seeks to purify itself, to slough off whatever is extraneous, to rid itself of polluting thoughts, memories, feelings, desires.

When I was young, I wanted to be strong, to stand firm, to live a healthy life, but the homophobic discourses in which my self-consciousness arose were debilitating to me; they sickened me, sapped my strength of will, finally even threatened my existence. My story fits the Nietzschean story quite well. Weakness generates the strength of a desire for purity—my desire for a unified and true account of myself, my desire for a new and unwavering self built on a solid epistemological foundation, my desire to remake myself as a self that could have been a hero. My ascetic desire for a truth about my sexuality was what enabled Foucault to lure me into his genealogical discourse. But once I was there, the very discipline that had driven me there threatened to tear me apart, because it refused to disregard the epistemological implications of Foucault's treatment of sexual subjectivity. For genealogy resists being appropriated as an object, an objective discourse, for the consumption of a subject who does not change. Genealogy does not allow a neat division between subject and object at all. Genealogy blurs that distinction. Genealogy corrupts. The fact that Foucault raised questions I'd always asked myself but never saw anyone else raise and the fact that the answers he gave were bolstered by evidence that replicated the world I saw all around me had pulled me into his discourse at the level of epistemic argumentation. I was engaged with this work; I was convinced by it; I'd stood in judgment of the text, and I'd concluded that Foucault was right. But what, exactly, was he right about? Me? How does an ascetic self—a self formed and sustained in a will to truth and true identity and transcendent knowledge and judgment, a self whose perpetuation depends upon the unity of its drives—begin to think the truth that some significant part of itself is heterogenous? that its true identity is diversity? that its ownmost history is really a genealogical series of others?

I had wanted to believe that my sexuality was innocent and that only society's attempt to incorporate it into a finalized and totalized, unchanging yet empty form and to identify me fully with that emptiness was cruel and darkly motivated. My sexual desires and dreams and longings were my own; they were natural things, things apart from the corruptive influences of power. But now nothing was innocent. The wagons had not stayed circled. The outside—history, power, evil—had crept inside. It wasn't just these stupid and reductive categories that were historically and socially produced; it was sexuality itself. The very desires that I so vigorously defended against my enemies, the very desires that made my life worth living, those desires—their intensity, meaning, value, and importance in my life—were not first of all mine; they were first of all the consequences of generations of social and political struggles, administrative realignments, reinterpretations, historical accidents, and petty reactions. My desire—the energy that drove me and the relationships it enabled—was a product of sociohistorical networks of power. And my sexuality was not the only desire that was historically formed, that had a genealogy; even my desire for knowledge of that sexuality had a history, as did my desire for knowledge in general; my will to truth had a malicious past that it hardly liked to admit. I was contaminated by and guilty of the very things I condemned and struggled against. I was but the child of forces that I could not control.

All I wanted was to be honest, to live an honest life, to be true to myself. I wanted to cast off all the lies that people told about me and display myself in shining purity for what I really was. But the more deeply I delved into (or was pulled into) Foucault's genealogy, the crazier that project came to seem. In the process of trying to discipline myself to the historical truths it told, a whole bundle of tensions—contradictory drives, alien forces, random interventions—began to emerge. Even that venerable old philosophical ideal of true identity—perfect and complete integrity, incorruptibility—once thought genealogically, began to reveal itself as a product of weakness and fear and myriad other drives and events. It is not something pristine that we recall from a disembodied former state or an impression that God the Potter has fortuitously installed in our minds. Our belief in it is grounded neither in experience nor in reason, but rather in desire. And so, on its own terms, that belief must destroy itself; the ungrounded and ungroundable must be purged from the ascetic self. The energy that sustained the belief now turns against the belief in a self-violating movement that dissipates the power of the ascetic drives. This is the moment, the movement, of self-overcoming, the moment that genealogy tends to generate.

I recoiled. But I also believed. My truth, the truth about me, was that I was at heart not only the one I took to be me but many others as well. That historical multiplicity was me. And I had to accept that, learn to believe it, act in concert with it, discipline myself to order my life accordingly. That is what one does with truths; it is only right. To refuse to live by a truth one knows is to forfeit one's integrity, and I sure didn't want to do that. But how to order my life accordingly? What would that even mean? This truth—the truth that all self-identity, all permanence, all incorruptible truth is a fiction, an error, a lie—was unthinkable, and yet something like that was coming to voice in my undergoing of Foucault's discourse.⌉

It is possible to make sense of Foucault's work in the language of traditional analytic epistemology without being forced thereby to dismiss it as illogical or self-violating. With careful analysis it is possible to treat Foucault's genealogical claims as truth-claims and to evaluate them as such. In other words, it is possible (although it may be difficult) to read Foucault's history of sexuality in the same way that Jonathan Katz suggests his history of heterosexuality be read; we can take the text as an object within the field of knowable objects, and we can master its moves and claims. And if we do that, we might live our lives a little differently; we might change a few of the things we think and do. Katz hopes we will stop giving credence to heterosexuals' assertions of right dominance. But we ourselves will not undergo much change. We will still be the same people we always were, though a little braver and a little better outfitted for battle perhaps. In contrast, the kind of transforming work that Foucault's texts tend to perform occurs most significantly at the level of the reader, the knower, the knowledge-seeker, and not at the level of the logic of beliefs or of actions grounded in beliefs. If we take Foucault's texts as collections of truth-claims to be deciphered and assessed, we miss something very crucial. In fact, I would suggest, in doing that we refuse something, suppress something, protect ourselves against something. On that subject (speaking of lineages), I quote my dissertation advisor, *meinen Doktor-Vater*, as the Germans say:

> To think in this way is difficult because our dominant structures of language encourage the posture of standing outside of the text, in an interpretive position that is actually quite different from the text, and understanding it from a quasi-transcendent perspective. Such a perspective protects itself from the process of self-overcoming by its seemingly neutral distance. It is *quasi*-transcendent in the sense that the thought stands outside of the process in the text that is to be thought and yet seems to ground or give connective meaning to the text's rendering. . . . [T]his traditional interpretive position is closely related to the ascetic ideal and the experience of transcendence that is affiliated with it.[23]

Taking up the stance of the analytic evaluator is taking up the ascetic ideal, which is a means of protecting ourselves from the way the text operates to bring the reader, the subject of knowledge, *under the reader's own power and authority,* to the point of self-violation, self-overcoming.

To make Foucault's texts safe for analytic epistemology is to refuse to think with the texts, to refuse the thinking that the texts seek to usher in. But to give oneself over to the text and think with it is to risk a radical loss. The kind of thinking the text sets in motion endangers the very subject who undertakes to think. To think with a genealogical text is to give oneself, as knower, over to the process of self-overcoming, self-violation, and live within the de-centering of a way of being whose existence requires constant centrality.

With religious dedication I the Knower had pursued knowledge of my own identity, hoping always that the question "who am I?" would be answered with the fact: who I am. I was diligent; I was scrupulous; I strove to become free of corrupting bias and the pollutions of desire. And my work was rewarded. I got an answer to my question. But the answer to the question "who am I?" was: who I am not. What the knower was given to know was: "I am who I am not." Which meant: I now had to be who I could not be. *That* was the answer. And my integrity as a knower demanded that I integrate that into my identity somehow. A fissure had formed at the heart of things. Something had begun to happen to me that no amount of knowing would enable me to control.

My sister Ann and I were bored a lot. We were always being made to stay put in places where there was nothing to play with. So we made up games—like the mocking game. To play the mocking game, you take the last few words spoken to you—usually part of a command from the adult who banished you to this toyless void—and you say them very slowly, carefully enunciating every syllable. (If there is more than one player, you say them in unison.) Then you repeat the words, gradually increasing the speed with which you pronounce them. After the nineteenth or twentieth repetition, the words aren't words anymore, just bizarre sounds, and you have dissolved into peals of laughter.

It was as if life had started to play the mocking game. Suddenly the sternest of commands, the most solemn pronouncements of duty, the most sacred of truths had degenerated into nonsense, and this catastrophe had occurred not because of some evil outside force but rather by the sheer repetition of those lofty intonements themselves. And, while part of me was terrified and indignant and ready to dismiss Foucault as a raving relativist lunatic, another part of me had completely dissolved into peals of laughter. It was all very injudicious, but I couldn't help myself.

There was another part of me, too. In addition to the scandalized me that was anxious to retain its authority and the me that was incapacitated with childish hilarity, there was a me that was just utterly fascinated. That part of me smiled with unself-conscious admiration and asked: How did *that* happen? and what makes that *work*? What is this practice, this genealogy? When I wasn't looking at the world with the eyes of a graduate student, this genealogy, well, it wasn't a totally unfamiliar thing. I knew one of its cousins, a version of genealogy with which every Southern child is personally acquainted. Genealogizing is, if you'll pardon the expression, in our Southern blood. Whether we're black or white, male or female, rich or poor, gay or straight, our genealogies are of vital importance to us.[24] Anti-abortionists may insist all they like that a life begins at conception, but we know damn well it begins at least five generations prior to that. In the South you can't introduce yourself without saying where your people are from— "people" meaning ancestors as well as living relatives, "from" meaning the name of the county and the nearest landmark. And this is no simple listing of begetters and begotten-upons; there's at least one story to be told with every name, and the stories are the most important parts. The admiring part of me began to ponder that fact.

Outsiders—yankees, foreigners, and Floridians—often mistake the family tree for the genealogy. They think genealogies are charts, like animal pedigrees, and they make fun of us for putting so much stock in them. They think we trace our bloodlines back and then imagine we've inherited à la Lamarck the acquired characteristics of whichever British monarchs or Cherokee princesses we turn up along the way. They think genealogies are teleological and self-aggrandizing. But as has long been noted, yankees, foreigners, and Floridians tend to be short of time, if not of listening skills, and our genealogies often get too long for them. They quickly see what they take to be the facts, but in doing so they overlook some crucial things.

The practice of genealogy is integral to Southern communities; it *operates* there. Its functions are legion, but maybe one of its most general effects is to create a place for the unfolding of our lives; it sets a scene; it links past with present through names and designated landmarks. It enables us to recognize ourselves in a network of relations—familial, communal, political, linguistic, geographic. It enables us to communicate and to reinforce the values that have defined us as a family or a community or a people or a region for a very long time. At the same time, though, it enables us to recognize the extreme contingency of those values and those networks of relations and, therefore, the extreme contingency of our own lives and even of our own selves. Genealogizing as a practice carries with it an acknowledgment that selves are not naturally occurring entities and that identities are the sorts of things that can be both formed and overcome. You can lose yourself—for instance, if you go off to college and forget your raising. To be oneself requires participation in a communal practice of ongoing narration. Thus does genealogy carry with it always an acknowledgment that who one is can change.

Very few Southerners can trace their ancestry back to the antebellum aristocracy, much less back to British monarchs, and of course there was no such thing as royalty among the Cherokee. The overwhelming majority of us are the descendants of sharecroppers and slaves and those Cherokees, Choctaws, Chickasaws, and Creeks who could pass well enough to escape the long march to the Oklahoma Territory. Our families' and communities' consciousnesses were formed in the midst of misery, injustice, economic exploitation, war, occupation, terrorism, and all of it accompanied right up until the time of my own birth by crushing poverty. In a technologically deprived rural landscape, in the absence of any more than the most rudimentary education and of a literary and artistic and architectural heritage that in other communities forms the nodal points of meaning and gives coherence and objective existence to values, Southerners told (and tell) stories. Very often the stories bespeak those absences and along with them "the memory of hostile encounters which even up to this day have been confined to the margins of knowledge" (TL, 83), the memory of the conflicts that resulted in so much of that deprivation. The stories give us ourselves as contingent beings, as fallible beings, as finite beings, as endangered beings, as radically alterable beings, and virtually never as heroic beings.

One of my points of entry into Foucault's genealogy of sexuality was my desire to know the truth about myself, my desire for an account of my true identity. But there was another, simultaneous yet quite different, entry point: my familiarity with this old and often ridiculed practice of Southern genealogy, which involves an intimate acquaintance with both the formative power of discourse and the ever-present possibility, even the inevitability, that all that has been formed will undergo dissolution and be lost. Thus I was no stranger to genealogy's critical and transformational value and power.

By the time I read Foucault's and Nietzsche's genealogies I had been questioning my old family stories for many years. Telling them and retelling them, engaging their silences, supplementing and embellishing them to myself and for myself, I looked to them to weave for me a new communal fabric that could give place to the experiences that rent the old. There were no queers in my lineage. And I am sure that the stories bequeathed to me by my family and community were not meant by the people who told them to me to serve my efforts to live a queer life.

The rules and values and truths they saw shining through those stories probably totally precluded a life such as mine. My life probably would have bewildered and horrified all of them. Still would.

But whatever the intentions of the storytellers, the practice of genealogy doesn't really preclude anything. Foucault once wrote that history is a succession of systems of rules. "Rules," he said, "are empty in themselves, violent and unfinalized; they are impersonal and can be bent to any purpose. The successes of history belong to those who are capable of seizing the rules, to replace those who had used them, to disguise themselves so as to pervert them, invert their meaning, and redirect them against those who had initially imposed them . . ." (NGH, 151). We don't make up totally new rules; we rearrange the ones already there until a new world emerges. And new selves emerge in the process. Let me change the word *rule* to the word *story* and finish Foucault's sentence: "The successes of history belong to those who are capable of seizing these stories, to replace those who had used them, to disguise themselves so as to pervert them, invert their meaning, and redirect them against those who initially told them; controlling this complex mechanism, they will make it function so as to overcome the storytellers through their own stories." There's no doubt that my good Southern family oppressed me almost to the point of death right along with all the other institutions that tried to exploit and then obliterate me. But the stories don't belong exclusively to them; the stories don't really belong to anyone. And the stories know that. They have no proper owner or place, no particular right order, no hidden or intrinsic meaning. Family stories are open-ended matrices of meanings constantly interpreting themselves through their tellers.

Human history, Foucault following Nietzsche tells us, "is a series of interpretations" (NGH, 152), a succession of re-told stories. Southern genealogy is an interpretive process, the undergoing of which makes and un-makes and re-makes selves as it makes and un-makes and re-makes communities and worlds. One may understand this as one engages in that practice and undergoes that process—or one may not. In Nietzsche's and Foucault's genealogical practices there are self-conscious attempts to make interpretive processes part of the ongoing process of interpretation. Nietzsche speaks of *"wirkliche Historie,"* "effective history." By this he means a discipline of historical enquiry that effects, produces, does something, that brings something about as opposed to a discipline of historical enquiry that aims only to record, in passivity, what is produced somewhere else.[25] Effective history is history that is a part of history, that is itself historical. If we want to think the Southern practice of genealogy, for example, to come to understand it and its place in a culture and among a collection of peoples, we will have to think genealogically, not epistemologically. We will have to stop looking for the definitive truth. We will have to let go of "a super-historical perspective," stop trying to engage in a discipline of historical enquiry "whose function is to compose the finally reduced diversity of time into a totality fully closed upon itself . . . whose perspective on all that precedes it implies the end of time, a completed development" (NGH, 152). In Nietzsche's and Foucault's discourses, the processes of interpretation are becoming self-conscious, are becoming self-interpreting. And in doing so they are becoming self-transgressive and are opening toward something they themselves cannot master and cannot be.

The undergoing of these discourses is transforming, and that is frightening. But if we want to resist slavishly trying to live the way others have told us we must, if we want to be different people from the people we have been made to be—and I wanted that far more than I ever wanted any truth—we must break the hold that the ideal of finalized and timeless truth has upon our souls. We must learn to think history genealogically. Awareness of the openness of matrices of meaning must play among the meanings themselves. That is what genealogy, as a philosophical practice, is about. Therefore, "[t]he purpose of history, guided by genealogy, is not to discover the roots of our identity but to commit itself to its dissipation" (NGH, 162). All claims to timeless identification are suspect in genealogical practice. Such claims are the enemies of genealogy, because they seek to foreclose interpretation or to deny its disruptive play. As the ascetic will to truth undergoes the genealogical movements of Nietzsche's or Foucault's texts, as it is made first to embrace its own "truth," the "truth" that it has no final truth, its own history comes to be exposed. As I read Foucault's genealogy of sexuality, my own desire for a real and final truth of my sexual self and of sexuality per se was exposed as itself an historically emergent desire bound up inextricably with the powers that it believed itself to be in rebellion against. As the impurity of that desire for truth revealed itself, its energy dissipated. In the midst of the self-overcoming movement of genealogy, I no longer felt compelled to know, once and for all, the essence of anything. And in the dissipation of that all-encompassing organizing compulsion, other concerns gained strength.

3

Why I Shouldn't Like Foucault . . .
So They Say

So there I was, in dissociating subdivisions, frightened and appalled by Foucault's genealogical assault on knowledge and the integrity of the knowing self, but simultaneously wickedly delighted by his disruption of established order and genuinely awed by the complexity and power of the mechanisms he used to do all that. I no longer read Foucault just because I wanted to know something about sexuality. Now I read Foucault for a whole collection of reasons, some of which were at odds with others. I read because I wanted to find a way out of the conclusions about knowers and knowledges that his works drove me to accept; I was caught up in the epistemological claims his discourse makes, and the only way out, if there was one, was just to go straight on through. I read for the same reason I watched Schwartzenegger movies: I wanted to see more things blow up. Just as the child was delighted by reducing the adult's words to absurdity, the former mental patient was delighted by the critique of psychiatric power, the felonious sodomite was delighted by the critique of criminological practices, and the feminist lesbian was delighted by the critique of sexual institutions. Finally, of course, I read because I was just plain fascinated by genealogy itself. I wanted to understand how it worked and to experience its transformative power—not with any particular end in view, but just for the sheer pleasure of understanding and of undergoing transformation.

In 1984, when I decided to write my dissertation on Foucault, many of my fellow grad students expressed skepticism. The men wanted me to explain why I thought Foucault's work was more valuable than Marx's or Rawls'; the women wanted me to explain why I thought Foucault's work was worth more of my time than the feminist theorists we were all reading then. I tried to avoid such conversations or get out of them quickly, because the truth was I couldn't justify my interest. All I could say was I felt that something important was happening there.

It was a little like going off to college and then going back home and having people ask you what you learned. You feel like some major transformation is underway in the depths of your soul, but with home folks you get tongue-tied. It just doesn't translate. After you are home awhile, you start to fear you haven't learned anything after all and college was just a dream. You can't justify to anybody why you're spending your time there anymore and why you're working so hard to pay for a private education when you could go to the community college or the voc/tech school. They say college ruins people. College-educated people can't speak plain English, can't relax, can't get along with ordinary folks. They say college will alienate you (only they don't use that word); it'll make you unfit to live in your own community. It'll rob you of your identity and your faith; it'll make you an atheist. \o \

I'm in no position to refute those claims. Education is transformation, and transformations are dangerous. Processes of transformation are in part processes of destruction. To be born again one must first die. Dionysus must suffer the agony of being torn to bloody shreds by those he most loves and trusts. To give oneself over fully to a transformative process is to risk absolutely everything with no guarantees. In any transformative process some part of us will cease to exist. Prudent people, therefore, resist giving themselves over to transformative processes completely. They don't immerse themselves in anything they don't fully grasp, at least in outline, in advance. Prudent people pay attention to criticism.

Foucault's work did not lack critics even in my small circle of acquaintances in 1985. They complained that the work is too hard to read; the prose is too dense and so is probably just a smoke screen for poor reasoning or no reasoning at all. "Why can't he write like ordinary philosophers?" they asked, and the question doubled as an accusation. Many were quick to tell me that Foucault's ideas are menacing to radical politics and the power of marginalized people. If I failed to find them so, then I failed to understand either my own interests or the real implications of his analyses. Foucault, they contended, attacks the very foundations of movements for women's and sexual minorities' rights, the cornerstone of feminist and of queer community, and even the conditions for the possibility of controlling my own life. They alleged that he attacks the very grounds of normativity, of moral judgment, which means he undermines the notion of justice; that he attacks the notion of identity, both personal and communal; that he attacks the notions of subjectivity and agency, and therefore he undermines autonomy. If we stop believing in justice, detractors ask, how can we demand that our oppressors respect us? If we stop believing in sexual identity, how can we come together to build queer community? If we stop believing in the sovereign subject, how can we claim responsibility for our actions and hold our oppressors responsible for theirs? They warned me that if I kept studying Foucault's work, I'd be fooled into repudiating the most basic aspects of my self: my identity as a woman, as a lesbian, as an autonomous agent, and as a philosophical seeker of truth. In other words, if I kept studying Foucault's work, I would become alienated from the only communities where I could ever expect to find any kind of emotional home. Worse still, I might actually further Foucault's cause, thereby doing to others what Foucault had done to me. I would participate in a project that, if successful, would destroy feminist and queer communities and along with them any possibility for liberation. For, if Foucault triumphs, critics assert, radical political movements will never be able to press their agendas to victory and transgressive individuals will never be able to come together and affirm themselves; society will remain as it is (or get worse), which means the radical right will win and those of us classified as sexual outlaws will live out our lives at the mercy of the likes of Jesse Helms.

The prospect of a future that resembles the present is extremely unpleasant. I live in a state that classifies most sexual acts as felonies and thus defines me as an habitual, hardened criminal[1]; this means that if I offend anyone for any reason I can be eliminated from the political playing field. I live in a state in which a parent who has not even been convicted of sodomy can lose custody of her child simply because she acknowledges having had sex with another woman[2]; a state in which same-sex couples are barred from applying for state-administered low-income housing loans and from filing cases in domestic relations court[3]; a state in which no citizen has legal protection from heterosexist harassment (in fact such harassment of gays, lesbians, bisexuals, and transgendered people is routinely carried out not only by skinheads but also by the police, the legal system's own agency)[4]; a state in which writing these words—which could be construed as confessing a crime—could cost me my job (and therefore my medical insurance and therefore quite possibly my life). The stress of daily life outside the social contract—in a marginal region that is exterior to the public, political sphere but where privacy is nonexistent under the law—takes its toll. Neither I nor anyone else occupying a similar position wants to prolong this state of affairs. And certainly we do not want a return to the past. John D'Emilio's account of queer existence during the Cold War makes the present seem by contrast like Gay Day at Disneyland. In 1953, soon after his inauguration, Eisenhower "issued an executive order that made homosexuality necessary and sufficient grounds for disbarment from federal employment. . . . Corporations under government contract applied to their workers the security provisions of the Eisenhower administration."[5] The military stepped up efforts to eliminate homosexuals from the services; thousands of people were dishonorably discharged. The Post Office undertook a campaign of extralegal harassment. "Postal inspectors joined pen pal clubs that were often used by male homosexuals as a way of meeting one another, began writing to men they believed might be gay, and if their suspicions proved correct, placed tracers on the victim's mail to locate other homosexuals."[6] The Post Office's objective was to inform the men's employers of their sexual orientation so that the employers could fire them.[7] Verbal harassment is bad enough, and verbal threats of physical harm are worse still, but surveillance undertaken for the purpose of denying American citizens a livelihood is a form of physical violence. During the Cold War the U.S. government itself visited that kind of violence on its own citizens.

I know my interests are better served by strong anti-heterosexist political movements and by strong queer communities than by any critique that would render those possibilities null. I just don't believe Foucault's work pushes things in that direction. Still, while the parts of me that were wickedly delighted with or deeply awed by Foucault's work were unconcerned that a successful Foucault might mean trouble down the road, both me the threatened subject-of-knowledge and me the wary self-preservationist-in-the-face-of-adversity decided some of those criticisms might bear looking into. Maybe if I could answer the critics, I could satisfy some of my own questions. Furthermore, the me who is annoyed-with-anyone-who-tries-to-tell-me-what-to-do thought maybe if I could answer the critics they might shut up and leave me alone.

Accordingly, I gave rein to the maliciously meticulous-scholar me, who proceeded to isolate three lines of criticism typically aimed at Foucault: (1) Foucault leaves us with no criteria for preferring one set of values or courses of action over another; thus we cannot justify our political agenda any more credibly than proponents of the status quo can justify theirs. In the absence of clear justificatory hegemony, since the status quo is almost always materially more powerful than its opposition, its policies will prevail. The main reason why Foucault's work leaves us in this undesirable position is that it undermines humanism and puts nothing comparable in its place. (2) Foucault's work destabilizes agency. It brings into question the very possibility of individual freedom, because it suggests that one can never get free of power relations and it gives no account of how to develop agency within networks of power. Foucault's universe seems to be fully deterministic. Thus, further, it offers no affirmation of the potential agency (freedom, self-determination) of oppressed people. Further still, since it denies agency even in our opponents, it eliminates our justification for holding oppressors responsible for their actions. (3) Foucault's work destroys the basis for community, which is the basis for political action. This worry typically comes to the fore when critics examine Foucault's suggestion that identities—both individual and collective—are the products of power and that subjectivity is subjection. On Foucault's view, they say, identity is something we ought to resist, not something we ought to affirm and reinforce by building communities.

If any of these criticisms hold, then my fascination with Foucault's work was a dangerous thing indeed. For although in the midst of genealogical movements of self-overcoming it might seem to me that there occurred a sort of expansive freeing as old ways of thinking and old demands and questions died away, if the critics were right then in fact my range of possibilities for thinking and acting effectively would really be constricting. My sense of freedom would be an illusion. Self-transformation would amount only to self-defeat. I didn't believe these criticisms could hold, but they were so widespread that I had to address them.

SECULAR HUMANISM AND THE QUESTION OF THE HOLOCAUST, OR WHY CAN'T FOUCAULT TALK LIKE ORDINARY FOLKS?

The first criticism—that Foucault leaves us with no criteria for choosing among competing sets of values—was common in the early 1980s. (This debate over criteria for ethical judgment in fact parallels the debate over criteria for epistemic judgment discussed in chapter 2.) Dozens of articles from that period present this criticism, and it still circulates. I've come to refer to it as "The Holocaust Question," because it was so often put in this way: "Foucault has no basis upon which to condemn Hitler and the Holocaust, right?" Of course everyone wants to be in a position to condemn Hitler and the Holocaust, so if Foucault's analysis prevents that, clearly we ought to reject Foucault. Not to be in a position to condemn Hitler and the Holocaust, so the subtext of this question seems to run, would be to be in a position from which no value judgments whatsoever could be justified. And that would certainly be a dangerous position to occupy, especially if one is already outcast and oppressed. Of all the works that make this criticism, I was most fond of two: Michael Walzer's 1983 article "The Politics of Michel Foucault" and Nancy Fraser's 1985 article "Michel Foucault: A 'Young Conservative'?"[8] For purposes of analysis, I take them as exemplary.

Michael Walzer makes his main criticism of Foucault most explicit at the end of Part IV of his essay:

> For [Foucault] morality and politics go together. Guilt and innocence are the products of law just as normality and abnormality are the products of discipline. To abolish power systems is to abolish both moral and scientific categories: away with them all! But what will be left? Foucault does not believe, as earlier anarchists did, that the free human subject is a subject of a certain sort, naturally good, warmly sociable, kind and loving. Rather, there is for him no such thing as a free human subject, no natural man or woman. Men and women are always social creations, the products of codes and disciplines. And so Foucault's radical abolitionism, if it is serious, is not anarchist so much as nihilist. For on his own arguments, either there will be nothing left at all, nothing visibly human; or new codes and disciplines will be produced, and Foucault gives us no reason to expect that these will be any better than the ones we now live with. Nor, for that matter, does he give us any way of knowing what "better" might mean.[9]

Since Foucault does not believe human nature is a given, a foundation on which to erect a stable set of values, there seems to Walzer to be no way for Foucault to establish any system of values at all and therefore no basis for him to make any moral decisions or take any political action. Without humanism, there is nihilism.

Walzer's reading operates by impaling Foucault's texts on the horns of a dilemma: Either they advocate the abolition of all networks of power/knowledge, including science and morality, or they are remiss for giving us no account of how to decide among various systems of power/knowledge. Initially Walzer seems certain that Foucault is not calling for abolition of every possible way of ordering the social world; for down that road lies . . . nothing at all, or at least nothing recognizably human, since Foucault holds that humanity is socially constructed. However, Walzer asserts, if Foucault believes we should resist some networks of power/knowledge and not others, he ought to provide some "principled distinction"[10] between good power/knowledge networks, those we ought to support or establish, and bad ones. But of course, as Walzer makes clear, making that kind of distinction seems to be ruled out since Foucault insists upon "blurring the line between guilt and innocence,"[11] between good and bad. Foucault isn't simply holding back his criteria for distinguishing between networks of power; rather, given his views, he can't possibly have any criteria. Thus, "Foucault's position is simply incoherent."[12] His work seems to be nothing more than an unreasoned reaction against whatever social order presently prevails. In other words, Foucault talks nonsense.

Walzer's interpretation of Foucault's reticence regarding normativity leads us right back to the first horn of the dilemma, and once again it seems that, if he is consistent, Foucault must really be advocating abolition of all social orders. We are going in a circle, then, whose motion Walzer attributes to Foucault. The next step, a familiar one because we have taken it before, is to notice that Foucault cannot really be an anarchist, because, unlike anarchists, he does not believe in a natural human being apart from social order; in the absence of social order there would be nothing human at all. So he owes us criteria, but his position precludes criteria, so he must be an anarchist, but . . . and on the circle goes. Walzer assumes Foucault does not advocate the abolition of all social order, because he would never advocate the abolition of human being.

But why assume that? I won't argue that Foucault wants to abolish all social orders; he doesn't. What he rejects is Walzer's call for universal criteria for moral judgment. However, in Walzer's (unacknowledged) assumption that preservation of the human is a categorical imperative lies an important clue to his reading of Foucault. Walzer's reading is carried on in the absence of any reference to Nietzsche, an absence so striking, given Foucault's close intellectual kinship with Nietzsche, that one might even call it a repression. Juxtaposed with Walzer's assumption, let us consider a passage from *Toward a Genealogy of Morals* where Nietzsche describes the birth of the modern soul: "From now on, man is *included* among the most unexpected and exciting lucky throws in the dice game of Heraclitus' 'great child,' be he called Zeus or chance; he gives rise to an interest, a tension, a hope, almost a certainty, as if with him something were announcing and preparing itself, as if man were not a goal but only a way, an episode, a bridge, a great promise."[13] For Nietzsche, man is never an end in itself to be protected at all costs. How, then, can we assume that anyone as steeped in Nietzsche's work as Foucault is unquestioningly committed to the preservation of "human being"? It is clear in his early book *The Order of Things* that Foucault, too, understands "man" to be a category generated within a certain power/knowledge network that is in the process of breaking down. Yet Walzer's construal of Foucault's position erases that line of thinking completely. Walzer's Foucault must have a surreptitious commitment to the eternality of the category "human being"; otherwise the dilemma he says Foucault is caught in simply doesn't exist. But whose commitment is this? Not Foucault's. It's Walzer's own, and his unacknowledged insistence upon the preservation of the category of "the human," his refusal to see it as questionable, is profoundly influential in his (mis)reading of Foucault.

It is especially repugnant to Walzer that Foucault describes power as both nonsubjective and intentional. (His annoyance is most evident when he implies that Foucault's description of power relations is nonsense: "I don't know what that sentence means. . . ."[14]) Foucault claims that widespread, complex disciplinary structures are not the product of any person's plan, an assertion Walzer finds incredible: "Foucault seems to disbelieve in principle in the existence of a dictator or a party or a state that shapes the character of disciplinary institutions" and, therefore, "Foucault desensitizes his readers to the importance of politics."[15] Clearly for Walzer politics consists, primarily if not entirely, in confrontations between subjects—the revolutionary against the dictator, the workers against the capitalists, the prisoners against the wardens. And in those confrontations, Walzer maintains, the subjects who exercise the most power are the ones who organize the political context; the dictators, capitalists, and prison officials are in control. In order to preserve this understanding of politics, Walzer goes so far as to personify (to subjectify) institutions, such as political parties and governments. However they occur—whether natural or socially constructed, individual or collective—subjects constitute politics, not vice versa; subjectivity is logically prior to power, so the category "the subject" can't be included in political critique.

It is because Walzer can't imagine questioning the category "the human" that he can't understand politicizing the subject as Foucault does. What is at work, then, in Walzer's reading of Foucault is an unselfconscious humanism that simply renders much of Foucault's analysis opaque. It is this humanism that leads Walzer into the circle of reasoning he attributes to Foucault. He thinks he has impaled Foucault on the horns of a dilemma and thereby pinned down and neutralized his work; he thinks Foucault is caught because he must reject the first alternative, since to embrace it means the abolition of the human, and he must reject the second alternative, since to embrace it means to abandon politics or sacrifice any claim to rationality—because in the absence of logical criteria for decision one cannot act *"with reason."*[16] But if we don't start with the humanistic assumptions that (1) political action is always the work of a logically prior subjectivity and (2) good actions are always premeditated, reasoned actions based on universalizable normative criteria, then the dilemma in which Walzer locates Foucault is no dilemma at all. Foucault is not going in a circle; he is just going boldly where Walzer does not want anyone to go.

I confess I take pleasure in seeing humanists sputter and protest. In that respect I am faithful to my upbringing. Every good Southern Protestant's eyes narrow at the words *secular humanism*. It's a reflex. Many of us have forgotten the cause of this physiological manifestation of suspicion, but there is one: The point of secular humanism is to do away with God.

Now, there have always been people who've done without God. They're called sinners. They have no morals; they smoke and drink and dance and cuss and make a mess of their lives. Therefore they're easy to pick out of a crowd and teach children to avoid. Secular humanists, though, are another animal. They are insidious, because they do without God and still act like moral, upright citizens. You can't pick them out of a crowd; they might turn up anywhere; and no matter how well you raise your children they might end up taking a secular humanist as a role model. (This is why you hope your kids will go to the community college or the voc/tech school rather than the private university, even the church-affiliated one.) Secular humanists set man up in place of God; they make man the repository and foundation of all values. Secular humanists are idolaters. So say my forebears. And so say I. No point in setting up yet another God. Besides, I figure if you're going to reject Jehovah, you at least ought to get to drink and cuss and dance. What's the point of atheism if you're still saddled with morality?

The humanistic framework that forms part of the background of Walzer's criticisms is brought into the foreground in Nancy Fraser's much more subtle treatment of Foucault. Fraser is willing to acknowledge that rejection of the category "the human" is a logical possibility. Her question is whether Foucault has realized that possibility in such a way that a reasonable person might be justified in following his lead. We must note that, explicitly at least, Fraser's question is not about whether a reasonable person might reject humanism; it's about whether Foucault is justified in *his* rejection of humanism. Her answer is no; Foucault has failed in at least two important ways: He has failed to show that a pragmatic, historically sensitive humanism is ineffective, and he has failed to provide an alternative theory of valuation, which means that he cannot ground his own nonhumanist critiques. In short, without humanism or some meta-ethical substitute, we have no way of answering the Holocaust Question, no way of justifying the high values we place on some things and the low values we place on others.[17]

Fraser implies that if we reject humanism, we must first have a good reason for doing so. Her critique of Foucault assumes that we must take our leave from humanism rationally; we cannot simply start somewhere else. Only two kinds of reason for departure are permissible: Either all forms of humanism are proven to be incoherent or ineffective, or some other way of grounding political action is proven to be more coherent or more effective. These assumptions, I would argue, leave us bound to humanism by making humanism itself, with its insistence upon a rational subject, the measure by which all other political theories, analyses, or approaches are to be evaluated. They effectively enshrine the values and methodological preoccupations of humanism and prohibit experimentation. Most importantly, they render humanism itself inaccessible to critique, since the only critique it would accept would be one carried out under the terms it imposes and controls.

But are Fraser's assumptions true? If we are to get out, must we *reason* our way out of humanism? And must we substitute something similar to rationalistic humanism in its place if we are to have a viable political strategy? In a 1981 article Fraser herself makes the following observation: "Foucault's analysis entails that modern power touches individuals via the various forms of constraint constitutive of their social practices, rather than primarily via the distortion of their beliefs. Foucault dramatizes this point by claiming that power is in our bodies, not in our heads. Put less paradoxically, he means that practices are more fundamental than belief systems when it comes to understanding the hold that power has on us."[18] Fraser seems to agree with this description of how power works. She sees "Foucault's vivid reminder of the priority of practices [as] a useful corrective to the potential one-sidedness of even more sophisticated versions of the politics of ideology critique."[19] Why, then, does she also seem to expect Foucault to exercise power through his texts primarily at the level of rational persuasion? Wouldn't it make much more sense, even on Fraser's reading, to look for political value in what his texts *do* rather than primarily in the arguments they advance?

The truth of Fraser's observation is perhaps clearest in *Discipline and Punish*, where Foucault describes two competing theories of punishment that emerged in Western Europe and North America in the late eighteenth century, both of them in opposition to the monarchical power that had been in effect for several centuries. Both models, in contrast to the old monarchical model, favored thrift rather than excess in punishment; both placed a high value on cost-effectiveness in several registers—that is, on punitive efficiency. The main difference between the two lay in the specification of the target of penal intervention. For the liberal advocates of judicial reform, efficient punishment aimed at the mind and its ideas or "representations"; a good penal system operated so as to create an automatic link between the idea of a legal infraction and the idea of its punishment and thus to deter any rational person from crime. But for the advocates of mechanical and later normalizing discipline, efficient punishment aimed at bodies and behaviors; a good penal system operated so as to produce docile bodies in the habit of obedience. Foucault argues that it is the second mode of organization of power that prevailed as penal institutions were established in the late eighteenth century and that this mode of organization of power quickly metastasized. Power in the institutions that developed through the nineteenth century tended to act not so much on the mind and its representations as on the body and its gestures, not so much on reasoning as on doing.

What if Foucault is right about this? Insofar as power still operates that way, would we not then always be doomed to fail if we always combat power networks solely or even primarily at the level of ideas? Might we not need to practice, rather than to reason, our way out of whatever it is that causes us debilitating pain? And if that is so, then might humanism, with its insistence on rationality and autonomy, simply reinforce the power networks that currently oppress people . . . like me? Maybe Foucault has good grounds for refusing to reason with humanism and for refusing to put in place something sufficiently like humanism to do the job that humanism does. Maybe humanism's job is a job better left undone. Maybe humanism just keeps us all impotently bound to produce interventions at the level of ideology, while politics is carried on by other means.

But whether Foucault is right or wrong in this hypothesis, his assertion of it is grounds for our reading Foucault's highly politically charged texts as something other than reports of careful reasoning or efforts at moral or political intervention at the level of ideas. I, for one, could see the political power of Foucault's texts as long as I read them in the context of my concrete history and corporeal experience. I experienced both the danger and the power of Foucault's works most directly and sharply not in those moments when I appraised them rationally, but in those moments when I let go of my insistence on objectivity and judgment and just let them do their work on the concrete, embodied, historical me. In the second volume of his *History of Sexuality* Foucault makes some important remarks that support my contention that it is practices, not ideas, that his writings address and seek to change. "There is always something ludicrous in philosophical discourse when it tries, from the outside, to dictate to others, to tell them where their truth is and how to find it, or when it works up a case against them in the language of naive positivity," he writes. "But it is entitled to explore what might be changed, in its own thought, through the practice of a knowledge that is foreign to it" (HS2, 9; UP, 15). This *practice* of knowledge—which Foucault contrasts with the mere construction, presentation, and critique of rational arguments—is "an 'ascesis,' *askesis,* an exercise of oneself in the activity of thought" (HS2, 9; UP, 15). This is a self-transformative, self-overcoming practice, whose purpose is "to learn to what extent the effort to think one's own history can free thought from what it silently thinks, and so enable it to think differently" (HS2, 9; UP, 15).

As practice, as exercise, this textual operation does not differ in form from the disciplinary power that Foucault describes in *Discipline and Punish,* which is figured there as transformative exercise whose target is the behavior of bodies (DP, 161; SP, 163). Thus, just as pedagogical intervention in the life of a schoolchild is an event of power, Foucault's own textual interventions in his (and perhaps his readers') thinking is an event of power. Power in both cases occurs as exercise and transforms behavior. After a program of repetitive but graduated tasks, the schoolchild has the ability to do new things; after a program of philosophical *askesis* the philosopher has the ability to do new things. In both cases there is an augmentation of forces, a strengthening, an empowerment. But in the latter case—as I have argued elsewhere[20]—disciplinary power, rather than reinforcing its own mechanisms of control, undermines and perhaps displaces itself in the self-overcoming movement that is its own disciplinary self-transformation. Whereas the disciplinary networks that ensnare the schoolchild or the factory worker operate primarily through transformative exercise that is supervised and enforced by some agent other than the child or worker and according to a known and specified goal, Foucault's *askesis* cannot have a known and specified goal since what is to be transformed is not only the object but also the very agent of *askesis* itself, and it is to be transformed in its very identity as knowing subject. I will return to this question of Foucault's *askesis,* but for now I simply want to emphasize that Foucault understands his texts to be exercises of power whose points of intervention are practices, behaviors, and gestures, not ideas, not representations, not reason stripped of corporeality. My reading of Foucault differs from Walzer's and Fraser's in that it does not expect that Foucault's political efficacy will emerge first of all or primarily at the level of good judgment, and thus it is not motivated by a desire for normative criteria. "How am I to judge?" has just ceased to be a question of paramount concern in my undergoing of Foucault's texts. Furthermore, the relative unimportance of that question does not rob the works of political force but may, on the contrary, enable the political force that they have. After all, I hardly need to *decide* I ought to resist heterosexism; I just find myself doing it; in fact, as I discussed in chapter 1, I was and am formed as a subject within resistance to it. If humanists require that *before* I resist I must justify my doing so—that I use *their* terms and concepts, speak *their* language—they subvert my political energy and annihilate my resistance altogether. What appears politically questionable, then, are the assumptions and requirements embedded in humanist critiques themselves. Indeed, *I* cannot reason my way out of humanism, since humanism precludes my particular existence from the outset. I cannot start with humanism, then, even as a departure point; it is imperative that I start somewhere else. The fact that Foucault starts elsewhere means new possibilities are opened and questions themselves—not simply answers—are transformed.[21]

AUTONOMY AND SUBJECTION: OR, THE FREE WILL V. DETERMINISM DEBATE REVISITED

A second type of criticism of Foucault is articulated in one of its more sophisticated forms by Linda Alcoff in her article "Feminist Politics and Foucault: The Limits to a Collaboration." Alcoff is specifically concerned with Foucault's value for, as she puts it, "an effective feminist emancipatory project,"[22] but she believes that the problems she sees in Foucault's work would be equally harmful "for any emancipatory project,"[23] feminist or otherwise. Presumably, then, if Alcoff's reading is plausible and her criticisms significant, Foucault's texts are of no more use to sexual outcasts than they are to heterosexual feminists and may even be detrimental to both political movements.

In an interview in the mid-1970s, Foucault made a comment that Alcoff finds extremely problematic and on which she focuses much of her critique. It concerns the analytic status of subjectivity in Foucault's genealogical work and culminates in this sentence: "One has to dispense with the constituent subject, to get rid of the subject itself, that's to say, to arrive at an analysis which can account for the constitution of the subject within a historical framework" (TP, 117). Subjectivity, Foucault consistently argues in his later work, is a power-effect. Subject positions, options for behavior, and even various modes of inner experience and self-identity arise within networks of power as consequences or correlates of their tensions and operations. Subjectivities do not preexist, and therefore do not construct or fully control, the networks of power in which they form. Thus, if one wants to analyze power networks genealogically, one must dispense with the notion of a ruling, sovereign subjectivity prior to any network of power.

Although Alcoff suggests that Foucault's primary predecessor in this process of displacing subjectivity is Martin Heidegger,[24] a more obvious and methodologically more immediate predecessor is Nietzsche. The very possibility of memory, of imagination, of any recognizably human type of interiority, Nietzsche argues in the *Genealogy*, must be traced back to exercises of power. Divided consciousness, the prerequisite for self-reflectivity, occurs when cruel drives are forced back against their source, when, because of political pressures, individuals internalize the drive to inflict pain, which is above all the drive to affect, to effect, to cause. Thus, the self, the subject of self-consciousness, is an effect of forces that it does not and cannot control. Foucault does not pass published judgment on the particulars of Nietzsche's account of the development of subjective interiority, but he clearly agrees with Nietzsche's general point: Subjectivities are historically emergent, which means they are effected in networks of power. As a consequence, subjects can't have analytic priority in genealogical work. This does not mean that subjects have no analytic role to play whatsoever, nor does it mean that subjects never exercise power. It only means that subjects are to be explained with reference to power networks rather than vice versa.

Alcoff, however, claims that Foucault's demotion of subjectivity to an analytic position posterior to power results in a conception of subjectivity deprived of agency.[25] She writes, "It is difficult to understand how agency can be formulated on this view. Given the enormous productive efficacy Foucault accords to power/knowledge or the dominant discourse, there could be agency only if human beings were given the causal ability to create, effect, and transform power/knowledge or discourses, but Foucault does not concede to us this capacity."[26] In the absence of agency, Alcoff believes, resistance to domination is impossible and even conceptually incoherent. Thus, "if Foucault's analysis of subjectivity is correct, a feminist emancipatory project is in trouble."[27]

This passage alone does not preclude agency, however; it only performs an analytic reassignment of a conceptual category. Alcoff's interpretation of the passage is only possible because she reads it in conjunction with a second passage from an essay written in the early 1980s wherein Foucault points out, "There are two meanings of the word *subject*: subject to someone else by control and dependence, and tied to his own identity by a conscience or self-knowledge. Both meanings suggest a form of power which subjugates and makes subject to."[28]

In this passage, Alcoff takes Foucault to be saying the only way to escape subjugation is to escape subjectivity altogether, and she takes this claim to explain and justify his analytic demotion of subjectivity in the mid-1970s. But Alcoff doesn't want to eliminate subjectivity:

> [T]hinking of ourselves as subjects can have, and has had, positive effects contributing to our ability effectively to resist structures of domination. Subjectivity can accord a sense of agency and authority over one's actions, needs, interests, and desires. It can create an obstacle to the instrumental appropriation of one's self for externally articulated ends. It can produce at least the potential for an ontological space in which the reflective reconstruction of one's social environment can take place, a site of relief from determinism and manipulation. In short, even though it may be a discursive construction, the notion that one is a subject can engender a repositioning of one's perspective from other to self (a very important act for women at this historical point) and a vigorous awareness of the possibility of critical reflection on demands that issue from an external source.[29]

Whether historically emergent or not, whether a product of power or not, subjectivity is important as a tool or mode of resistance to domination, according to Alcoff; Foucault is wrong to cast it aside.

As I read Foucault, however, these two passages, separated in time, are not related to each other as thesis and justification. They simply address two different levels of analysis. When Foucault said in the 1970s that genealogy dispenses with the constituent subject as an analytic category, he was just acknowledging and espousing an analytic move that Nietzsche had already made. Genealogy, as Foucault notes, "is a form of history which can account for the constitution of knowledges, discourses, domains of objects, etc., without having to make reference to a subject which is either transcendental in relation to the field of events or runs in its empty sameness throughout the course of history" (TP, 117). His point is not that there are no subjectivities, but that one can engage in genealogical analysis without *necessary* reference to them. In other words, subjectivity does not function in genealogies as a first cause. In contrast to genealogy, most liberal and marxian histories ultimately refer to some kind of subjectivity that preexists power (even if, as in most marxian theories, it does not survive the advent and subsequent unfolding of power unchanged).[30] For such histories there was always a time before, when power had not yet come into being. It is power, not constituent subjectivity, that must first be accounted for; power must have a cause. Genealogy differs from other kinds of history in that it begins with a different assumption. But this is nothing new; Nietzsche said it over a hundred years ago. And there is no reason, on the face of it, that this assumption should preclude the development of causally efficacious subjects within the interplay of networks of power. In fact, Nietzsche describes the historical emergence of just such relatively potent agents, as does Foucault.

Foucault's first passage only seems problematic in light of Alcoff's reading of his apparent equation of subjectivity and subjugation in the early 1980s. That second, later passage bears repeating here: "There are two meanings of the word *subject*: subject to someone else by control and dependence, and tied to his own identity by a conscience or self-knowledge. Both meanings suggest a form of power which subjugates and makes subject to." Clearly the first claim that Foucault makes here is uncontroversial; one meaning of *subject* is "subject to someone else." In this case subjectivity (or subjection) seems incompatible with agency; insofar as one is in someone else's control, one is not an agent (though of course there are degrees of being in someone else's control). The second claim seems equally uncontroversial; another meaning of *subject* is "tied to [one's] own identity by conscience or self-knowledge." This latter, surely, is not antithetical to agency; it is one of the conditions for the possibility of it. One cannot be a deliberating, choosing, blame- or praiseworthy being if one has no capacity for self-reflection, no "conscience or self-knowledge." Agency requires the latter form of subjectivity as its prerequisite. We are left, then, with the third claim, which concerns "a form of power which subjugates and makes subject to." This, I think, is what leads Alcoff to believe that Foucault denies the possibility of agency. It appears that, if the power that establishes and maintains conscience or self-knowledge is a subjugating form of power, then agency is an illusion, for subjectivity, in Alcoff's words, "has made us more, not less, vulnerable to domination."[31] If this is the case, the only alternative to domination is the destruction of subjectivity, which is how Alcoff interprets Foucault's project.

The difference between my reading of Foucault and Alcoff's turns on our differing understandings of the meaning of *power* in his discourse. Foucault says quite clearly that there is no entity named *power* (OGE, 219). Power exists only in its exercise; that is, power exists as an event, not as a thing. Networks of power are, then, repeating circuits of events. The language of event is extremely important here; it is designed to displace the language of cause and effect at the most basic analytic level. Foucault does not speak of power as a cause whose effect is some state of affairs or set of relations external to it. There is no outside to power. Rather, power is—occurs as—the events that are sets of relations. Power does not hold us in its grip; rather, we emerge historically within repeating circuits of events. We are events of power. We are shaped by power networks, and our identities remain dependent upon them. When a network shifts, when events fail to repeat, when a circuit of repetition clashes with exogenous forces, identities dependent on that set of power relations undergo change and may even collapse and disappear.

Foucault speaks of power as the cause of social structures, personal identities, laws, systems of thought, and so on—"power produces"—but, as I have argued elsewhere,[32] the word functions merely as a placeholder in a grammatical sense, much as the *it* functions in the English sentence, "it is raining." Some entity named *power* wholly prior and external to the event of production does not actually effect force relations among people or communities that are then separable from power networks; force relations arise, form networks, and reinforce or conflict with one another. Foucault states very explicitly: "power must be understood in the first instance as the multiplicity of force relations immanent in the sphere in which they operate and which constitute their own organization; as the process which, through ceaseless struggles and confrontations, transforms, strengthens, or reverses them; as the support which these force relations find in one another, thus forming a chain or system, or on the contrary, the disjunctions and contradictions which isolate them from one another; and lastly, as the strategies in which they take effect" (HS1, 92–3). One must not make a distinction between, on the one hand, power as cause and, on the other, dominations and submissions as separable effects. "[P]ower is not an institution, and not a structure; neither is it a certain strength we are endowed with; it is the name that one attributes to a complex strategical situation in a particular society" (HS1, 93).

Alcoff, I believe, reads Foucault's notion of power as if it were an entity, a cause external to its effects.[33] She reads power as it if were in fact what it is in grammar, a subject. Thus she collapses all types of subjugation into the type Foucault mentions first in the passage she cites: "subject to someone else by control or dependence."[34] Then, on her reading, the someone else the subject is subject to is power, which functions as another subject, a super-subject. But the second type of subjugation ("tied to his own identity by a conscience or self-knowledge") is simply an event of subjection; what subjects and what is subjected are not external to one another. The subject simply *is* subjected; that is what it is to be a subject. Foucault doesn't think we ought to cease to be subjects in that second sense. Quite the contrary, in many of his later essays and interviews he is interested in the cultivation of some kinds of subjectivity, not the destruction of all of them.

In no sense, then, does Foucault's analysis preclude or destroy agency. Except insofar as I am to differing degrees at different times subjugated by the actions of others, I can exercise agency despite (and even because of) the fact that my very existence as a subject is a form of subjection. Alcoff's mistake is actually a refusal to demote subjectivity as a causal category from its position of analytic priority. As I read Foucault, he in no way compromises my ability to act as a politically engaged agent to minimize the forms of subjugation I suffer at the hands of others or my ability to criticize others and hold them responsible for what they do. Furthermore, by placing subjectivity squarely within historical power networks, Foucault is able to offer rich analyses of the subjugations I daily undergo and is thus able to supply valuable resources for resisting and opposing at least some of them. He is even able to initiate new political strategies and set the stage for the emergence of new political realities.

ON THE POSSIBILITY THAT FOUCAULT WILL MAKE YOU LOSE YOUR IDENTITY AND ALIENATE YOU FROM YOUR COMMUNITY

A third kind of criticism of Foucault's work is that it militates against political action by questioning the basis of gay and lesbian community. Since it is on the basis of a shared identity that individuals come together in a community to support each other, engage in cultural production, and fight for their civil rights (so this criticism runs), any threat to the reality of identity is a threat to marginal communities and their political struggles. There are several questions a maliciously meticulous scholar might ask about this criticism. One is whether Foucault actually does undermine or destabilize identity as critics claim, a question that has much in common with the one just examined regarding Foucault's alleged destabilization of agency. Another is whether community actually does require the existence of a shared identity in order to ground and maintain itself. Another is whether political action to end oppression really requires the existence of a community of those who are oppressed. What exactly are the relationships among these three phenomena: identity, community, and political action? Is political action really dependent upon each of the other two in turn?

I argued in the preceding section that Foucault's work historicizes subjectivities but that it does not thereby expose subjectivities as illusions or advocate their destruction. The same can be said for identity. Foucault claims that sexual identities are historically produced, but he never suggests that they are unreal; on the contrary, our sexual identities may be among the most real things about us. (The global economy is historically produced, too, but my knowing that does not make me stop believing in the reality and the importance of the greenbacks in my wallet. Money matters; likewise, sexual identity.) Foucault does imply that sexual identities are dangerous. The production of sexual identities has laid waste to a lot of lives over the last couple of centuries, and my own was very nearly one of them. There are grave dangers associated with the requirement that we all accept, perform, and cultivate sexual identities. However, Michael Walzer to the contrary, Foucault does not suggest that all dangerous things or even all hurtful things are things to be destroyed. "My point is not that everything is bad, but that everything is dangerous, which is not exactly the same as bad" (OGE, 231). The question of whether or in what ways to resist or reinforce or dismantle or elaborate upon sexual identities can only be answered in contexts, in relation to strategic situations. It doesn't make sense simply to oppose or favor sexual identities without reference to the local power networks in which they are embedded at a given time. Foucault offers no blanket rejection of sexual identities and proclaims no categorical imperative to resist believing in them. He does, of course, refuse the notion that sexual identities are a necessary, ahistorical feature of society, and he implies that we might want to work toward displacing them. That refusal and its implications bring his work into conflict with some activists and theorists who assert that such identities are a permanent and essential feature of all human societies and that individuals who are born with homosexual identities are the only ones who could possibly establish gay and lesbian subcultures or communities. This conflict—this disagreement over the question of the status of homosexual identity through history—brings us face to face with one incarnation of that beast generally known as the essentialism/constructionism controversy.

This ongoing controversy is a very difficult one to sort out. As Diana Fuss points out in her book *Essentially Speaking*, there are many different kinds of essentialism and many different kinds of constructionism; there is a single essence of neither position, and we should be careful not to posit one. However, in an effort to get at least some handle on what the terms of the debate are, Fuss offers a "classic" definition of essentialism: "belief in true essence—that which is most irreducible, unchanging, and therefore constitutive of a given person or thing."[35] Likewise she offers a more or less classic definition of constructionism: belief that "essence is itself a historical construction."[36] Given these working definitions, it is at least provisionally possible to assert that most adherents to sexual essentialisms would likely accept all or most of this claim: "Homosexual identity preexists homosexual communities and institutions, the discovery of homosexuality by medical science, the development of linguistic categories to name homosexuals and homo-sexual practices, and even any individual's self-awareness as a distinct type of sexual person." Of course, some constructionists might affirm some of parts of this claim as well; many would be happy to acknowl-edge that homosexual identity existed before medical science's discov-ery of homosexuality. There are, then, some possible points of agree-ment, but the disagreements maintain a significant distance between the two positions.

Probably the most persistent disagreements between essentialists and constructionists come to light when each camp articulates what it takes to be the relationship between community and identity. For most essentialists, identity comes first and serves as the basis for community formation; people find each other and unite because they are what they are. But for many constructionists, community comes first and serves as the basis for the formation of identity. Shane Phelan states a version of the latter position: "The construction of a positive identity requires a community that supports that identity."[37] People come together on the basis of shared interests and gradually devise a shared self-understand-ing. The interests that bring them together do not necessarily initially amount to an identity.

From a constructionist perspective these two claims about the rela-tion between identity and community seem antithetical. However, from an essentialist perspective, they are not; they can be easily reconciled if we simply distinguish between having an identity and being aware of having an identity. Perhaps it is possible that people have an identity that is unknown to them, that underwrites, so to speak, their demeanor or behavior. (Readers of eighteenth-century novels will be able to think of countless fictional examples of this. *Joseph Andrews* comes to mind. Eighteenth-century British people of a certain social position and out-look apparently believed in class identities.) It may be their common demeanor and behaviors that bring a group of people together; but once their community is established, they may begin to think about those commonalities and formulate some awareness of their shared identity. Self-awareness and the development of a vocabulary to express it may well require the existence of a community, but that doesn't mean identity itself requires one. It may appear to some queer historians that identity depends on community and is established after or in conjunc-tion with it; but, essentialists would hold, identity really preexists the community and enables its formation.[38]

One reason for the difference of opinion between essentialists and constructionists is that the word "identity" has more than one meaning in this dispute. Queer identities can be analyzed as historically emerging and evolving phenomena because we have records of individuals and groups of individuals working through the process of developing vocabularies and senses of self. If we hold, with constructionists, that identity just amounts to a certain kind of self-awareness, then people who lack that self-awareness lack that identity.[39] But for most essentialists, the process of developing self-awareness is the process of learning about something already present, a self who already is homosexual, lesbian, or gay. It is possible, therefore, for people to be one of those things and not know it or to have imperfect understandings of themselves or to be in denial of what they are. It is even possible for huge numbers of people over long periods of time to have little or no knowledge of their identity, and yet still have one.

To see what's really at stake, we need a vocabulary that distinguishes between these two meanings of *identity*. Fortunately, Fuss, following Aristotle, supplies one. She writes:

> To locate the identity of an object, for example, entails in analytic philosophy determining both whether that object is itself and not a different entity and whether that object remains the same over time. In Aristotelian logic, essence and identity are closely related but by no means synonymous: a person or object possesses an essence which determines its identity, but identity, rather than operating as a substitute for essence, functions as its effect.[40]

What an object is in itself is a matter of its essence. That the object is able to remain "the same" over time is *an effect* of its essence. Thus, identity in the sense of maintenance of oneself in the selfsame is an effect of essence.

Perhaps I may be allowed to deform Aristotle (if not also Fuss) a bit and use this distinction between essence and identity to clarify the terms of the above dispute. Let's say that essentialists posit a homosexual (or lesbian or gay) essence, something that is what it is to be queer. Let us say further that for essentialists it is this essence that enables some people at some times to recognize themselves and others, to acquire a knowledge of their identity. This identity, this possibility for self-recognition, then, is an effect (though not a necessary one) of essence, but it is not the same thing as essence. Thus, even if essences exist, it would still be possible to examine the phenomenon of self-recognition or self-awareness apart from essence and hold that the conditions for the possibility of self-recognition or self-awareness as queer are historically produced. Given this distinction between essence and identity, it's clear that constructionists and essentialists could agree that homosexual identity appeared at a certain point in history and was conditioned by economic, social, and political factors. But the two groups would disagree about the factors that were collectively necessary and sufficient for that identity to appear. In addition to the cultural and economic factors the constructionists point to, essentialists think that there also must be a foundational essence of homosexuality; the social, cultural, and economic factors alone would not have been sufficient to produce people with homosexual identities.

How would we go about trying to settle this dispute about whether a homosexual essence exists? One way would be to point to one, which would settle the matter immediately just as my pointing to the azalea settles the question about whether there are azaleas in my yard. The problem with that approach is that by definition an essence cannot appear directly to the senses; the things senses perceive are changeable, and an essence is precisely that aspect of a thing that is not changeable.[41] We're never going to stumble across a homosexual essence at a party or in a laboratory.[42] But, since we can't point to or otherwise locate a homosexual essence in principle, can we assume that homosexual identities can be effected and supported entirely by sociocultural and economic factors—that is, can we safely and responsibly assume a constructionist position on the issue? Fuss raises this question herself immediately after her mention of Aristotle: ". . . is it possible to base identity on something other than essence?"[43] In other words, what conditions are necessary for something like homosexual self-recognition? Do those conditions include the real existence of a homosexual essence? Much social constructionist literature comprises efforts to understand how sexual identities were constructed, which implies a belief in their reality. The ability to recognize oneself as homosexual (or gay, lesbian, queer, etc.), then, is both logically and for some people practically independent of belief in essential natures, as is the ability to recognize the sexual identities of others. But might not identities still really be effects of essences even if some people don't recognize them as such? What, other than an essential nature, could possibly generate and sustain a particular identity in the first place? Could socialization alone ground identities?

Having spent a great deal of my life in a region of the U.S. where one of the most salient aspects of anybody's identity is his or her religion, I insist that the answer is yes: Sometimes socialization alone is enough to create very deep kinds of self-awareness and a fundamental sense of one's identity and place in the world. No one is born a Christian; no one inherits Christianity through the genes. Yet in Alabama to identify or not to identify as a Christian is not something a person can deliberate about. Alabamians are raised on Christianity; it pervades our lives from the day we are born. College ruined me, so I repudiated Christian doctrine and left the church, but in many senses I remain Christian. My speech bears the mark of King James' English, of gospel rhythms and pulpit exhortations; my brain forms words to hymns when I hear classical music; like most Southerners, I muse in parables; I believe that love of money is the root of most evil and that one should always go the extra mile; whenever I witness a person's claims dismissed with an ad hominem argument my mother's voice sounds in my head: "Truth can show up anywhere; Jesus was born in a barn." Though Christianity doesn't have the central place in my life that it once had, it hasn't dropped away just because I might like for it to. I perceive the world like a Christian, I talk like a Christian, and in many ways I think like a Christian. Christianity is far more than just a belief-system that can be repudiated. If I'd stayed in Alabama in the ranks of the working class, my sense of self would still be as rooted in my relation to right religion as it is rooted in my relation to sexual norms, and I would have very little control over that.

Back in the days when my deepest sense of self was inextricable from Christian community and tradition, it never occurred to me that such a sense of self and such a community were not possible unless each of us somehow bore within us an essence of Christianhood. On the contrary, we precisely did *not* believe that. We believed that a Christian sense of self was something one had to acquire through conversion, prayer, and self-discipline, and absolutely anyone could acquire it. At its best a congregation is a group of people who understand themselves to be engaged in the long and arduous process of instilling that sense within themselves and each other. That's why there are churches—at least in part and theoretically; the main purpose of a church is to cultivate and sustain the Christian identities of its members, to create jointly and offer to one another a world that would support their sense of themselves as followers of Christ and children of God. We had to work at being Christians; we had to construct ourselves as Christian individuals.

Even though we believed, however, that a Christian sense of self was something we had to work at, we did not believe there were many alternatives to it; you had to be either a Christian or a sinner; you had to be either a Christian or a violator of Christian doctrine and practice.[44] Nobody in that subculture had the freedom to choose not to be either one. Christian discursive practices structured absolutely everybody's

life. The categories they gave us gave us ourselves and all our possibilities for thought and action. Everyone had a religious identity, even
those people who ventured the farthest outside the fold. Even the most
desperately lost sheep still belong to the Good Shepherd's flock.[45]

In the case of Christian religious identity the most central aspects of
who a person is and takes him- or herself to be come about in the
absence of an essential nature. No one disputes that Christian identities
are social constructs, least of all Christians themselves.[46] Therefore, as
the religious example shows, constructionist views of identities as
historical and contingent are not logically incoherent or controverted by
the fact that most of us could not change our identities if we tried. Some
of the most important aspects of all our identities may be historically
and socially produced but still may not be the sorts of things that any of
us have the power to change very much at all. It isn't absurd, then, to
maintain that our social positions as homosexuals are the product of
at least two hundred years of public discourse and, further, that our
personal identities as gay or lesbian or bisexual or queer people are
learned, either through the process of being labeled by others or of
subjectively organizing our own behavior and experience with regard
to a certain cluster of sexual concepts or through a combination of both
processes. In the absence of essences or belief in essences, identities
don't just disappear, nor do they become ephemeral enough to be
changed like a whimsical opinion. They remain what they are: reified
personality types, coagulations of comportments and communicative
styles, social positions carrying certain penalties and privileges, ways
of distinguishing oneself from others, ways of orienting oneself in the
world, ways of designating the practices and relationships that have the
most significance for one's daily life. And they can maintain their stability through time; in fact, they may be impossible to shake in some
places for quite long stretches of time. Thus, there is no reason to think
lives can't be built on the basis of contingent and socially produced
sexual identities and no reason to think stable communities can't be
established on the basis of an historical sexual identity or even on the
process of creating a sexual identity. (I leave aside for now the question
of whether it's possible to build lives and communities on some basis
other than identity altogether.[47]) Foucault's genealogy goes on in the
absence of any belief in essential natures or essences. It does not go on
in the absence of any belief in subjectivities or identities, and thus even
if communities require identities as prerequisites, Foucault's work does
not undermine them.[48]

The next question is whether communities and/or effective political
action can go on in the absence of any *belief* in essential natures or

essences. Can gay and lesbian communities be formed and sustained under such conditions? Can people, either as individuals or as communities, engage in political actions to reduce or end their own oppression once they lay claim only to contingent, historically emergent identities? Many people have answered that question negatively, I think, which is why so many theorists back away from constructionist understandings of sexual identity—and which is why colleagues still issue warnings about my interest in the work of Michel Foucault. Certainly my concerned colleagues are right that gay and lesbian political action sometimes operates as essentialistic identity politics. But I'm convinced that it doesn't have to, that it doesn't always, and that identity and community and political action are in practice separable phenomena that function at least sometimes relatively independently of one another. Examination of some historical and sociological data will prove my point.

I start with the question: Is the existence of or at least the belief in transhistorical sexual identities grounded in essential natures necessary for lesbian and gay community? Well, it doesn't seem to be so in my community. Some members of my community do believe that there is an essential homosexual nature. They talk about "coming out" as if it meant "self-discovery," and they think it's really cool to read that there might have been homosexuals among the ancient Egyptians or the Hopi. We are everywhere, they say, and they mean it. They believe that if DNA tests can eventually determine sexual orientation, the blood of our prehistoric ancestors trapped in the bellies of mosquitoes encased in stone-age amber will reveal that there were homosexuals among the Cro-Magnons. There are other members of my community, however, who believe they chose to be who they are; for example, there are women who say they gave up on men after being battered or psychologically abused and decided to find fulfillment with women instead. And there are still other members of my community who say we are made to be who we are through socialization—who say people are born bisexual but are formed by society into hets and homos, and many lament that fact. Most of the members of my community do identify as lesbians or gay men, but there is absolutely no consensus among them on whether their identities are inborn, socialized into them before they were old enough to choose, or completely and self-consciously chosen.[49] Nor does this lack of consensus seem to bother anyone most of the time. Those who say they chose dance cheek to cheek with those who say they were born that way, and those who think they were socially constructed buy the next round of potato skins. Virginians don't like to argue.

At the very least, then, a community can exist without agreement on the question of homosexuality's nature or cause. What matters is participation in and loyalty to the community. One's membership in the community is more a matter of what one does than of what one is—or, therefore, of what one believes about how one got to be what one is.

The community doesn't require agreement on the nature of homosexuality, but it does promote some kinds of commonality. Whoever we are and whatever condition we arrive in, a lot of our socialization goes on after we get inside the community. Because homosexual self-awareness is generally formed under conditions of oppression and brutality and because there is a dearth of information available to children growing up with the stigma of homosexuality attached to them by others, many of us arrive at the doors of the bar the first night with that same old question on our lips, "But how do I *be* that?" And we rely on the people inside the bar (or the student group or the Metropolitan Community Church) to teach us. We learn over time how to dress, talk, dance, decide whom to ask out, and interpret and react to all kinds of signals from all kinds of people, including heterosexuals. The community doesn't make people's personalities from scratch, but it does shape them significantly. Over time one is marked by membership in the community; one's very body comes to signify that membership. In significant ways, then, homosexual communities do create and shape homosexual identities.

Probably most of us arrived at the bar doors that first night with the label *homosexual* already slapped across us. In one way or another we recognized the label and knew we had to grapple with it; that's probably what we were *doing there.* It's likely that most of us developed a rudimentary sense of gay or lesbian identity before we were part of a community. We formed our senses of self out of the fabric of hatred and abuse threaded through with whatever bits of literature we might find in medical journals or porn shops. We pieced together a sense of who we must be. So for most of us the community isn't the first or only source of our identity. But it's also possible for a person to develop a gay or lesbian identity because he or she *becomes* part of a community, for the community to be the first source of identity. I've seen it happen that way too. Some people just enjoy the thrill of transgression and hanging out with transgressive, creative, gutsy people and are gradually drawn into a life they would probably have had little interest in if they had never been exposed. This possibility for choice is something the radical right knows and fears. Very often our communities are exciting and attractive. They are communities people who had a real range of choices might actually choose to join. They offer forms of freedom, acceptance, affirmation, respect, and challenge that fundamentalist Christian communities, for example, offer none of their members.

Over time it doesn't matter how we got there, though; all of us, different as we are, are the community. We are united in cultural and political practice. One of the reasons why homophobic people, organizations, and institutions work hard to homogenize us, to render our cultural experimentation trivial, and to depict us as practitioners of a single lifestyle instead of as the varied individuals that we are is that they don't want to face the fact that in spite of our differences we've come together to associate with, support, and often even love one another as fellow community members by choice. Our enemies don't want to acknowledge our freedom, our creativity, and our hard work, so they pretend we're all just alike and congregate out of blind instinct like herd animals. But the fact is that we are not herd animals. As individuals we are not related by history or by biology. We've come together and built communities with few resources, still fewer models, and no "natural" ties like kinship or marriage. Our communities are among the most diverse of any currently in existence, and we have to work to make them work. Membership in the community is both a choice and a project.

Just as it's important to remember that there is great diversity within queer communities, it's important to remember that there is not one community; there are many different ones. Even in Richmond, with a metropolitan population of about 600,000, there are a number of distinct communities. Some are most easily recognized as loosely attached to one or another building. For example, the Metropolitan Community Church clearly includes those who attend worship services in that building and clearly excludes those who never do; the Richmond Lesbian-Feminists clearly includes those who attend potlucks at a few particular suburban homes and clearly excludes those who never do. Other communities are a little harder to pick out since they don't have obviously marked territory, but they are distinct communities even so. Richmond's queer communities are distinguished from one another by the same kinds of things that distinguish Richmond's various heterosexual communities from one another: race, class, age, gender, religion, and recreational interests. If we pay attention to the multiplicity of communities, another fact becomes clear: Homosexual identities alone are not sufficient by themselves as a foundation for a community.[50]

If having a gay or lesbian identity were all it took to form a community, then there would be only one community in a city no larger than Richmond. The existence of several communities and the easily recognized existence of individual queer people not affiliated with any community is ample evidence that communities are not related to identities in any simple way. A gay or lesbian identity is not a sufficient reason for an individual to become a part of a lesbian or gay community. It is also not a necessary prerequisite, as I've already mentioned; some people come to the community before their identities are formed. We often speak and act as if all lesbians and gay men were members of communities and as if the members of a given community share an identity from the word go. But neither of those propositions is true in Richmond. I would argue that the major impetus for gay and lesbian community formation—though not the only impetus by any means—is not gay or lesbian identity; it's a common set of interests, including but not limited to an interest in same-sex relationships and genital pleasure. As long as there are people who enjoy same-sex genital pleasure and/or life partnerships and as long as people are persecuted for that or for their gender-transgressive styles of dress and gesture, there will be reason to affiliate with one another for the purposes of fun, comfort, and mutual support. We become friends and allies because we understand each other, enjoy each other, and care for each other even when nobody else in the world does. What else is a community, and what else is a community for?

Some people seem to think that queer communities are also for political action and even that effective political action is impossible outside such communities. I think the first part of that claim is debatable and the second is false.

Queer communities—like all communities—perform a lot of functions, many of them related to the survival and well-being of their members. Some theorists—particularly lesbian feminist theorists (often called "cultural feminists")—hold that the very performance of these functions amounts to political action. Insofar as queer people live in a society that wants us dead, our survival could be construed as a political act, like holding up under torture; therefore everything we do to ensure each others' well-being could be construed as a political act. But I don't think that's a helpful way of understanding either communities or politics. In fact, most Americans don't want us dead; they just want us to shut up and stay away from their kids. If we happen to die, they won't care, but it's not something they'll take any trouble to effect. If a member of my community is sick and the rest of us organize to bring her food, we're not engaging in political activism; we're just doing what all communities do for their members. The balance of power is not affected by what we do, and we're not trying to affect it. For most of us in queer communities, day to day survival is not heroism, and it doesn't change the power networks that shape our world. People who say they're politically active simply because they are good neighbors to other queer people are deluding themselves and shirking the obligation they obviously feel to engage in action to change the world for all of us.

Some would counter by asserting that the very existence of visible queer communities has a political impact on the rest of society, so as long as a person acts to promote the visibility and permanence of her community then she is engaging in political action. This is partly true; visible lesbian and gay people and communities have had a political impact on American politics. Activist Urvashi Vaid attributes Tennessee's 1996 decision to strike down its anti-sodomy laws to the visibility of gay and lesbian people both in Tennessee and across the country; she says the court's refusal to take seriously the idea that a gay or lesbian "lifestyle" is harmful to the individual living it is a direct result of the visibility of happy, healthy, upstanding gay and lesbian citizens in public media over the past several years.[51] Certainly Vaid is right that the existence of queer communities can change the political landscape. But there are those who would use that fact to assert, in turn, that one's visible participation in such a community amounts to working to change the political landscape. Again, I think that's a dilution of the meaning of politics and a trivialization of political action. It's just not the case that when I pull on my boots and head to Babe's on Country Night, I'm going out to change the world; I'm just going out to dance and, hopefully, not to think about politics or oppression very much. My community very often is my escape from a politically charged and dangerous world, not my engagement with it. I believe that's the case for most people in my community. As a community we are precisely *not* a locus of political activity, even if our actions do sometimes have political effects.

Despite its relative lack of interest in political engagement, though, there are times when my community becomes politically active in direct, self-conscious, chosen ways. For example, in the spring of 1996 the city of Richmond decided to deny the Women's Softball League access to Humphrey-Calder Field, where softball games had been played for years. The field was given over to the Little League, and the women were reassigned to a field in the far north side. The Richmond Parks and Recreation Department claimed the reason was that the women tended to hit the ball over the back fence and into traffic on Interstate 195. None of the women took that claim seriously; they assumed it was because the neighborhood had protested the presence of so many lesbians on summer evenings. Several groups, including the Metropolitan Community Church and the Richmond Lesbian-Feminists, issued appeals to their membership to write to the Parks and Recreation Department, the mayor, and city councilmen in protest.[52] The women circulated petitions and eventually acquired more than eight hundred signatures. On June 24 they took their petitions to the City Council and spoke during "public comment time." Following this action, Richmond Mayor Leonidas Young directed Councilman Tim Kaine to meet with the women and with the Director of Parks and Recreation.[53] By the opening of the 1998 season, the field had not been returned.

In this case, a community mobilized to take political action because one of its cultural activities was in danger from bureaucratic authority. Even if effective, however, the action will have a very limited impact on both Richmond politics and the future of women's softball. Richmond has no statutes that forbid discrimination on the basis of sexual orientation; it is legally defensible for the city to deny citizens access to public facilities on the basis of their sexual orientation. Therefore the women are not able to complain that they are being discriminated against *as lesbians*; they can only appeal to tradition and procedural irregularities in field assignments to support their claim to Humphrey-Calder Field. Should the Parks and Recreation Department state that the presence of lesbians in large numbers on any city softball field is detrimental to civic life, all use of such fields could be denied to the women. Effective action in the long term would actually have to transcend the community. Instead of arguing for the use of a particular softball field, lesbians might organize to change the Richmond City Code to outlaw discrimination on the basis of sexual orientation; then they could show that they had been denied access to the field on that basis.[54] But so far the community has not mobilized for that purpose.

There are of course classic examples of entire gay and lesbian communities rising up to fight oppression. The Stonewall Riots were a community's response to an ongoing police threat to its territory and cultural activities. The White Night Riot in San Francisco following sentencing of Dan White, the murderer of City Supervisor Harvey Milk and Mayor George Mascone, moved John D'Emilio to write:

> What I witnessed that night, and over the succeeding days, allowed me to read my historical research in a new light. I saw how dependent the movement was on the subculture; in reality, the subculture, or community, was the sea in which activists swam. Much of the crowd that gathered in front of City Hall had poured out of the bars when they heard about the jury's verdict. Many of them were the much maligned "clones" whom many activists criticized—those allegedly apolitical gay men with short-cropped

hair and mustaches, wearing the uniform of flannel shirt, Levis, and bomber jacket, and having Nautilus-perfect bodies. In the collective experience of the bars and larger subculture, political consciousness clearly germinated, ready to flower under certain conditions.[55]

D'Emilio contends that successful political action is intrinsically related to subcultural development. Even so, however, he does not assert that communities are intrinsically political or even that they should be.

Most gay and lesbian people know they're oppressed for their sexual orientation, and most are angry when they're forced to confront that oppression in stark ways. Communities do turn out spontaneously and protest or riot when they feel threatened. But "community" is not synonymous with "political action group." The relationship between communities and sustained, organized political activity is extremely complex. Political activity is no more and no less dependent upon the community than the community is dependent upon political action; nor are they interdependent necessarily and in all cases.

Insofar as the community as a unit responded in a sustained and organized manner to a threat to its activities, the Humphrey-Calder Field protests were very unusual in Richmond. For the most part, those queer people in Richmond who participate in political activity in any sense do so as individuals, not as members of a community. Communities often serve as conduits of information for political rallies, fundraisers, and legislative actions, but they seldom serve as the rallying point for political counterattack against the governmental systems that oppress us and they even more seldom serve as the rallying point for seizure of the legal or extralegal means to limit the power of homophobic individuals and private organizations. It is as individuals that we donate money to or respond to letter-writing directives from national gay and lesbian advocacy organizations; it is as individuals that we support broadened nondiscrimination statements or argue for domestic partner benefits at work; it is as individuals that we do the time-consuming and often disheartening work of moral education among the straight people in our personal lives; it is as individuals that we do our volunteer work with Virginians for Justice or various HIV/AIDS organizations; it is as individuals that we challenge child custody decisions or domestic relations law in court. Political action doesn't arise directly out of the community most of the time. There is no clear correlation between community membership and political action, although without some recognized political organization and discourse many of these individual actions might not be seen as political activity at all, or at least not as queer political activity.

One might argue, still, that political activity is dependent on the community's existence in the sense that state and national political movements and organizations originated in local communities, that communities were necessary in order for such organizations ever to come into existence and, further, that they themselves constitute communities. No doubt in some cases these claims are true; some political action groups did arise out of communities and some do function as communities. But these claims do not hold in all cases and so are not necessarily true. D'Emilio's description of the Mattachine Society is instructive.[56] Harry Hay, one of the founders of the Society, worked alone for two years before he was able to recruit two allies, Bob Hull and Chuck Rowland, to support him in his idea for an underground homophile movement. Still more time passed before the three found their other two allies, Dale Jennings and Rudi Gernreich; the five began working to found a homosexual rights organization in November of 1950. They saw themselves as building a political movement, not an affective community. The Mattachine Society didn't grow out of a community, and it wasn't set up to function as one. It was organized on the model of U.S. Communist movements; members of different "cells" didn't necessarily even know each others' names, and those in lower ranks weren't told the names of superiors. Had there been no homosexual communities, there would have been no way to spread the word about the formation of the organization—no way to locate potentially interested people. But the communities themselves were not the locus of political action in such a dangerous time.

In Richmond in 1998 the distinction between community and movement still holds, much as it did in Harry Hay's Los Angeles forty-eight years ago. Sustained political action is most often undertaken within corporations or professional organizations by queer employees or members or, in more public forums on issues of more general concern, by the state civil rights organization, Virginians for Justice. Communities may or may not actively support these activities, and these groups may or may not use community infrastructures to publicize themselves and their aims. But even when there is a clear convergence of community and movement activity, it is still clear that the community and the movement are working in cooperation rather than as one unit.

The separation between community and movement is easy to see if we examine the activities of the state civil rights organization, Virginians for Justice. Founded in 1988, Virginians for Justice is the only organization in Virginia whose mission is to work within the state General Assembly and the judicial system to gain equal civil rights for lesbian, gay, bisexual, and transgendered citizens of the Commonwealth as well as for people with HIV/AIDS. Its current objectives are few, but ambitious: It seeks the repeal of the Crimes Against Nature law, the reduction of crimes committed against people because of their gender or sexual orientation, and a prohibition on job discrimination. In addition, it stands ready to oppose any heterosexist legislation that might be introduced into the General Assembly during any session. These four objectives address major aspects of the problems faced by all non-heterosexual people in Virginia—our vulnerability to police and penal incursion into our private lives; our legal helplessness against the homophobic policies of employers, creditors, landlords, and courts; and our violation at the hands of bat-swinging, torch-bearing skinheads. There are other problems that queer Virginians face, but most are unlikely to be resolvable as long as the law criminalizes us and we can be denied jobs and access to public facilities and services just because we are not heterosexual. Virginians for Justice is doing some of the most important political work that is going on in the Commonwealth at the present time.

Yet, Virginians for Justice is not the brainchild of a politically engaged Virginia community.[57] The organization was established by a small group of Maryland and District of Columbia activists with an initial bankroll of $5,000. The group appointed a Board of Directors whose sole purpose at that time was to hire a professional lobbyist to work in General Assembly sessions. There was no provision for grassroots organizing and no Board member from any region of the state except for the suburbs just south and west of Washington, a part of the state that differs radically from the rest. The aim was not to build a statewide organization but simply to change a few state laws. The group expanded slightly during its first year to include at least one Richmond resident on the Board. It then hired a professional lobbyist for four months during the 1990 General Assembly session, a heterosexual woman who worked simultaneously as a lobbyist for the tobacco industry. A few months later, dissatisfied with the performance and the high price of its lobbyist, the Board decided to change tactics. It broadened its base of support by initiating elected Board positions that would be representative of congressional districts throughout Virginia and, with an almost completely new Board in place, began a year-long reassessment of the political situation. Sometime in 1991 the Board decided that hiring a professional lobbyist who then had to be educated on queer issues was a mistake; instead they hired a lesbian already knowledgeable about the issues but who had no experience as a lobbyist. Her job was both to learn how to lobby and to teach the members of the Board what she learned. This she did over a period extending from January of 1991 until the close of the G.A. session in 1993. After 1993 the

Board restructured the organization a second time, hired an executive director, and began working with volunteer lobbyists and then with a part-time lobbyist who is paid a nominal salary. Only one of VJ's initiatives has succeeded to date—abolition of the part of the Alcohol Beverage Control Board's code that made serving a "known homosexual" grounds for loss of an establishment's liquor license (this occurred late in 1991)—but support in the General Assembly for repeal of the Crimes Against Nature law and for adding sexual orientation and gender to the state's hate crimes law is growing, as evidenced by the growing numbers of co-sponsors these bills have received.[58] By 1998 membership had grown to about 1,500, with contributors, volunteers, and board members drawn from across the state (although the best represented areas are the suburbs of DC, Richmond, and Norfolk and Virginia Beach). These members often have little contact with one another, however; most Board members seldom see one another between monthly meetings, and even among those most active in the organization, interests beyond the legislative initiatives in question are divergent, as are their living arrangements, socioeconomic status, and—most significantly—sexual orientations. Membership in VJ does not require that one even disclose one's sexual orientation, much less that one have any particular sexual identity. Many members and in fact one recent member of the Board identify as heterosexual; some, including a member of the Board, are transgendered; and some members are bisexual. In short, it is not necessary for members to have anything in common beyond a commitment to working to obtain civil rights and personal safety for all individuals regardless of gender or sexual orientation. Virginians for Justice is neither the outgrowth of a Virginia homosexual community, nor does it now function as one.

The organization is perceived by many legislators and others as an interest group, and it works in much the same way as other interest groups—like the National Rifle Association and the tobacco industry—work; it lobbies for legislation that its Board deems beneficial to its members and against legislation it deems harmful and unfair. No doubt most people outside the organization believe those members are all part of a "gay and lesbian community" and all share a "homosexual" identity, but that perception is simply erroneous. Insofar as the law and social custom mark certain people as sexual outlaws and appropriate targets for abuse, those so marked and those who care for them have common interests, whether they have common identities or not.

The relationships, then, between sexual identity, community, and political action are various and complex. While for some people and groups identities probably do come first and then those with common identities build an affective community that engages in political activity to protect itself and further its aims, for others there are other paths and other priorities. There is no clearly right or necessary way for political action to come about. Thus, there is no reason to posit an essential homosexual nature that doesn't change through time to account either for the creation of homosexual identities or the creation of homosexual communities or the creation of homosexual political movements. These things have emerged in different ways in different places for different people. Foucault's refusal of the notion that there is an essential, unchanging homosexual nature does nothing to preclude the formation or furtherance of any of the three.

CONCLUSIONS

In this chapter I've given free rein to my maliciously meticulous scholar-self and have examined three major political objections to Foucault's work: that it robs us of all possible criteria for moral judgment and thus for political action, that it diminishes our freedom by declaring that we cannot act as responsible agents, and that it destroys the basis for collective political action by challenging the notion that sexual identities are transhistorical. I've shown that these accusations are untrue. Individual agency is still intact. Political judgment and action can still occur, albeit in ways somewhat different from those humanists might prefer. The possibility of collective action, too, remains. Hence, despite my long Foucaultian sojourn, I have not lost my identity or become alienated from my community, nor have I become inactive, apathetic, or impotent. On the contrary, I am more actively involved in the world, more concerned and caring, and much more powerful than I was before. Not all of those changes are the consequences of any kind of philosophical engagement, to be sure, but reading Foucault's work has made me stronger in several ways.

First, through study of Foucault's work I have come to see that humanism—though it promises justice and equality for all—actually is a source of oppression. Humanists insist that the only way to justify political action is to ground it in transcendent values and universal rationality. The values and rationality have to come first, and then you have to use them to arrive at your decisions for action. Only then can your actions be right or good and worthy of humanist support. What that really means, though, is that my actions will never earn humanist support. Homosexual people don't begin to resist heterosexist institutions and homophobic acts because we've first come up with some analysis or theory that tells us that resisting is morally right. We find ourselves in the midst of having to protect ourselves. We come to self-consciousness as gay and lesbian and bisexual and transgendered and queer people because we are persecuted or at least threatened with persecution for the behaviors we engage in or refuse. Who we are, our very identities, are formed in the violence of deep social conflict, fear, and hatred, and they change as we undergo initiation into or disillusionment with or expulsion from whatever variously embattled communities we move through in the course of our lives. We don't have the luxury of standing apart from the fray and musing about what would justify intervention in it; we are just *in* it. In our lives there is no politically neutral space where we can retreat to deliberate. Therefore moralistic humanism just won't work for us. Try as we might—and many of us try really hard—to speak and act as if our political and moral judgments issued from pure rationality rather than from concrete, worldly queer experience, our enemies see through us. They know we don't take up our political and moral positions after and because of dispassionate deliberations made on the ground of universalizable, politically neutral, normative criteria. They know we have high stakes in the judgments we make and exhort others to make; they know our lives depend on the outcome of public debate; thus, they know they can discredit us as biased at any turn, at which point the humanists will condemn and abandon us. We can't meet humanism's standards. Humanism requires that decision-making occur in a space that people like us can never occupy. It requires us to start thinking and working in a place where we are not and never were. We can never stand on the firm ground of politically neutral reason as we take our stands, so we'd better find some way to shift the site of struggle. Foucault's work offers techniques for doing that.

Second, in recognizing both that and, to some extent, how my sexual identity is historically formed, and in coming to understand that who I am occurs as resistance to certain networks of social forces, I have also come to understand that my freedom, my capacity to act and effect, is intimately bound up with my subjection in myriad ways, and that any analysis that bifurcates freedom and power damages me by obscuring the milieux in which I must live. I am not hoping and working for an apocalyptic moment that will bring an end to all earthly power; I am hoping and working for disruptions in networks of power that have all but calcified and therefore tend to close off experimentation, thought, and change; I am hoping and working for intensifications of freedom, which is not the same thing at all as a reduction of the amount of power in the world. In that work, Foucault is my ally.

Third and most important, through these years of reading Foucault's work I have come to respect my own lifelong resistance to the label *homosexual* and to the status of those who bear that label. I have come to understand that my earliest responses to the label and to the oppression that accompanied and depended upon it were good, appropriate, and healthy and that my earliest flickerings of knowledge about how that oppression worked were real and valuable insights. Those early insights and actions can serve as the basis for more mature and systematic understanding and resistance. That is not, of course, what most analysts, even gay-friendly ones, would say. Most people would view my youthful refusals, concealments, and silences as the very opposite of a self-affirming, positive political response to heterosexism. Practically every day I hear both gay and straight people speak disparagingly of non-heterosexual individuals who refuse to name themselves *homosexual* or *gay*, as if refusal of the label is synonymous with self-hatred and cowardice. Practically every "gay-positive" account of homosexual identity development I've ever seen insists that I rid myself of my loathing for the label *homosexual* or *gay* and embrace my homosexual identity as if I had chosen it myself. In effect, then, they all press me to concede that my childhood tormentors were completely right about who and what I was except that they didn't know that "gay is good"; such accounts push me to acknowledge that the homophobes who tortured me had the facts right but just had their values all wrong.

If I listen to very much of that kind of "gay-affirmative" rhetoric I almost feel ashamed of my long rebellion against sexual classification and identity, as if it was a stupid, pathetic enterprise and I was a weak, stupid homophobe for engaging in it. Then I have to remind myself that rhetoric that makes queers feel ashamed is not "gay-affirmative" even when it claims to be. Analyses that berate victims of homophobia for "internalized homophobia" are the tools of homophobes. Foucault's analysis, by contrast, allows me to remember my early resistance: No, I didn't stand opposed to my tormentors' *appraisal of homosexuality*. I stood opposed to their *drive to identify everyone on the basis of sexuality*. I stood opposed to the very idea that sexuality is a domain of facts before it is a domain of values and powers. The issue was never simply overcoming the stigma attached to homosexual identity. I was never interested simply in convincing those around me that gay people are just as good as straights. I was suspicious of the whole damned sexual and gender identification project. I believed it served dangerous interests and was perpetuated precisely because of its power to limit the freedom of all people—not queers only but straight people as well. Foucault's analysis lets me affirm these suspicions and explore them, and, by allowing and foregrounding them, it taps into the profoundest reaches of my lifelong, life-forming resistance to homophobia. Other analyses cut me off from the knowledge and strength that first made my resistance possible. Foucault's analysis puts me in touch with that knowledge and that strength. It helps me remember where the sources of my deepest and hardest and strongest resistance to my oppression actually lie.

4

Disorientation

Or, Beyond Sex-Desire

What is to be resisted, Foucault's *History of Sexuality* implies, is sexual identification. I knew that—with all my being. Sexual identification and classification were what I had been resisting ever since childhood. Before I read Foucault's analysis of sexuality, that knowledge of mine had rarely if ever before been seconded by any other human voice. Yet even without reinforcement, it informed almost every aspect of my life. I was who I was in great part by virtue of my resistance to that ubiquitous tangle of power and values that Foucault calls the deployment of sexuality. My existence was resistance.

In an important sense, though, my resistance was futile; I had always already been assimilated. There was no part of me that I could withhold from the *dispositif de sexualité*. All my feelings, thoughts, dreams, actions, and physical self-presentations were available for categorization at any time to any one of the system's representatives (including me) in thoroughly sexual terms. I had no being apart from what could be sexually classified. There was no outside to the sexual identification system, no place for me to be a human being without any sexual identity at all. At the same time that resistance from within sexual networks of power seemed futile, though, "from within" was the only possible location for resistance, for it was only as an embodied sexual identity that I could've had the self-awareness, motivation, and strength to resent and rebel against the word that named me and the box/closet/coffin in which I was supposed to live. It was as Foucault said: "Where there is power, there is resistance, and yet, or rather consequently, this resistance is never in a position of exteriority in relation to power" (HS1, 95; VS, 125–6). Had there been an outside, I would have gone there; I would not have remained within that system long enough to have resisted it. But of course, once outside, I would no longer have been I.

My resistance took at least three forms. The first, which was the most natural but also the least possible to sustain, was simply to refuse to incorporate any sexual identity into my self-image; the second was to refuse to do anything that would enable a sexual label to be attached to me by others; and the third was to point out the political investments and historical variability of sexuality and sexual identification in order to discredit whatever claim any sexual label might exercise over me. Though at different times I favored one or another of these strategies of resistance, I maintained all three to some degree more or less simultaneously for about eighteen years.

The first strategy, refusing even private acceptance of any sexual identity whatever, was at first the most natural for me, since for a time even after I began engaging in genital sex acts (until that day I asked my mother what the word *homosexual* meant) I didn't know that acts or desires formed the basis of a purely sexual classification system. I was introduced to the fact that I had to be the subject of my sexuality—and to be so in a certain well-defined way—only after I had acquired a fair amount of sexual experience. The initial relation between my sense of self and my sexual activities was not that of being a homosexual (or any other kind of sexual) subject at all. Sexual acts initially seemed to me to be no more definitive of me than any other act that I engaged in. Assuredly, they had an impact on what kind of moral subject I took myself to be, but they were no more determinant than other actions, sexual or nonsexual, that might be taken to fall within a moral domain.

Very quickly, as I have already discussed, I was made to understand that society would not allow me *not* to be a sexual subject and that if I persisted in engaging in homosexual acts I would have to be a homosexual subject and be outcast and ridiculed as such. What kind of moral subject I might be was exhaustively defined by my homosexuality; nothing I might do would mitigate society's moral condemnation of me. My sexuality, not my morality, determined who I truly was. But instead of experiencing this prioritizing of my sexuality as a recognition of the real truth about me, I experienced it first as an imposition. Previously I had experienced myself as a subject of religious discourse, ethical discourse, and familial discourse, but not as a subject of sexual discourse except as sexual acts could figure into one of those other subject-constituting domains. This subsequent imposition of sexual subject-hood felt like a profound violation of my selfhood, of who I already was, and even after I could no longer remember how it felt not to be primarily a sexual subject, I still remembered that violence and resented having been made to be what I had become. Often, especially when I wasn't involved in any overtly homosexual activity for a stretch of time, I engaged in this strategy of sexual indeterminateness and refused to acknowledge that I had any sexual identity at all.

Of course, whether I accepted the fact or not, society did place sexuality and sexual desire at the center of my life. Therefore, the strategy of maintaining sexual indeterminateness required me not merely to avoid centering sexual identity but constantly to de-center it, which is not an easy task. Most people would say it's impossible, for, if sexuality just is fundamental to human selfhood, a project such as mine was nothing more than sexual repression. But if so, it was a repression I undertook not out of fear of or disgust with sex but out of a need to protect my sexual practices and my self from the damaging effects of sexual reductionism.

To hold off the horrible weight of the dominant discourses of sexual subjectivity, I tried to construct a self-image and a life that did not place sexuality and sexual desire at the center. I was aided in this endeavor to de-center sexuality and construct some other center for my life by a variety of relatively sexless models of female adulthood that were still alive in my subculture of origin when I was growing up. In those days there were women—women from a different era living in rural communities not well-connected to mass media—who probably did not have the kinds of sexual identities I and my age cohorts eventually came to incorporate. For example, my grandmother, born in rural Alabama in 1905, probably never had a very highly developed sense of heterosexual selfhood. She probably didn't even have the concept of heterosexuality until she was middle-aged, if then, since, as Katz tells us, the word *heterosexual* wasn't commonly used until the 1930s. I have no idea what kind of a relationship she had to her own sexual desires, or if she ever experienced herself as the subject of sexual desires. I do know, though, that according to the tradition in which she was raised and which she and others of her generation tried to impart to my generation, adult females (at least those of the white race) were not the subjects of heterosexual desire. Boys and men were. Boys and men wanted sex. Girls, however, only wanted men. According to that tradition, for girls, sex, like good culinary skills, was merely a means to an end, and that end was primarily social, economic, and emotional—that end was marriage. All girls wanted to get married and have children. Failure to marry was failure in every sense. An unmarried woman was condemned to be a scorned servant of condescending relatives with no home of her own for the rest of her life and no one to provide for her in old age.[1] Grandmotherly advice always assumed that we girls wanted to get married, and, more significantly in this context, that we didn't want to have sex. The parts of that discourse that look nowadays like condemnation of sexual wantonness—such as condemnation of promiscuity or premarital sex—were condemnation all right, but the girls condemned were still not necessarily thought to have wanted the sex they had. When a girl got pregnant out of wedlock, for example, she was condemned for failing to restrain her boyfriend or for trying to trap some poor man into marrying her; in other words, she was condemned for failing to stand her ground or for engaging in manipulation and deceit. She was not condemned for wanting to have sex for sex's sake. We were taught, through her negative example, to stand our ground, refuse men's advances, and not to be so foolish as to expect a man to marry us if we didn't succeed. We were never given any advice on how to control or manage our own desires; the possibility that we might have them was never entertained. Even the extreme example of the condemnation of the proverbial "slut" had nothing to do with the idea that a woman might want sex. Au contraire, a slut was not a girl who liked sex; a slut was a girl who craved men's attention so much that she would actually submit to physical risk, pain, and degradation to get it. She was condemned for having no self-respect and for being stupid (because every smart woman knows no man will pay attention to a slut for very long). This was the lesson we were supposed to learn from the negative example of sluts: Don't bother enduring sex if in the end you aren't going to get anything for your trouble.

Clearly adult females in this discredited discourse of my grandmother's era were not the subjects of heterosexual desire, even if they might sometimes have experienced physical desires and sexual pleasures with men. Sexual desire was not an essential part of their identities. Women who recognized themselves within this discourse differed from me first of all not in that they desired sex with men whereas I desired sex with women but rather in that they desired men rather than sex whereas I desired sex rather than men. In the early stages of adolescence, I experienced my homosexual self as freakish first of all because I sometimes got sexually aroused and desired carnal intercourse. The fact that my arousal occurred in relation to females seemed less anomalous than that I had desires at all. I differed from my grandmother's contemporaries not in my *sexual* orientation but in my orientation to the entire relational, affectional, and carnal universe.

We can laugh at these outdated claims about female sexuality, or rather the lack of it, but I'm fairly certain they were not simply the ravings of repressed old ladies in denial. If Jonathan Katz has it right—

that is, if in the nineteenth century people really did experience sexual and gender identity and well-being differently from the ways most of us experience them now—it stands to reason that in places where electricity, plumbing, and paved roads were all but nonexistent before 1945, female heterosexual and lesbian identities may well have been all but nonexistent too. The nineteenth century hung on in such places long after 1901. When I was growing up in Alabama there were still remnants of discourses of female adult identification alternative to the now-dominant sexual ones, and it did not seem impossible to draw upon some of those remnants to construct an identity that did not place sexuality at the center of my being.

So I tried, ultimately unsuccessfully to be sure, but lack of success was not due to the impossibility of there ever being a human identity for which sexuality is not foundational. The problem with those alternative discourses—the reason they turn out not to be viable for someone like me—is that what they make foundational instead of sexuality is kinship and commitment. My grandmother's identity was bound up with her place in a relational network made up of religious, economic, and kinship components that simply is not available to me or to most other people in the U.S. today, even in the South. It just doesn't exist anymore. Without that kind of network, wifely devotion is hardly more than self-sacrifice, for it occurs in the absence of the emotional support, community and family rewards, and economic significance that once made wifery a potential identity in itself rather than merely an extension of the identity of a man.[2] That potential, however, is nearly impossible to duplicate outside a preindustrial farming community. As a result, the only part of that pre-sexually identified identity that an individual woman can recapture nowadays is the dedication to family (now merely nuclear) that it entailed. Like most other women of my generation, I tried that. But about all it really amounted to, for me, was a subordination of sex to love. I tried to make sex-desire irrelevant by substituting religious and then familial devotion. I tried to build an identity on the basis of a love relationship designed to de-sexualize my life. But I was never able to center commitments of this sort—religious commitment at first and then commitment to love a man and create a home—and simultaneously to nurture and protect my homosexual desires and practices. While not all such commitments preclude sexual practices altogether, they typically do preclude or severely limit homosexual practices, and since my homosexuality was precisely what those attempts to construct an identity not centered on sexuality were supposed to protect, my project was doomed.

My second strategy, that of silence, was equally doomed. Refusal to own up to any particular sexual identity didn't exempt me from having one; it just left the labeling to people other than me. In other people's eyes I was either a closet queer or an honorary het—neither of which I wanted to be. Eventually, silence gave way to a strategy of misinformation. Instead of saying and doing nothing to give anyone any clue to my sexual desires or self-understanding, I intentionally said and did contradictory things. Unfortunately, though, true liminality was beyond the imaginations of all concerned, and I still ranked among the pathetically closeted and ridiculously repressed in the estimation of most of my acquaintances. Alone I could not evade sexual identification, and my society was simply not going to cooperate in my project of defiance.

The third strategy, that of placing sexual identification in question by investigating and pointing out the historical variability and political investments of sexual classification, held some promise as a means of influencing the social environment in which my self-understanding and presentation had to unfold. Maybe if I could change people's minds about the nature of sexuality, I could create a social space in which sexual identities could at least be somewhat fluid if not nonexistent altogether. Through graduate school and my first years as an assistant professor I worked especially hard on this project. However, change, if it is forthcoming at all, is exceedingly slow, particularly if the means used to effect it are almost exclusively cognitive.[3] No matter how many questions I raised about the alleged naturalness of sexual identities, no matter how much evidence I presented that sexuality is a social construct that could be otherwise, I could not create even a small, localized society in which enacting neither a heterosexual nor a homosexual identity was truly an option. I just didn't have the power, alone, to resist sexual classification, and I certainly didn't have the ability to create alternative ways of thinking and living for others that I couldn't maintain for myself.

So the time came when, nearing thirty, I decided the only sane, reasonably healthy thing to do was to take on the label that in fact fit me quite well, get with the program, jump on the bandwagon, and affiliate myself (at least in name) with the queer community (which at the time was no more than an idea embodied only in books and magazines as far as my experience was concerned). Of the options available to me, that one seemed the least likely to be perpetually lonely, the least costly to myself and others, and the least complicated; I believed in the long run it would afford me the greatest amount of security, pleasure, and self-respect. Given that the world is how it is, I chose over the next few years to forfeit virtually every aspect of the life I had built for myself, to name myself lesbian as others had already done so often to me, and to affirm my homosexuality and live my life openly and proudly in accordance with the standard dictates of what was coming to be known at that time as the lesbian/gay/bisexual/ transgender ("lgbt") movement. In other words, I decided to come out.

Though in some ways the decision was a great relief, in many ways it was also a betrayal of all I had been and had worked for for most of my life. My sense of self for nearly twenty years had been bound up with those projects of resisting and refusing a sexual identity. To take one on, no matter how much doing so simplified and promised to enrich my life, was to abandon the only way of being that made any sense to me and to give in to all the people who—like my ninth-grade biology teacher—insisted that I play their game and define and live my life by their rules. It was to capitulate to the power of discourses that I knew had constructed sexual identities along with their alleged "naturalness" as a means for justifying extensions of surveillance and mechanisms of control throughout a population and its individuals' life spans. Coming out as lesbian to friends and relatives and colleagues when I was a thirty-year-old college professor felt not very much different in many respects from coming out as queer to psychiatric technicians when I was a high school senior. It was a "confession" that I felt forced to make only because all other courses of action were already exhausted. Coming out was not a liberating experience for me—or rather, it was only liberating in some ways and for some parts of me; in the main, I experienced it as an acknowledgment of defeat and as a surrender to a socially constructed identity that brought with it a set of strict limitations, expectations, and requirements over which I had little control. I chose it because I finally admitted that I had no choice. My resistance had been futile in the face of such vast networks of social power. I had failed.

It might appear that Foucault had failed as well. After all, was it not precisely these sorts of strategic resistances that his analysis of sexuality suggested? Wasn't I supposed to try to build a life in rejection of sexuality as the foundation of my identity? Wasn't I supposed to try to render sexual classification systems unstable by refusing to confess and by attacking their grounding in claims of natural givenness? Hadn't I done my Foucaultian best? And now it looked to be all for nought—right in theory; impossible in practice. Apparently my only real option all along was not to challenge the deployment of sexuality as a network of power but just to try to influence the content of our society's sexual knowledge, just to join with all those squeaky clean gay Republicans who insist that good gay people, like good straight people, are really just plain old middle Americans and should be treated as such.

I couldn't help being a little angry that twenty years of struggle had seemingly come to nothing. Foucault had insisted: "The rallying point for the counterattack against the deployment of sexuality ought not to be sex-desire, but bodies and pleasures" (HS1 157; VS 208). And that was exactly what I had been doing, wasn't it? I had been trying to refuse, ignore, de-center, contest, and even attack the notion of sex-desire as the founding truth of a human life, and at the same time I had been trying—contrary to my grandmotherly models—to maintain a genuine connection to my bodily well-being and to my homosexual pleasures. Wasn't that right? Didn't I have it right? Well? Didn't I?

Maybe not.

I had just assumed that I more or less knew what the terms in that vague little sentence really meant. I mean, I can read, and they weren't foreign words, right? Surely it's perfectly obvious that the problem with sex-desire as a rallying point for the counterattack against the deployment of sexuality is that sex-desire is a key element in that deployment, since it is the current basis for the division of humanity into hetero and homo, which is in turn a key component of sexual oppression. If we make sex-desire our rallying point and so emphasize and reinforce our homosexual (or heterosexual) identities, we won't be in a position to mount a truly radical challenge to the apparatuses of power that hold us in their grip; we will have to affirm and hold onto the very element in those apparatuses that stabilizes and unifies them. We've got to avoid doing that and look elsewhere for the places within sexual networks of power where we can stand and launch our assaults. Okay, bodies and pleasures sound like reasonable starting points. And I had been affirming them both. Hadn't I? So why did it all fall apart?

Either something was wrong with that sentence from Foucault's book, or something was wrong with the way I'd been reading it. As discouragement, fatigue, and inexorable logic moved me toward the decision to come out, simultaneously I moved toward a more subtle and complex understanding of what resistance and counterattack might turn out to be. Heretofore I had thought that resistance and refusal of sexual identity were the bases of revolt and revolutionary change, that the former led directly to the latter. If you want to undermine the system, then you've got to stand opposed to it. But I began to see that that wasn't necessarily the case, and even the contrary might sometimes be true. In some instances counterattack might only become possible once resistance had been foregone. These were new thoughts, brought about by the crisis of eminent failure and loss as much as by continued meditation on Foucault's work. But Foucault's work played a crucial role: If I had not begun to attempt a revision of my interpretation of Foucault's assertion, I don't think I would have been able to admit defeat and relinquish that old sense of self and the resistant way of life that I had built around it.

As I looked back over Foucault's texts, my reading of them, and the pieces of the life that was coming apart around me, three heterogeneous elements began to form a kind of pattern, almost like a pulsating neon sign saying: "Pay attention!" Eventually these three converged in a way that provided the energy for the transformation I needed to undergo. First, there was that vague little sentence itself: "The rallying point for the counterattack against the deployment of sexuality ought not to be sex-desire, but bodies and pleasures." Gradually I realized I didn't know the meanings of any of those terms. Foucault's assertion separated bodies and pleasures from desire, as if such a thing were possible, but I couldn't really think bodies and pleasures apart from desire. Interpreting that sentence, which I had assumed to be fairly clear, was going to take a lot of work. Second, over and over again—not in the books but in the interviews in the gay press—there was Foucault himself not shunning or evading a sexual identity but accepting and even boldly claiming one. In several interviews in the three years before his death, he labeled himself homosexual, outright and without equivocation. What was I to make of that? What kind of resistance to sexual categories and identities was he advocating? It certainly didn't seem like he practiced what he preached. Yet a careful reading of those interviews is revealing. While he did clearly label himself *homosexual* or *gay,* very often in the same breath he reworked that label in ways designed to divorce and free it from its pairing with heterosexuality as its opposite. "Being gay is not, I believe, identifying oneself with the physical masks and psychological features of the homosexual, but rather trying to work out and evolve a lifestyle" (FL, 5B; AMV, 165). He wasn't just capitulating; he was claiming his homosexuality in order to recast gayness, to take it up not as a kind of being but rather as a kind of practice: "It's now up to us to step forward into a gay asceticism, which would involve working on ourselves and inventing—I don't mean discovering—an as yet uncertain way of being" (FL, 5A; AMV, 165). Taking on the label, he seemed to be saying, need not consist simply in coalescing with the sexually outcast masses nor in contributing to an ever-growing body of clinical sexual truth. "The problem is not trying to find out the truth about one's sexuality within oneself, but rather, nowadays, trying to use our sexuality to achieve a variety of different types of relationships. And this is why homosexuality is probably not a form of desire, but something to be desired. We must therefore insist upon *becoming* truly gay, rather than persist in defining ourselves as such" (FL, 4A–B; AMV, 163). Was Foucault advocating surrender?

Maybe. But not surrender to a power/knowledge network that would identify, subsume, and use me for its own clearly tyrannical ends. Surrender, rather, to a new, open-ended set of ascetic practices.

Third and finally, an element emerged from late childhood, a part of an ancestral story. Unaccountably, for the better part of a year, over and over in my head I heard the first line of the sixth chapter of the book of Isaiah[4]: "In the year that King Uzziah died I saw the Lord sitting upon a throne. . . ." This line is the opening passage in Isaiah's description of the vision wherein he was given his holy mission and the gift of prophecy. Isaiah is terrified; no one sees the face of God and lives. Yet Isaiah does live. He lives because a seraphim cleanses his mouth with a burning coal. After he has undergone this near-death experience and purification, he is able to hear Yahweh's request for a messenger: "Whom shall I send, and who will go for us?" At that point Isaiah makes his famous reply: "Here am I! Send me." Isaiah's vision is life-transforming; thereafter, he is never the same.

Finally, after months of hearing this passage from Isaiah in my head, I began to remember a sermon I had heard in childhood. It took that first line as its text: "In the year that King Uzziah died I saw . . ." The sermon, as I recall it, was about how the good things in our lives—the accomplishments, gifts, triumphs, the mainstays, all the things that we value and that give our lives meaning—very often only obscure our vision and prevent us from seeing what it is that we must do. As long as Uzziah was alive, as long as there was a strong and benevolent king upon an earthly throne, as long as there was stability and some hope for a progressively better world, Isaiah could not see the path that his life should take. It was the crisis, the grief, and the fear brought on by the death of the sovereign Uzziah, the guarantor of order and meaning, that opened Isaiah's eyes. Or so the preacher told us that Sunday years and years ago.

In the year that I watched all that had given order and meaning to my life pass away, somehow out of the ashes of discarded and disdained memory that story resurfaced. From out of my own distant and almost forgotten past, a voice reminded me: "Even what is good may be a hindrance. All that is must be relinquished. One must give oneself over to what is as yet unknown." Black snakes of abysmal thoughts, threatened survival, heralds of a life transformed. It was time to give up, let go, sacrifice the work that had defined my life and provided it with order for so many years. For most of my life I had made a virtue of refusal and of independence. And I had called those things my truth over against the lies that others insisted were my truth, the truth of my being. But, right as I was, good as that was, I had to admit to myself that

I had gotten weary, mired down; I had gotten stuck. I was, as Nietzsche says, stuck to my own virtuous wilfulness and fast becoming victim to my own strength.[5] My independence of mind and self-definition were illusions, because in reality I was in deadlock, gripped even in my resistance by the powers I opposed. And not only the strength of the opposition, but my own strength held me prisoner there.

It was time to let go. But I was afraid. I knew—or at least I believed I knew—what would happen to me if I stopped refusing sexual labels and self-conceptions: *I would become a reified pervert, thoroughly discredited and unable to speak.* That was what had started my career of dissidence in the first place. But Foucault's avowals of his own gayness undermined my assurance on that point. Maybe I didn't know exactly what would happen to me. Maybe if I stopped resisting sexual categories something would happen that I couldn't even imagine. On the one hand, that was cause for hope. But on the other, it was cause for a new kind of fear. I found myself having to admit that one of the reasons I was so terribly afraid of giving myself over to the label *gay*—which had nothing to do with the primary reason, namely, that my previous experience told me that enforced confinement and malicious, hateful assault on my physical and mental integrity were likely results—was that I was still thinking in terms of master plans and reasons and arguments. I was still all tied up in the idea that political action takes place only after a plan has been laid out. Since I couldn't see where declaring myself gay would lead me, I was afraid to declare it. I wanted to understand the plan, the complete set of directions, *before* I started moving at all. Though I was suspicious of secular humanisms, I was still engaging the world like a humanist engages it: I wanted theory to master and direct practice; I wanted to have rational and complete guidelines and a set of guarantees; I didn't want to plunge blindly into a transformative process. But it was time to let go of my desire for mastery and to give myself over to life beyond my control, because the fact was I was never going to go anywhere if I insisted on seeing the destination in advance. Even Foucault's little assertion about how to launch a counterattack, his political "directions," would never make sense in advance; they would only begin to make sense once I started moving, trying to follow them.

There are two parts to those "directions": We must (1) reject desire and (2) affirm bodies and pleasures as rallying points for radical political action. I had spent years paying a lot of attention to the first part of the sentence but not much attention at all to the second part. I had vigorously rejected self-definition by sex-desire but had allowed the terms *bodies* and *pleasures* go largely unthought. After all, I reasoned (when I reasoned at all), everybody knows what bodies and pleasures are, so why worry about them? They would take care of themselves. Strangely enough, my way of reading Foucault's little sentence had just the reverse bias of most commentators' readings. The usual interpretive approach is to ignore Foucault's warning against basing politics on desire totally and then to decry his recommendation of bodies and pleasures.[6] Most commentators, in other words, spend very little time wondering why Foucault warns us away from desire and loads of time wondering how bodies and pleasures could possibly serve as rallying points for anything. Elizabeth Grosz is an exceptional reader in that she has puzzled over both parts of Foucault's assertion. She asks: "[I]s it that bodies and pleasures are somehow outside the deployment of sexuality? Or are they neuralgic points within the deployment of sexuality that may be strategically useful in any challenge to the current nexus of desire-knowledge-power? Why are bodies and pleasures a source of subversion in a way that sex and desire are not?"[7] Grosz's third question points to the very heart of Foucault's last works on sexuality and suggests the direction in which an answer lies, the direction I think Foucault in fact takes and compels his genealogically enthralled readers to take. Once we start thinking genealogically, we do begin to see major differences between desire on the one hand and bodies and pleasures on the other. Bodies and pleasures are not outside the history and deployments of sexuality, as some commentators assume Foucault intends to claim. But their histories within those deployments differ significantly from the history of sex-desire. In turn, those historical or genealogical differences give bodies and pleasures a different place in current sexual networks of power. That means that there are also major strategic differences between bodies and pleasures and desire. In the rest of this chapter I'll trace Foucault's genealogical account of desire, and then in the next two chapters I'll take up the question of how desire's genealogy makes it a very different phenomenon than are bodies and pleasures.

As avid readers of Foucault's work know, the *History of Sexuality* series announced in the introductory volume published in French in 1976 and English in 1978 was never finished; moreover, the last two volumes, coming eight years after the first, completely reoriented his study, refocusing it both temporally and thematically. In these later two books we are not given the promised analyses of the hystericization of women's bodies, the pedagogization of children's sex, the socialization of procreative behavior, or the psychiatrization of perverse pleasure (HS1, 104–5; VS, 137–38)—all of which I had really looked forward to getting; we are not even given an analysis of events within the eighteenth and nineteenth centuries, where Foucault had focused his attention before. Instead Foucault turns to classical Greece and imperial

Rome and to the place of sexual practices within dietary regimes and techniques of self-discipline in those time periods. These changes (along with significant stylistic changes as well) are more than a little surprising, and for me they were upon first reading in the mid-1980s way more than a little disappointing.[8] I wanted to know more about how sexual subjectivity had emerged in the nineteenth century, but that's obviously not what interested Foucault for the last eight years of his life.

As I took up the project of reworking my interpretation of that sentence in *The History of Sexuality*, I began to think about the reasons why Foucault might have made this major change in his philosophical, historical, and literary plans. No doubt he had many reasons, but the one he articulates most clearly and simply is this:

> [I]t seemed to me that one could not very well analyze the formation and development of the experience of sexuality from the eighteenth century onward, without doing a historical and critical study dealing with desire and the desiring subject. . . . [T]he idea was to investigate how individuals were led to practice, on themselves and on others, a hermeneutics of desire. . . . [I]n order to understand how the modern individual could experience himself as a subject of a "sexuality," it was essential first to determine how, for centuries, Western man had been brought to recognize himself as a subject of desire. (HS2, 5–6; UP, 11–12)

Clearly, Foucault sees an historical distinction between desiring subjectivity and sexual subjectivity, a distinction that is obscured in current deployments of sexuality. Desiring subjectivity, it would seem from these passages, is one historically necessary condition for the possibility of the emergence of sexual subjectivity—without which a deployment of sexuality is now virtually unimaginable. But the two are not necessarily identical.

That there is some historically conditioning connection between the two forms of subjectivity may not in itself be enough to disqualify desire as a rallying point for attacks against sexuality—although it should be enough to give us pause—but Foucault's analysis suggests that there is much more. As I'll try to make clear in this chapter and the next two, desire and sexuality's most oppressive deployments are often more than merely accidentally entangled, and the conditioning relation runs more than one way. In contemporary deployments, discourses of desire thoroughly permeate and are thoroughly permeated by normalizing sexual discourses; the two sets of discourses are inextricable. Thus, we can presume, sexual subjectivity and desiring subjectivity are, in our day, likewise inextricable.

That certainly seems to be true for us queers. Our sexual subjectivities and our desiring subjectivities seem to be one and the same.

Surely (many people would assert), given the tremendous diversity among homosexual people, the only thing that makes us *us* is the alleged deviance and the particular direction of our desire. After all, the only way, definitively, to tell a gay person from a straight person is to note the type of desire each has, isn't it? Gay and lesbian people are no different, morphologically, from straight people. Our pleasures are no different, either; an orgasm is an orgasm, whether it's had in the company of a woman, a man, or oneself alone. Even sexual acts and practices will not definitively distinguish homosexuals from hetero-sexuals. Not only can a straight couple do most of the things we do, but lots of straight people have done all the things we do, because they have had sex with someone of the same sex at some point in their lives.[9] That doesn't mean—as many of us gay folks know the hard way—that those people are not still straight. But if neither bodies, nor pleasures, nor practices will serve to differentiate straights from gays, then surely it's only desire that makes us different from heterosexuals. Therefore, homosexuality (like heterosexuality) is a matter of desire alone, isn't it?

In fact, I don't think the difference between heterosexual and homo-sexual people can be reduced to a difference of desire; I think it's dangerous and dishonest of anyone to insist that it can be. But this question of the relationship between desire and sexuality will have to wait. First it's important to reconstruct Foucault's genealogy of "desir-ing man."

A GENEALOGY OF DESIRE

Much as Nietzsche's genealogy of morality begins with a time before evil, before moral subjectivity, Foucault's genealogy in *The His-tory of Sexuality* begins with a time before sex, before sexual subjectivity. In *The History of Sexuality, Volume 2* (more commonly called *The Use of Pleasure*), however, Foucault goes back even farther in history in order to describe a way of being a human being that did not include an experience of being, fundamentally and inevitably, a subject of desire, much less an experience of being a subject of sexuality. We go back, then, to classical Greece, to the city states around 400 B.C., the time of Socrates, Plato, Alcibiades, and Sophocles. Foucault contends that these men, along with their contemporaries, did not experience themselves as sexual subjects just as he contends that people in the sixteenth century in Europe did not, but even more surprising, he also contends that these Greeks did not experience themselves as subjects of desire.[10]

Now, this may seem a little far-fetched, since of course these men had desires, as we understand the term. They wanted all kinds of things from food to wine to sex to fame and glory and right relationships with their gods. But in order to be a subject of desire as Foucault uses that phrase, a person has to have a certain kind of relationship to his or her longings and a certain conception of desire. To be a subject of desire means to view desire as a central issue in one's life and to conceive of desire separately from other kinds of concerns. The ancient Greeks didn't conceive of desire, even desire for sex, in the same way that we post-Freudians do. For them, Foucault asserts, desire was not a particular, individual event or thing. Instead, it was just one part of a dynamic (shifting, changing) ensemble that also included pleasure and act. These three elements formed one thing, according to the ancient Greeks; they were inseparable from one another and equally important. They named this thing *aphrodisia*. Free Greek men were ethical subjects concerned not with desire but with various issues including *aphrodisia*.

Furthermore, according to Foucault, not only did the Greeks have a very different conception of desire's place in relation to other concepts, feelings, or things; they also had a different definition of *desire*. To them, desire was not just that feeling one gets as part of the experience of privation or lack—as it might be said to be for psychoanalyst Jacques Lacan, for instance. If they had seen it that way, of course, the ancient Greeks would have had to view desire as more fundamental to the human being's natural state than either pleasure or actions are, and, as already pointed out, they did not. Instead, they understood desire as a longing that comes only after pleasure has been experienced and at the moment when memory of pleasure is invoked through a depiction or mental representation of the acts that are likely to bring it about. (A virgin, therefore, cannot experience sexual desire, nor can a lifelong teetotaler desire a good wine.) Desire is neither logically nor chronologically prior to the pleasurable acts that nowadays we might see as its satisfaction.[11]

When we think about what we have to do to be good citizens or parents or neighbors or friends or spouses, one of the first and most important things we think about doing is controlling our desires, by which we often mean denying them; mastery of desire is a fundamental concern for those of us in our culture who strive to be ethical. Not so for the ancient Greeks. The work of the Greek citizen who wanted to be strong, healthy, and good focused not on desire but rather on questions about exercise, diet, and this ensemble, the *aphrodisia*, and consisted not of learning to squelch desires but of learning to manage or administer these ensembles of impulses, needs, and practices so as to be respected in the city state and fit to lead others, so as to shape a beautiful life.

It is important to note, as Foucault does, that this sort of ethical project in ancient Greece could only be undertaken by a relatively small number of people, the citizens, a group that did not include women, children, or slaves.[12] Subordinates could not exercise this kind of ethical self-control, because they had to be under the control of other people. This is yet another indication of how different from our own the Greek conception of desire and subjectivity were. Whereas we tend to believe every individual has sexual desires and is defined by those desires regardless of that person's social standing, the Greeks believed that the relation a woman or even an adult male slave had to the *aphrodisia* could never be the same as the relation a citizen could have, and thus desire could not be the same thing for a citizen that it was for a noncitizen. Furthermore, the most important period of ethical self-formation for a Greek citizen was young adulthood, because that was the period when the child, who was not an ethical being, passed away and gave place to the man, who had to be an ethical being. The Greeks believed that if the personality or character was well formed in relation to the *aphrodisia* during this period, one did not need to spend much time worrying about it in middle and old age.

The idea was to create oneself, so to speak, during one's young manhood. A young man worked on himself, his feelings, thoughts, attitudes, and physique in order to become the kind of person others could appreciate. That is what ethics consisted of; it had little to do with obedience to prohibitions and nothing to do with self-abnegation. Ethics was *ethos,* a way of life. Regarding the *aphrodisia,* the point was not to abstain from pleasure or refuse to engage in courtship of either women or boys and young men; the point was to pursue potential lovers and to enjoy their bodies and one's own in ideal, manly, appropriately measured ways. One should avoid passivity, for example; one should be the active partner (the lover as opposed to the beloved) in everything from courtship to intercourse. One must not allow oneself to be penetrated, for that would be to lapse into unmanly passivity. Likewise, one should not allow one's fondness for the beloved to become a tool by which the beloved could exercise control, for that too would be to lapse into unmanly passivity not only in relation to the beloved but also in relation to one's own sentiments. To be manly (and therefore virtuous) required that one be master over all facets of the *aphrodisia* as well as all other points of ethical concern.

In the five hundred years between the time of Socrates and the time of Epictetus, from classical Greece to imperial Rome, major concerns and therefore ethical problematizations shifted. Foucault describes both the continuities and the differences in the third volume of the *History of Sexuality* series, *The Care of the Self* (HS3, 44ff; SS, 59ff). The Greeks had practiced something Foucault calls "an art of existence"; that is, they worked hard in young adulthood to shape their characters and to become the sort of men that others would recognize as ethically beautiful. Similarly, Roman citizens also wanted to create beautiful lives for themselves that others would respect. But, in imperial Rome what is at the center of the practice of the art of existence is something Foucault calls the "cultivation of the self," a lifelong enterprise rather than, as formerly in Greece, the work of young adulthood.

Among the Romans, the individual self came to be seen as fragile and vulnerable throughout life. It was in constant need of protection, nurturance, discipline, and therapy. During this time, care of the body as an integral part of the self became absolutely paramount; everything that was believed to unbalance the body was suspect, including violent exercise, wine, and rich food. Likewise, Foucault asserts, "there was greater apprehension concerning the sexual pleasures, more attention given to the relation that one might have with them. In a word, there was a more intense problematization of the *aphrodisia* . . ." (HS3, 39; SS, 53). This intensification led to what might be seen as greater sexual austerity in light of a more painstaking delineation of the body's more and less healthy states. The Romans thought it was bad to experience sexual pleasures very often because of the bodily changes, including exhaustion, that accompanied them. They did not, however, condemn sexual pleasure of any kind; they simply thought it was a good idea, for one's own sake, to be careful when and how often one indulged.

This problematization of bodily health, in turn, was closely connected with two other major features of Roman culture and thought. One was the development of an incipient quasi-universal account of human health. We can contrast two very different ways of understanding human health. One way would be to assume that a healthy person is one who feels good and is able to engage in any kind of physical activity he or she wants to engage in. This way of defining good health makes healthiness relative to individuals. A different way of understanding health would be to assume that a healthy person is one whose body is in a certain specifiable and measurable state—a person whose internal body temperature is 98.6 degrees Fahrenheit, whose blood contains a certain balance of elements, and so on. This latter way of defining health presumes that all human bodies are significantly alike and that health is not a relative term but rather a universal or constant term. The Romans began to think of health in a way that resembles the latter more than the former. Therefore, they began to measure themselves as individuals against a kind of quasi-universal norm to which they hoped to conform. The individual Roman body did not set the terms of its own well-being, then; more and more, Romans felt a need to be obedient to general principles and prescriptions for taking care of themselves in order to achieve that ideal of well-being.

A second major development in Roman culture that makes it different from ancient Greece, Foucault asserts, is a growing concern with the fragile body/self's relations with other people. In order to have a good life, a person must be ever vigilant to make sure that he or she (wives of Roman citizens were thought to have at least some ability to be ethical subjects) is not becoming too dependent upon others. Dependence renders the self vulnerable; to need others is to lack control over one's own life and to be subject to pain inflicted either by those others or by circumstances that might take them away. Psychic rather than physical dependence is what is most to be avoided, though both are important; one must police the boundaries of one's psyche so as not to allow it to become too enmeshed in the psyches of others.[13]

Even here, in imperial Rome, Foucault insists that there is no subject of desire. Romans are still ethical subjects concerned with self-mastery in relation to a variety of concerns including the *aphrodisia*. Desire is still merely an element in the *aphrodosia*; it is not problematized independently of the other elements in that ensemble. Roman citizens were not especially concerned about regulating or controlling or exploring desire as people in later cultures were and are. But in ancient Rome, unlike ancient Greece, there is a kind of subjectivity that begins to look more familiar to us than the subject of the Greek *aphrodisia* did. Sexual pleasure, whose kinship with convulsive seizures is now highlighted, is increasingly shunned as a danger, while acts increasingly are measured against a common "nature." And this means that whereas for the Greeks the three elements of the *aphrodisia*—pleasure, desire, and act—were inextricable from one another, among the Romans they are beginning to be thinkable separately from one another. Eventually, this will make possible the conception of desire as a specific thing independent of pleasure or act, and that will open the possibility for desire to become the foundation of people's self-conception.

Apparently Foucault had planned to carry on this study of the slow development of the subject of desire. Unfortunately, he died before he finished. He did draft manuscripts on Christian morality and on the sixteenth century,[14] but they have not been published. There are only brief studies and scattered interview comments available, so one can only speculate on what would fill the historical gap between Rome and the eighteenth century.[15] Nevertheless, this much is clear: According to Foucault, the subject of desire comes into existence only after Christianity has begun to establish itself. Only then do human beings—and now this activity is not strictly limited to elite males and the wives with

whom they stylize their marital relations—come to understand themselves fundamentally as desiring beings and come to understand their
ethical work as the interpretation, the confession, and often the slow
eradication of sensual desires. Action is now relegated to the realm of
obedience. Pleasure, as Foucault says jokingly, no longer exists; that is,
it occupies no significant ethico-theoretical space and is mentioned only
to be dismissed.[16] Desire becomes paramount, for it is through a hermeneutics of desire (undertaken under the guidance of one's confessor)
that one seeks to expose and reverse the Fall into disobedience, evil, and
deathliness. One must purify oneself of all sensual desires in order to
satisfy the only desire a mortal, finite, dependent, and essentially
lacking being should have: the desire for God, who is Truth.

People often assume that the early Christians dedicated themselves
to something as ambitious as complete mortification of the body, that
their goal was to stop engaging in any kind of sensual bodily functions.
But, as Foucault demonstrates, that was not quite the case. Bodily
functions themselves were not slated for eradication; they were viewed
as, perhaps unfortunately, inevitable. What was to be eradicated instead
were the desires that one might feel in association with the performance
or undergoing of those functions. The body might have to go on
functioning in certain ways—eating, drinking, sleeping, excreting—but
the movements of the body didn't have to have any impact on the mind
or soul; a person didn't have to desire the performance of those functions, look forward to them, or encourage them in any way. Though he
does not formulate or endorse it explicitly, Augustine sets the stage for
this project of eradication when he argues in *The City of God against the
Pagans*, Book 14, sections 16–24,[17] that in paradise (before the Fall)
human beings had complete voluntary control over the excitation of
their genital organs and so did not experience lust as a precondition for
procreation. Augustine's successors reasoned that if human beings did
not experience lust before the Fall, redeemed and purified human
beings after the Fall need not experience it either. Foucault quotes
Cassian (a younger contemporary of Augustine's who lived from 360
until 435) as saying: "We have to repress the reactions in our minds and
the emotions of our bodies until the flesh can satisfy the demands of
nature without giving rise to any pleasurable feelings, getting rid of the
excess of our bodily humors without any unhealthy urges and without
having to plunge back into the battle for our chastity" (BC, 237–8; CC,
305). The issue is not mortification of the body per se, then, but purification of the soul, elimination of those agitations the soul usually
experiences in response to bodily functions—which in Cassian's text is
the need of the monk's body to excrete excess semen. Nocturnal emis-

sions are not expected to cease, but they need not jeopardize the monk's chastity if he does not allow pleasures or desires for intercourse and fantasies thereof to accompany them.

It is important to notice here that, according to Cassian, a monk's battle for chastity extended, in the final rounds, to control over his dream life. He might fend off impure fantasies during waking hours, but eliminating them from his dreams was perhaps the most difficult feat of all. Nevertheless, there were techniques for doing so. One should be careful not to indulge in overeating or in any impure thought during the day, because these would surely affect one's dreaming. Impure dreams are a sign of hidden lust, according to Cassian, "a sign of the corruption that festers within, and not just a product of the night. Buried in the depth of the soul, the corruption has come to the surface during sleep, revealing the hidden fever of passions with which we have become infected by glutting ourselves all day long on unhealthy emotions" (BC, 237; CC, 305). One might convince oneself during waking hours that one was pure, but in dreams the truth comes out and the real state of the monk's soul reveals itself.

As Foucault points out, Cassian's fifth-century advice and admonitions to monks is far removed from later medieval and early modern Christianity's codes and practices, but in his writings we begin to see the shape of things to come. Exactly how Foucault would have traced the transformations of Christian ascetic practices through the next several centuries is unknowable, but we do know that the mid-sixteenth-century Council of Trent (1545–1563) constitutes in his view something of a turning point. The Council of Trent laid down a detailed set of new procedures for the examination and purification of the clergy, but, perhaps more importantly for Foucault's work, these techniques were then imposed on the laity as well,[18] and the ideal of purity came to be applied to married people as well as celibate ones. At that point, even people who were expected to continue having sex had a Christian duty not to allow the necessity of sexual performance to give rise to desire for it; one could have sex, but one couldn't enjoy, want, fantasize, or even think about it. The body was not to be allowed to influence the mind. People who thought about it or wanted to engage in it when they weren't and didn't have to were sinners in need of confession and absolution.

Clearly after the Council of Trent the issue for Christians was not so much intercourse itself, a bodily function, as the agitations of the soul that its performance, necessary for the health and well-being of the individual and the society, might provoke. Mind/body or soul/body dualism was a central feature of Christian thinking by this time. Therefore, what was at issue now wasn't the bodily act (whatever it might be) but the desire for pleasure that might become a motivation for committing the act when commission wasn't physically necessary. The soul could remain aloof from the body if it tried hard enough, and aloofness was one of its goals. What was problematized, therefore, was desire. The most important concern a good Christian had was how to master and eradicate his or her desire. In this developing Christian discourse we witness a movement toward establishing and maintaining a strict separation between the immortal soul and the flesh that is its temporary housing. Flesh will be flesh, but a Christian must not allow the mechanics of flesh to give rise to impure thoughts. A Christian must obey, not desire.[19]

Despite the familiarity of this way of thinking, Foucault insists that these ascetic discourses and practices are not yet the discourses and practices that he marks out as constituting sexuality. Sex is not the central issue here, even though desire is. And sexual desire is not an enduring feature of one's essence or identity. As a Christian, one constitutes oneself as a desiring subject only to forfeit oneself so constituted. The desiring subject is transient; the self as a deathly bundle of longing is identified only in order to be overcome. The manifestation of desire in Christian confession, then, is a necessary prelude to a sort of exorcism; it is not the bringing to light of a permanent truth of the self that one must accept and perhaps even cherish. A medieval or renaissance Christian is a subject of desire, but not yet a subject of sexuality.

Sexuality, Foucault asserts, begins to emerge in the eighteenth century.[20] From that point on, the "techniques of verbalization" refined throughout the Christian period (the techniques of extracting and giving a confession) are "reinserted in a different context by the so-called human sciences in order to use them without renunciation of the self but to constitute, positively, a new self."[21] This is the beginning of the constitution of the subject of sexuality, a slow and uneven process across class, age, and gender groups that will require decades of extension and consolidation before producing types of selves familiar to us (see HS1, 116–18; VS, 153–56). This new kind of self became possible because, on the one hand, people already experienced themselves as subjects of desire and, on the other hand, people began to move away from the Christian doctrines and practices that made it incumbent upon them to try to eliminate desire from their lives. Desire was a very prominent feature of most people's experience now, but they began to change their valuation of it.

In the eighteenth century, as we learned in *The History of Sexuality*, officials began to concern themselves primarily with the medicalization of the bourgeois family, infant mortality, and masturbation among male schoolchildren. Around 1800, hysteria takes the stage, and along with it the nineteenth century focuses attention upon masturbation among female children, and then upon perverse sexualities (beginning around 1840).[22] Just before mid-century authorities and charitable organizations also begin to extend such discourses to their analyses, policies, and practices regarding the lower classes. Foucault sees these events as the beginning of the creation of sexuality as a concept and as the presumed foundation of human culture and personality. Of course this change doesn't take place all at once. Sexuality's development took more than a hundred years, as did the development of sexual subjectivity within it. Its culminating point, Foucault suggests, occurred around the turn of the twentieth century with the emergence of psychoanalysis and its "procedures that set sex and truth in relation. In our time," Foucault asserts, "there isn't a single one of the discourses on sexuality which isn't, in one way or another, oriented in relation to that of psychoanalysis" (CF, 219).

Foucault does not make clear exactly how the subject of desire, for whom what is problematized is the flesh, gives way to the subject of sexuality, for whom what is problematized is sex. But the gaps are not terribly difficult to fill. Among the many shifts that might be significant, I will suggest two. One is the slow secularization of the knowing subject, beginning, as Foucault points out, with René Descartes. The other is the relatively rapid constitution, within the multifarious emerging discourses of sexuality in the early nineteenth century, of the unitary epistemic object "sex."

Descartes, a layman, offers the western world a methodology of knowing intended to replace the methodology taught in the schools, which were almost completely controlled by the Christian clergy. For centuries, the dominant mode of reasoning in the schools had been based on Aristotle's logic. Aristotle held that reasoning in its most fundamental form is syllogistic. His classic example is this:

All men are mortal.
Socrates is a man.
Therefore, Socrates is mortal.

If the syllogism is properly constructed and the premises are true, the conclusion must also be true. Syllogistic reasoning only works, though, if the reasoner has a stock of true propositions to use as premises. This means that it can work very well in situations where one is given a set of categories and principles and required simply to determine which items fall under those categories or principles. Syllogisms lend themselves to interpretive or hermeneutic endeavors, in other words. They are useful, for example, if one is attempting to determine whether a given act is an instance of law-breaking under a certain legal or biblical code. They are less useful when no set of categories or principles is given at the outset—such as when one is attempting to justify a new scientific theory, as Descartes and many of his contemporaries sought to do. Thinkers before Descartes' time didn't distinguish between hermeneutic and natural scientific enterprises, because they understood nature to be a book, readable just as the Bible is readable by those skilled in esoteric hermeneutic arts. Descartes does see a distinction, so he suggests what he terms a "geometrical" rather than a hermeneutic method of reasoning for scientific tasks. Like most others in his day, Descartes uses the locution "the book of the world," but in practice he no longer treats the natural world entirely like a book in need of interpretation. Scientific truth is not to be sought through more or less esoteric interpretive practices. It is available through deduction to anyone. The would-be knower need undergo no rituals of purification. All one must do is discipline oneself to the evidence that any subject has available to him or her.[23] In making this sort of claim, Descartes is going against the Church, which held that real knowledge is only possible for people (mostly men) who take holy orders and live celibate, highly ascetic lives. He is implying that anyone can know whatever there is to know if they use a method like his; he is holding out a new, secular key to knowledge. As Foucault puts it, "The relationship to the self no longer needs to be ascetic to get into relation to the truth. . . . Thus I can be immoral and know the truth" (OGE, 252). Anyone can be a subject of knowledge.

Descartes' work was wildly popular in his own time, even though it was eventually banned by the Vatican and by some Protestant officials as well. Over time, it helped to create a whole new way of thinking about knowledge and of relating to one's own beliefs. An individual lay person could experience him- or herself as a knower and could begin to order his or her life with regard to that experience. Thus, a new kind of human subjectivity came into being. This new secular knowing subject did not replace the desiring subject; those who were knowers did not cease altogether to experience their desires as they had before. The two ways of understanding one's self simply coexisted—often very uneasily.[24] For the Christian subject of desire, the self was in the end to be renounced. Not so for the secular subject of knowledge. For the latter, the self, as the site and foundation of knowledge, was to be disciplined, not eliminated. Thus, the moment of self-renunciation receded, and in the meantime, the desiring subject remained caught up in and identified by its desire.

As we saw in chapter 1, in the eighteenth century, with its ever-increasing nationalistic concerns, the incipience of capitalism, and burgeoning imperialism, the discourse of the flesh begins to diminish in importance in comparison to pressing organizational issues. How can a large standing army be maintained and controlled? What resources against our enemies might we expect from within our own populations? How can we organize those populations so as produce efficient soldiers, hardworking laborers, successful merchants? How can we keep the numbers of sick and idle down? These issues led to a variety of new practices such as population surveys, adaptation of scheduling techniques from monastic settings for use in secular contexts, studies of procreative practices and birth-control methods among common people, campaigns to insure maternal health and strengthen the family unit, and the development of disciplinary techniques that treated bodies like machines that could be retooled. Many of these concerns and innovations look, in retrospect at least, like a new concern among eighteenth- and early nineteenth-century officials with sexuality. However, Foucault warns us, we must not impose a unifying conceptual framework upon these disparate innovations. The various discourses and techniques that had begun to emerge by the beginning of the nineteenth century were basically ad hoc responses to local administrative problems. As yet they had no unifying principle of their own. Not until the epistemic object "sex" emerged did they come to constitute one unified domain of human concern. Foucault writes,

the notion of "sex" made it possible to group together, in an artificial unity, anatomical elements, biological functions, conducts, sensations, and pleasures, and it enabled one to make use of this fictitious unity as a causal principle, an omnipresent meaning, a secret to be discovered everywhere: sex was thus able to function as a unique signifier and a universal signified. Further, presenting itself in a unitary fashion, as anatomy and lack, as function and latency, as instinct and meaning, it was able to mark the line of contact between a knowledge of human sexuality and the biological sciences of reproduction; thus, without really borrowing anything from these sciences, excepting a few doubtful analogies, the knowledge of sexuality gained through proximity a guarantee of quasi-scientificity; but by virtue of this same proximity, some of the contents of biology and physiology were able to serve as a principle of normality for human sexuality. (HS1, 154–55; VS, 204)

The object to be investigated—discovered, understood, and managed—within these heretofore disparate disciplines is now sex, sex as it manifests itself and develops through time in the lives of the individuals and populations that constitute a nation.

Sex, Foucault claims, was invented; it is a concept designed to give order, unity, and the status of natural inevitability to a bundle of discourses and administrative policies. There is no naturally existing single thing that every instance of the word *sex* actually names.[25] Once it emerges as an epistemic object, sex can be used to explain all kinds of things about people's behavior. Eventually, it becomes the explanatory principle par excellence, used to explain virtually everything about most of us, especially those of us deemed sexually deviant. It also makes possible one solution to the dilemma of how to reconcile the subject of knowledge and the subject of desire. Foucault writes,

> By creating the imaginary element that is "sex," the deployment of sexuality established one of its most essential internal operating principles: the desire for sex—the desire to have it, to have access to it, to discover it, to liberate it, to articulate it in discourse, to formulate it in truth. It constituted "sex" itself as something desirable. And it is this desirability of sex that attaches each one of us to the injunction to know it, to reveal its law and power. (HS1, 156–57; VS 207)

Sex is the object of both knowledge and desire. Because we desire sex—because we are driven toward it and therefore our development is governed by it—sex is something we must understand. Because the power of sex is most clearly manifested in the way it governs the development of our desire, desire is the key to knowledge of it. Hence we reactivate hermeneutic discourses of desire, now not in order to eradicate desire and sacrifice the desiring subject but in order to see through desire to that which it lacks and to which that lack always points: sex, sex itself. Sexuality is the contemporary correlate of concupiscent desire. Sexual subjectivity is the child of the subject of desire.

We can go back now to Foucault's claim at the end *of The History of Sexuality* and to Elizabeth Grosz's question about it. If we want to attack the deployment of sexuality, why should we follow Foucault's advice and turn to bodies and pleasures rather than sex-desire? Why might bodies and pleasures make better rallying points for counterattack than desire would make? If I have adequately reconstructed it, Foucault's answer, in part, is this: Through the course of recent history, the concept of desire has been narrowed to sex-desire; desire in essence (and this is most obvious in psychoanalytic discourses[26]) *is* desire for sex; it *is* sex-desire. Sex is the linchpin of sexuality. The desiring subject, once the self-sacrificial subject of Christian discourse, is now the ever-present and insistent subject of sexuality. Therefore, affirmation of desire, even in the plural, will do nothing to counter the *dispositif de sexualité.*

It is for good reason that Foucault warns us away from desire, but does he have equally good reasons for directing us toward bodies and pleasures? In chapters 5 and 6, we will work toward an understanding of how bodies and pleasures, as elements within the *dispositif de sexualité*, might differ positively from desire. But before turning to that task, we need to take a careful look at a way of thinking that at first *appears* to de-center desire in favor of bodies but in fact *actually* retains desire as paramount and construes bodies only in relation to desire. We must be careful not to make the same mistake.

THE DESIRE TRAP AND THE BODY ENSNARED

Since its "invention" in the nineteenth century, homosexuality has been construed primarily as a form of desire, and only secondarily (and often not at all) as a practice or embodiment. Very often homosexual people have resisted the idea that our "identities" amount to our desire alone, however, and for a number of good reasons:

1. Homosexuality as we live it is not merely a matter of desire any more than heterosexual desire is the only thing that makes straight people heterosexual. A person who had occasional homosexual desires but never had homosex, had frequent heterosex, and lived his or her entire life as a participant in heterosexual institutions would be class-ified by most of us as a heterosexual. Similarly, though many gay people have occasional heterosexual fantasies or desires, as long as we don't act on them and we remain active in our homosexual relationships and communities, we and everyone around us still classify us as gay. Desires matter. But it also matters what a person does and which institutions a person participates in.[27]

Anti-gay militants know this fact and fear it, because it cuts both ways. They know that if they can destroy our communities and institu-tions, they can undermine homosexuality, but they also know that if we are allowed to participate as gay people in the communities and institu-tions they claim as theirs, our presence will change those institutions and practices enough to undermine their preferred version of hetero-sexuality and, in turn, they themselves will not be the same. They are right, for example, that if same-sex couples get legally married, the institution of marriage will change, and since marriage is one of the institutions that supports heterosexuality and heterosexual identities, heterosexuality and heterosexuals will change as well.[28]

2. In the very classification of homosexual desire as perverted—as sex-desire turned aside from its appropriate object or aim—we confront the glaring problem: Desires are mobile; they can be made to turn, to change. Therefore, if who we are is based upon the nature or direction

of our desire alone, our identities can never be rendered completely stable and invulnerable to malicious and destructive influences; hostile (and even kindly) psychoanalysts, psychologists, pedagogues, and parents will always be able to assault our integrity and our senses of self by pressuring us to reorient our desires.

3. Even desires that cannot be modified need not be respected or fulfilled. Former smokers say the desire for a cigarette never goes away, no matter how many years have passed since they last lit up. Some desires are ineradicable, and yet the actions they inspire are prohibited or chosen against anyway. And why not? Isn't it better to suffer from an unsatisfied desire for a hit of nicotine than to suffer from lung cancer? The fact that a person has an ineradicable desire is not in itself an argument for the free and uninhibited satisfaction of that desire.

As long as we base our calls for justice, equality, and respect on the fact of our homosexual desire, we face the inevitability of defeat, if not at one turn, then at another. Therefore—and quite understandably—for at least 130 years homosexual people and their allies have repeatedly claimed that homosexuality is not fundamentally and merely a form of desire but instead, for some people, is a manifestation of a bodily state. Homosexuality has a biological origin, they insist, and so it is not the sort of thing that can be condemned or prohibited by religion or law. It must be allowed, because it is embedded in the bodies of those who manifest it. Thus does the body typically enter discourses of homosexuality. It is introduced as what is natural, what is least amenable to societal intervention, what is least subject to historical change. The body comes on the scene in the role as the true origin of desire, its true cause and source, and therefore as desire's redeemer.

Although this conception and use of "the body" is extremely misguided, it is easy to understand why so many homosexual, gay, and lesbian activists have made this discursive move. As I write these words I recall the February, 1997, bombing of the Other Side, an Atlanta lesbian bar. Five patrons were injured in the initial explosion, and police and paramedics narrowly escaped injury from a second bomb discovered just a few minutes after rescue teams came on the scene. The following week a group calling itself "The Army of God" claimed responsibility for the crime. The "Army" promised more attacks on homosexuals and "declared war" on the government that (allegedly) protects us.[29] While obviously the Army of God is not representative of the population at large, it isn't alone in its violent condemnation of lesbianism. We—nonheterosexual people—are under attack. There are violent assaults on queer people; weekly, daily, physical assaults are perpetrated against us for no reason other than that we are identified as "fruits," "dykes," "fairies," or "faggots" and our very existence is deemed offensive. But in addition to the growing number of people attacking us with bombs, guns, knives, or fists, an even larger number of people are attacking us with words. They are telling us that we are criminals, unfit mothers and fathers, enemies of religion and family, threats to national security. They are telling us we shouldn't be who we are. These are words only— though some may be decreed by judges or codified by legislatures—and words are not bombs. Yet, with terrorism against us on the rise,[30] we can hardly help but hear these words as attempts at moral justification for the bombs. It becomes hard to tell the difference between physical and verbal assault, because as the bombs fly, the words are telling us we should cease to exist.

We scramble to defend ourselves, to put out the fires of hatred being set all around us. We snatch at anything, any means of protection near to hand in reaction against the violence and the threats. Because the rhetoric of those who say they would maim or confine us or take our children away is the rhetoric of Christian fundamentalism, we focus our attention on countering what those people—the Pat Robertsons and Ralph Reeds—have to say. The Christian fundamentalists insist that homosexual identity is a matter of behavior alone; all of us who are homosexual could cease being homosexual this very minute just by giving up our sinful ways. And since they claim we'd be better off if we did that, they feel perfectly justified in criminalizing anal and oral intercourse, outlawing same-sex marriage and other forms of recognition of our relationships, closing our bars and community centers, and banning our literature and art. Against this kind of extremism, what tools do we have nearest to hand? Because *they* pose the threat, they set the terms of public debate. Because *they* argue that homosexuality is merely a question of behavior, of practices, we assert that homosexuality is not in fact a set of practices or form of behavior at all, but a form of *bodily desire*. We argue that giving up our homosexual behavior (including our relationships and cultural productions) would not change the fact that we are homosexual. Under such conditions we would just be unable to express our homosexuality and would, therefore, just be miserable. The desire for homosexual activity and homosexual erotic relationships would still be present, merely unsatisfied, *because it is present in our bodies,* as part of our bodies' functioning. Therefore to attempt to force us to give it up or to punish us through anti-sodomy laws, systematic legalized discrimination, and unchecked extralegal violence is cruel and unjust. Since bodies are not chosen, sexual desire is not chosen and does not disappear when sexual behavior is prohibited.

In order to argue against the fundamentalist Christian assertion that our behavior is all our homosexual identities amount to, we emphasize the elements of our identities that are rooted in desire. But, at the same time, we know that defense of any expression of desire on its own merits and without further qualification is very difficult—and maybe impossible—in a culture so thoroughly shaped by Christianity. In many places in Western culture the expression of heterosexual desire (outside of marriage and for reasons other than procreation) is hardly more defensible than the expression of homosexual desire. So we have to bring in the body to bolster our case.

Heterosexuals would have exactly the same trouble defending their desire as homosexuals do if the world were ruled by people who had never experienced heterosexual desire. Remember being eight years old and coming to the realization that all married people had intercourse? Most of us at that age found that realization almost unbearably disgusting. If the world were run by eight-year-olds and all the poor adult heterosexuals had somehow to convince them to lift the anti-intercourse laws and recognize the validity of their sexual relationships, whatever would they say to justify satisfaction of their incomprehensible desires? With a little reflection, the answer is obvious: They would say what the Pope says. (In other words, they would appropriate the explanation of someone who, like the eight-year-olds, doesn't understand the phenomenon's intrinsic good through personal experience either.) "Intercourse is important and must be allowed because that is how our species perpetuates itself." Now, apart from the fact that eight-year-olds generally don't give a rip about the species and have little interest in sharing their material goods with younger brothers and sisters, this kind of argument might work. Intercourse has an instrumental if not an intrinsic value. Of course in this day and age—given overpopulation and advanced reproductive technology—we really don't need intercourse anymore if that is its only purpose. We could outlaw it without harm to the species, and in fact the species, along with the planet's entire ecosystem, might benefit as a result. But, even so, heterosexuals would still have another argument at their disposal—the argument from evolution.

Sex-desire (allegedly at least) is not just a bizarre sui generis occurrence. It comes from somewhere. Our beleaguered heterosexuals confronting the eight-year-olds might explain that their desire—though perhaps evolutionarily passé—is an ineradicable part of their lives because of the thousands of generations of evolutionary development that gave rise to it. Heterosexual desire was an extremely beneficial aspect of an individual's genetic makeup, so it was selected for. In other words, it is deeply embedded in human bodies. As a result, it's a very strong desire whose denial results in tremendous pain for the unsatisfied. For society to inflict that much pain on any individual is unjust. Therefore it would be better for society to search for ways to offset the bad effects of intercourse rather than to eliminate intercourse itself. The eight-year-olds would still be skeptical. They might point out that many people have chosen celibacy without ill effect. They also might point out that sexual fulfillment does not actually require penetration or even a partner. And they might well refuse to allow their tax dollars to be spent to promote the heterosexual lifestyle. But at least the genetic argument has some chance. Without it, no doubt, the heterosexuals would be at a total loss.

Desire is almost always a contested field of power relations in our culture. The issue is always how the energy of desire will be directed, invested, or spent—and who will benefit. Heterosexuals are no better off than homosexuals on this score. Where heterosexuals have an advantage over homosexuals is in the way that they can deploy "the body" as explanation, justification and, therefore, redeemer of their desire. Like the heterosexuals confronting the dictatorial eight-year-olds, homosexual people confront hegemonic regimes that cannot or at least will not comprehend our desires at all, much less understand the high value we place upon fulfillment of them. But unlike heterosexuals, we have trouble explaining our desires in bodily terms. Since homosexual desire seems unlikely to have contributed to the perpetuation and strengthening of the species over hundreds of thousands of generations, we can't argue as easily that the desire is ineradicable or persistent or even terribly strong. Thus, homosexual desire seems not to be on a par with heterosexual desire, since it is not a characteristic of the naturally evolving human body. Therefore, it could be eliminated without harm to the species. Instead of protecting the rights of homosexual people, we could just work to be sure that no more of them emerge in the world.

This apparent lack of parallelism between heterosexual and homosexual desire (which amounts to the claim that heterosexual desire has a bodily source whereas homosexual desire does not) has captured the imaginations of homosexual activists for decades, and many allegedly biological theories of homosexual desire have been advanced. Recently some gay scientists with expertise in genetics and brain physiology have added to this stock of theories by attempting to prove that homosexual desire is caused by something heritable in our DNA, just as heterosexual desire allegedly is (though that assumption has never been conclusively proven either).[31] Of course a lot of things not considered beneficial are supposedly heritable—cystic fibrosis, for example—

so it isn't enough to prove that homosexuality comes from the body or the genes; scientists must also show that homosexuality is beneficial to the species just as heterosexuality allegedly is and that it has been selected for and thereby strengthened through human evolution. If that could be shown, then we homosexuals would have exactly the same kind of argument at our disposal that the heterosexuals in the above imaginary example had. We could argue that our desire was physiological and natural (not social in origin and not pathological) and at least at one time so beneficial to the species that it was intensified through evolution to the point that, even if it does not serve any evolutionary purpose now, repression of it would cause tremendous pain. Like the eight-year-olds, the heterosexuals will be skeptical. But maybe they would buy the genetic argument, if someone made a good enough scientific case.

I don't believe a good enough scientific case has yet been advanced, but it is important to examine the best candidate so far, Dean Hamer's 1993 study, which lent credence to the notion that some forms of male homosexuality might be genetically based. This examination is pertinent here for two major reasons. First, Hamer's efforts typify attempts to make "the body" a "rallying point" for gay politics *without* problematizing sexual subjectivity or desire. His work shows us what "the body" looks like inside sexuality's discursive regime; in other words, Hamer shows us "the body" un-genealogized, and by doing so he (inadvertently) shows us "the body" fully caught up in, subordinated to, and defined by "sex-desire." Second, there are commentators who claim that when Foucault advocates a turn to "bodies and pleasures" as an alternative to sex-desire, he is advocating just this sort of move, a return to nature, a turn to some sort of pre-discursive natural body that stands outside of history. If we are to see why the commentators are wrong, we must see how Foucault's work in fact differs from such a move. In that endeavor, a contrast with Hamer's work is very instructive.

Hamer published his now famous study in the journal *Science* on July 16, 1993. Within days newspapers and magazines across America hailed him as the man who had discovered the biological origins of homosexuality. Although Hamer did not claim in his 1993 article to have found a "gay gene" or even to have proven conclusively that one must exist, in his 1994 book he does claim to have discovered the true origins of homosexuality. He writes, "No one had been able to *prove* that homosexuality was swayed by genes, however, until our study offered the most convincing evidence to date that sexual orientation was genetically influenced. . . . We didn't invent a new idea, we just showed it was true."[32] And in a 1997 article in *The Advocate* Hamer asserts that "my own laboratory and others have already discovered genetic information involved in determining whether we are born male or female, whether we are gay or straight, and how many sexual partners we will have."[33] Gay activists had mixed feelings about Hamer's conclusions; some saw his work as irrelevant to their struggles, a few thought it might even be detrimental, but many believed that once the world accepted the idea that homosexuality is a natural, bodily condition, equality and respect would be forthcoming. Hamer himself seems to think his work will further the gay cause. He mentions in his book that after his study appeared he was asked to testify as an expert witness in hearings concerning the constitutionality of the infamous "Amendment 2," which prohibited the state of Colorado from ever enacting any legislation to protect people from discrimination based on their sexual orientation. As Hamer explains, the attorneys who called upon him "reasoned that if they could prove being homosexual is a deeply ingrained characteristic—and better yet, genetic—the courts would have to protect gays' civil liberties and access to the political system."[34] And in fact, the judge in the case did make reference to evidence that suggests homosexuality is biologically based when he struck down the amendment.[35]

Hamer's conclusions are founded on two types of study. For one study he located seventy-six men in the Washington, D.C., area who identified themselves as gay. He recruited these men through four institutions—the HIV clinic of the National Institute of Allergy and Infectious Disease, the Whitman-Walker Clinic (which he chose because it serves gay alcoholics and substance abusers and he believes gay people may have a genetic predisposition to addiction), the Triangle Club (a D.C. center that houses chapters of AA and Narcotics Anonymous), and a D.C. gay Christian Scientists organization. He included no women in his study and made no effort to put together a selection of gay people that was representative of the diversity of our communities. More than ninety percent of the men were white and non-Hispanic. Average age was thirty-six. Most had attended college. And all these men were willing to talk to complete strangers about their sexual orientation and to allow interviewers to discuss their sexual orientation with members of their families.[36]

Hamer asked these men whether they had any gay relatives. Some of them, 13.5 percent, reported having gay brothers, and 7.3 percent reported having gay maternal uncles. Hamer takes this as evidence that homosexuality is passed from mother to son. Of course, a big factor here is how many gay men there are in the population at large. If two percent of the male population is gay (which is what Hamer assumes[37]), these numbers would be significant. But suppose fifteen percent of the male population is gay.[38] Then the numbers probably only reflect a greater likelihood of disclosure between gay brothers and between a gay nephew and maternal uncle than between a gay and nongay brother or between nephews and paternal uncles. Nobody knows how many gay men there are. But two things we do know from our own experience: (1) Gay people usually know if their relatives are gay, whereas straight people often don't, and (2) since straight women tend to be more accepting of male homosexuality than straight men typically are, it's more likely that a mother will disclose her brother's gay sexual orientation to her son than that a father will disclose his brother's sexual orientation to his son. The fact that gay men know more about the sexual orientation of their mothers' relatives is no surprise.

Hamer's other study involved forty pairs of gay brothers. Again, most were white, well educated, upper middle class, and at least one of each pair lived in the D.C. area. Of these, sixty-four percent had in common a certain strip of DNA on their X chromosomes. Hamer has no theory about how that strip of DNA might actually cause homosexual feelings or behavior; he has only a correlation, not a causal account that explains that correlation. The correlation itself gives Hamer a multipoint LOD score of 4.0. (The LOD is the logarithm of the odds ratio.[39]) For simple Mendelian inheritance—for traits that are produced by only one gene—that score is extremely significant. But even if homosexuality is inherited, as Hamer notes, it is not a Mendelian trait.[40] Instead, he suggests, it is a complex trait that probably involves a number of different genes acting in combination and interacting with the environment. Recently some scientists have proposed that a LOD score of 5.4 should be obtained before scientists claim to have established a highly significant linkage between strips of DNA and complex traits,[41] and in that case Hamer's statistics fall far short of proof. Hamer offers a couple of caveats himself. He speculates that even if some forms of homosexuality are inherited, not all are.[42] Furthermore, he points out that even in cases where one identical twin is gay, his twin, who has the same genes, has more than a fifty percent chance of being heterosexual.[43]

Thus far, then, Hamer's evidence does not warrant our concluding, even in the case of those gay brothers known to share strips of X chromosomal DNA, that homosexuality is inherited. But even if we accept the idea that there is some genetic linkage, we are still a long way from showing that homosexuality is the type of genetic trait that must be expressed if it is present and that ought to be valued and protected by a society that has benefited from its presence at least through some earlier phase of human evolution. In other words, we are a long way from being able to produce an argument against our heterosexist hegemonists that would be comparable to the argument they could produce against their own uncomprehending eight-year-olds. People assume that heterosexual desire is bodily, even without scientific proof; but they're skeptical of the claim that homosexual desire is bodily, so we still have to show how or why homosexuality has been selected for if we are going to show that its expression and the legal and social protection thereof is inevitable or necessary.

Hamer offers a couple of hypotheses as to how a gene that seemingly would reduce fertility might in fact benefit the individuals who bear it and thus perpetuate itself. (1) Maybe the "gay [by which Hamer means 'gay male'] gene" is expressed both in men and women; in men it expresses itself as attraction to other men and hence decreases the bearers' fertility, but in women it expresses itself as intensified attraction to men and hence increases its bearers' fertility, perhaps more than enough to compensate for the loss of fertility of the male bearers.[44] Or (2) maybe the "gay gene" expresses itself differently in different men, so that in some men it expresses itself as homosexual desire and thus decreases their fertility but in others it expresses itself as effeminacy but not as homosexual desire and thus increases those men's ability to sneak into women's lives and impregnate them without their husbands' knowledge.[45] If one or another of these hypotheses holds, Hamer reasons, homosexuality is not pathological at all but is in fact evolutionarily beneficial. Of course, he has no evidence to support either hypothesis.

Thus, a close look at Hamer's research shows that it won't do the political work some activists and sometimes Hamer himself claim it will do. The scientific evidence isn't strong enough to support the contention that homosexuality is the type of trait whose expression ought to be allowed, much less respected. In fact, the scientific evidence isn't even strong enough to support the claim that homosexuality is a natural occurrence rather than just an aberration brought on by social forces, perhaps acting on some sort of physiological vulnerability. Such explanations of homosexuality as natural are not going to win us our civil rights or stop bashers from beating us to death or convince taxpayers to support programs for gay kids in public schools.

But more important to note than the work's scientific and political shortcomings is the extent to which Hamer's "turn to the body" fails to be a turn away from sex-desire. Hamer's route to "the body" is entirely via desire. He cannot imagine a body except as a vehicle for desire and as a container of the encoded desire that animates and defines it. The body that Hamer investigates, then, is already caught up in the very discourses of sex-desire that Foucault's work urges us to resist and undermine. Hamer's gay body is in no sense a body freed from the normalizing disciplinary power invented and consolidated over the last three centuries. On the contrary, the body Hamer articulates may be the highest expression of normalizing sexual regimes. Its sexual identity is almost literally "written across" it, just as Foucault describes the inscribed body of the invert in nineteenth-century sexology. In Hamer's discourse, to see the body is to see nothing more and nothing less than the chemical code of sex-desire.

I suspect a body like Dean Hamer's is an inevitable outcome of non-genealogizing attempts to resist sexual oppression. But, conceived though it may be by the very strongest of our instincts to resist sexual networks of power, this body is and must remain a docile body, a normalized body, a body that can never overcome.

As long as we place our hope for a better world on finding a better *apologia* for homosexual desire, like Isaiah before King Uzziah's death, we will be blind to other possibilities and unable to develop the tools and skills and networks of relationships that might actually change our lives. Sex-desire—even, perhaps especially, when it is considered as a physiologically based phenomenon—is a concept that only has meaning within an inherently oppressive arrangement of institutions, knowledges, and practices. Why waste our resources and give our lives to defend it when we could dedicate ourselves to protecting and nurturing what we really care about: our queer relationships, our queer families, our queer communities, our queer cultures, institutions, pleasures, and practices? And if "bodies and pleasures" are to be our rallying points in that effort, then we need to reconceive bodies in ways that do not place them in the service of or make them conceptually subordinate to desire. Defining ourselves and defending ourselves on the basis of our sex-desire ultimately just traps us in the very discourses, conceptions, and cultural practices that created and hold us in our pain-ridden places in the world in the first place. Rather than maintaining our defensive posture, we have to attack what oppresses us, and we can't attack heterosexism effectively without attacking the deployments of sexuality that make it possible and sustain it. As Foucault's genealogy of desiring subjectivity demonstrates, one of the most significant and powerful of those deployments is the construction of human beings as in essence subjects of sex-desire—that is, the creation of the sexual self as an epistemic object to be categorized and known and (in the case of us deviants) identified with a sexuality. If we are going to engage in queer practices and enjoy queer pleasures yet also be free of heterosexist oppression, we cannot start with our desire; we have to start elsewhere. If elsewhere is going to be bodies and pleasures, the first order of business is to be very sure that we are not thinking bodies in ways that subordinate them once again to the domination of sex-desire.⟩

5

Natural Bodies

Or, Ain't Nobody Here but Us Deviants

Now, granted, it sounds more than a little odd to declare that until I started coming out I didn't have a clue what Foucault means by *bodies* or *pleasures.* Surely by my late twenties I knew what bodies and pleasures were. After all, I knew how to use the words more or less systematically and consistently. I knew what I had and I knew what I liked, and I knew how to get what I liked from what I had. Can it be more complicated than that?

Eventually I had to face the fact that it could be more complicated than that. Bodies and pleasures have genealogies too, just as desire does; they aren't nearly as simple as current usage of the terms might lead us to believe. Coming to understand bodies and pleasures in part means coming to understand those genealogies and through them coming to see the ways in which bodies and pleasures as both concepts and realities play into and help construct the world we live in—and also some of the ways in which they might help us alter that world. This chapter is an attempt at a sketch of a genealogy of my body and of some of that body's movements of self-overcoming.

A GENEALOGY OF MY BODY, PART 1: DUALISM

One significant moment in the genealogy of bodies like mine occurs in Meditation Two of René Descartes' 1641 work *Meditations on First Philosophy* wherein the great philosopher-mathematician discusses, much to the consternation and perplexity of many commentators, a ball of beeswax. It is an irritatingly difficult little section, coming in the narrative as it does after Descartes has allegedly suspended his belief in everything that he cannot know intuitively or by deduction but before he has demonstrated the existence of anything like a physical world. At this point Descartes knows only that he thinks and so a thinking thing must exist; there is as yet no reason to believe even that more than one thinking thing exists, much less that spatial, nonthinking things like beeswax exist. There is no philosophical consensus on what this passage signifies, which leaves me free to speculate.

As I interpret the famous "ball of wax" passage, Descartes is making an extremely important point about bodies and knowledge—namely, that the two don't completely coincide, that bodies never have knowledge, that even if bodies are knowable and known, they never know themselves. Take this ball of wax on Descartes' desk, for example. It is whitish, sweet-smelling, solid, and makes a low, dull sound when thumped. But put it near the fire and soon it is no longer whitish but colorless, no longer sweet-smelling but odorless, no longer solid but liquid, and no longer audible when thumped. The wax has absolutely none of the sensible properties that it had. Yet, in spite of that fact, we know (if we know anything about physical objects at all, which is still an open question at this point in Descartes' story) that it is the same wax whether in its solid or its liquid state. We know it, but we don't know it through any bodily sense, or so Descartes implies. As far as the senses are concerned, a different object lies before us in a puddle on the hearth than the object that sat with integrity on the desk. The body cannot discern the truth of the identity of these two different appearances of the same substance. Hence, the body—the human body—cannot know the essential truth of bodies. Only the incorporeal mind can truly know.

This claim that Descartes makes about bodies—that they cannot think, judge, or know—is far from a universally accepted and obvious fact, even though by Descartes' time many people had been making similar claims for several centuries. The claim is contrary to much of our ordinary experience. We assume that others think because of the ways they behave, and we experience their behavior only in the presence of their bodies or artefacts their bodies produced. It would seem natural to assume, then, that those bodies are doing the thinking they express; that would at least be the simplest hypothesis. Further, the fact that we expect different types of thinking from different types of bodies— juvenile versus adult bodies, for example—is an indication that under ordinary circumstances we act as if we understand mentation to be a function of embodiment. Descartes was aware of these ordinarily operative assumptions, aware that in order to overcome them and act in accordance with the belief that minds and bodies are distinct we need some philosophical help. His argument and his example of the beeswax are meant to give us that help.

Descartes' project has been enormously successful. Despite some philosophical dissent (from Spinoza and Nietzsche, to name two philosophers who refused to conceive of the body and the mind as separate types of entity), something close to a Cartesian account of the body has prevailed, at least insofar as the Cartesian body is an unthinking thing. And this has been true not only in proverbial ivory towers where metaphysicians float detached from the so-called "real world"; since Descartes' time most ordinary people in the West have thought of their bodies as unthinking objects essentially different from their souls or minds. Whatever else the word *body* has signified, for hundreds of years it has fairly consistently referred to something other than the power to understand. Consequently, it has also named something other than the power to judge or choose, something other than volition or free will.

As I'll describe in a later section of this chapter, some of the specifics of Descartes' account of the body have not survived. For example, Descartes thought bodies could be completely explained in algebraic and geometrical terms as spatially related bits of matter in motion. He thought bodies were analogous to machines, collections of parts whose configurations resulted in their sensible characteristics and capacities. Most of us don't think of or experience our bodies in that way these days. In this cybernetic age, we hardly even conceive of *machines* as machines anymore, in Descartes' sense of the word. But what has stuck with us from Descartes' time is the idea that bodies are objects rather than deliberating selves, the idea that the self is somehow responsible for a body but at the same time not perfectly identical with it. I grew up within the domain of that meaning of the word *body*, and it has had a tremendous influence on every aspect of my life. It wasn't that I always experienced my body as an unthinking object. I remember, for example, that my fingers learned to play a few pieces on the piano and that they retained their knowledge even after my consciousness could no longer dredge up any pictorial or verbal information about the sheet music. I remember that my feet used to calculate the trajectory of a softball the second it rebounded off a bat, and I would dash to my place at first base or skip backwards to catch a pop fly before a single thought registered in my mind. But I tended to disregard experiences in which my body seemed so thoughtfully attuned to the world and pay attention to the ways in which it was merely an object separable from what I took to be me. I lived my embodiment for the most part within the force of that Cartesian conceptualization. Most of the time I behaved as if my body were a mere thing under the control of a mind that was distinct from it, a mind whose exclusive job it was to think and, through thinking, to be in charge.

When my sister Ann and I were very small—so young as to be hardly more than extensions of "the maternal body"—just before we all went out to attend a church function or visit a relative, our mother would invariably say to us: "Do not embarrass me." This meant: (1) Make no loud sounds of any kind via any orifice; (2) make no sudden movements that might bring skin and bone into contact with fragile furnishings; and (3) neither excrete nor secrete wantonly. Within a decade I had completely internalized those commands; before going out in public I would suffer that same little wave of anxiety my mother used to suffer as she washed our faces one last time, and I would say to my body: "Do not embarrass me."

Who was "me" in this little interchange? Clearly the one who would suffer embarrassment did not take itself to be identical to the body that would embarrass, and clearly that "me" wanted to exercise control. By early adolescence I defined myself and understood myself as precisely not a material body but rather as a mind in charge of a body—and I measured myself very often by whether I managed that body poorly or well. And that meant that I defined and understood my body as precisely and only a material object that was never rightly in charge and that could not choose or plan or even think either poorly or well.

As a mind, I did not have "good success." I got control over excretions as early as any other child, but secretions were always more problematic. There is a reason little working-class Southerners are known as "snot-nose kids": Like my siblings and neighbors with no better diet and hygiene than my own, I had an almost perpetual respiratory infection. Then came menarche. It's a cruel joke that at an age when you can barely remember to shine your shoes for assembly tomorrow you are supposed to be able to remember to take a sanitary napkin to school twenty-eight days from now. And if you don't, the consequences are dire.

Feminists have been pointing out for years now that, while our culture tends to equate women with materiality and men with mentality or rationality, women are actually called upon to exercise mental control over our bodies to a much greater extent than men are. For example: Women are expected to learn about nutrition and devise and follow dietary regimes to manage both their own weight and health and that of their husbands and children; women are expected to abstain from extramarital sex and be discreet in manner and dress so as not to arouse men to savage passion; women, whose bodies are often depicted as dirty and disorderly and foul smelling, are expected to give no evidence that any biological process is going on inside us while brothers, husbands, boyfriends, and colleagues discuss their farts and hold belching contests at festive gatherings. Being a woman in our culture means, among other things, that you live out your life in subjection to the virtually constant demand to police your body, to keep it always under strict mental control—lest it become too fat or too thin, too pale or too dark, too wrinkled, too hairy, too provocative, too needy, lest it be obtrusive or loud, lest it smell of sweat or blood or garlic, lest it leak vaginal secretions or break a nail.[1] You must master that body and keep it under strict surveillance at all times.

As a result of this injunction to police, I suspect women tend to live out a Cartesian sort of mind/body dualism even more than men in our culture do. But, at the same time and by the same token, women may well be more aware than men are of how tenuous the alleged distinction between mind and body really is.[2] The more we are called upon to make our bodies subordinate to our intellects, the more attention we must pay to our bodies and the more intimately connected to them we may feel and take ourselves to be, despite the mind/body dualism that project itself assumes and implies. No doubt this is why mind/body dualisms have been among feminist theory's most prominent problematizations, to use Foucault's word.[3] Such dualisms structure all aspects of most Western women's lives; yet all aspects of our lives also belie mind/body dualisms and call dualistic conceptions of selfhood into question. We find ourselves in the grip of mind/body dualisms, but we also simultaneously find ourselves in the midst of their continual instability and threatened disintegration.

I contended with more than the usual obstacles to total bodily management for a child of my sex and class, however. There were also grand mal epileptic seizures, guaranteed to compromise any mind's confidence,[4] and then sexual arousal at the sight of semi-naked classmates in the girls' locker room. While gay boys have a more obvious reason to fear their arousal will be detected, arousal itself was enough to terrify me even if immediate detection was unlikely. The basic fact of the matter was that I was never in control of my body. Since I believed the people around me who said I was supposed to be, I felt guilty. But inside that sense of guilt, wrapped up with it somehow, was a very different incipient belief; along with the guilt at not being able to control my body was the gnawing notion that my body "had a mind of its own." And that strange little thought is the first tremor that heralds dualism's self-overcoming.

A GENEALOGY OF MY BODY, PART 2: NATURALISM

Just as René Descartes' conception of the body forms part of the genealogy of the body I call my own, so does the body as described by seventeenth-century political theorist John Locke. According to Locke, whose work directly influenced many of the documents that ground American law and politics, disposition of one's body is one's right, within certain limits, just as disposition of one's real estate or one's cattle is one's right. The body is explicitly construed as a piece of personal property. Violation of the body amounts to violation of a person's natural and inalienable property rights, which makes self-defense just a special instance of the defense of one's possessions.[5] This body, furthermore, is my property before the advent of property law, before the advent of the civil state, before political history even begins. There are minds and bodies, Locke asserts, before there is power or politics. Minds and bodies are naturally existing givens. In history and politics, they have a crucial role to play, but their origin and source lie outside historically emergent networks of power.

It is the natural desire to protect one's property, Locke says, that eventually leads people in the pre-governmental state of nature to band together and establish an agreement, a social contract, to create a government. The government's job is to protect its citizens' property, especially their bodies. In order to provide that protection, the government requires obedience, conformity to the terms of the contract, which means citizens must give up some of their natural right to administer their property as they wish—although they may engage in the duly established political process to negotiate for as much control as possible. Government—and the freedom from the uncertainties of the state of nature that government brings—can't come into existence unless individuals relinquish some power. If they don't, the government will have no power and the contract won't be enforceable; such limits on liberty are the price of freedom from the vicissitudes of the natural state; a limit upon natural freedom is necessary if we are to have civic freedom.

But with civic freedom there comes a new cause for anxiety: government itself. There is always the danger that the government (or sovereign, in Locke's terms) will act contrary to the spirit of the original contract and put citizens' property at greater risk than they faced before. In other words, government might start acting as if it owns the citizens' property rather than as if it simply regulates disposition of that property so as to maximize citizens' freedom from chaos and interference. If that should occur, then it is necessary that citizens stand against their own government and rebel.

In the Lockean tradition, politics always involves negotiation and rule-governed struggle for control over some piece of property. Rebellion is the vanishing point of politics. Rebellion occurs when people attempt to retake property they believe was, in some original sense, theirs to control and exploit. Liberation, the goal of rebellion, always involves eliminating or minimizing the government's (or some other person's or group's) control over property one perceives as one's own. Individuals are liberated when they are freed from whatever physical (and sometimes also mental or emotional) constraints have been imposed on them and therefore are able once again to dispose of their bodies and other property as they choose. One rebels in order to regain control of something over which one exercised control previously; one rebels in order to liberate oneself from current circumstances and reinstate an original condition of autonomy. Liberation is always a restitution, restoration, or return.

Since this way of thinking about power, politics, and freedom is so familiar to us, we may not always see how tightly it binds us to a conception of bodies as ahistorical givens distinct from minds. Nevertheless, it does.[6] According to this way of thinking, my body is originally my possession (that is, it is the property of a mind to be used as that mind sees fit). In an original state of nature, before others intruded into my life and usurped control over my body, I was free to use my physical capacities and resources as I chose. This idea of the body as a piece of naturally given property in and of itself indicates a strong sense of mind/body dualism. Add to this Locke's assumption that a body has no standing as a political agent on its own—my body, for example, doesn't have the right to vote; I only have that right if I am of sound mind, and it in fact doesn't matter what condition my body is in—and it seems fairly clear that our Locke-inspired tradition of public debate reinforces a basic mind/body dualism. Further, in Locke's version of this dualism, both minds and bodies are natural entities, givens rather than social constructions or creations of power. I—my mind, my true self—already exist before I enter the political realm, and so does my possession, my body. I enter into the political realm because I want to protect my body, which is valuable to me as property, as resource and tool. The mind is the true citizen, the autonomous individual who enters into the social contract, into politics, to protect its bodily, material investments.

Without knowing the history of this way of conceiving of human being—of minds and bodies—most Americans still think about politics almost exclusively in Locke's terms. Most frame their opinions and demands in terms of property and ownership, even when those opinions and demands have to do with issues apparently unrelated to material property. We can hear echoes of Locke in debates over questions like abortion, drug use, or suicide. For example, advocates of legal abortion contend that women should have the right to control their own bodies, and neither governments nor individual men should be in a position to exploit women's reproductive capacities; proponents of legalization of controlled substances contend that the government should allow people to do whatever they like to their bodies as long as they don't harm another citizen; many who support a legalized right to die insist that people should be able to dispose of their bodies as they see fit, and contest the power of the medical profession and of government to dictate the circumstances of a body's expiration, while those who oppose such a right sometimes defend government's interest in the bodies of its citizens as resources and occasionally go so far as to assert that our bodies are not our property but in fact are ultimately the property of God.

It is in part because Americans customarily conceive of bodies as naturally given property and politics as negotiation or struggle over property that I had such a hard time understanding Foucault's proposal to make bodies a political rallying point. Bodies descended from the bodies of Descartes and Locke are not political agents or well-springs of political strength; they are simply sites of domination, much like geographical territory or natural resources. The only relevant political question regarding such a body as the one I learned to claim is: Who is in a better position to exploit that body's natural capacities, me or someone else? Am I in control of my body and do I reap the benefits of that control, or is someone else in control or in a position to reap the benefits of my control?

This is not the political question that drives Foucault's analyses; it is antithetical to Foucault's project and operates as an obstacle even to understanding it. Foucault rejects the ahistoricity of mind/body dualism that gives these questions their sense. But from early adolescence well into adulthood (since I did not set the terms of the power networks in which I found myself), the question of who was in control of my body was the most pressing political question in my life. As youngsters we're led to believe that if we take responsibility for and learn to be good managers of our bodies—stay out of people's way, attract no attention, and give no offense—someday we ourselves will be the ones to enjoy the benefits of our bodies' capacities. Unfortunately many of us, as we grow older, learn a hard truth: Our physical and emotional control, our so-called "self-control," doesn't empower us; it just plays into the hands of others who turn it against us. Once we learn to exercise mastery over our bodily functions, impulses, and passions, we might expect to earn a place of respect in our communities and participate in the decisions that affect us, but what happens instead is that we are simply expected to go through the rest of our lives staying out of people's way, attracting no attention, and giving no offense. How infuriating it is to realize that being a nice girl only makes it easier for sexist pigs to insult and injure you, that being a conscientious laborer only makes it easier for the bosses to pay you less and work you more, that shouldering as much responsibility as possible for coping with your disabilities only makes it easier for tight-fisted taxpayers to say you don't need social services at all, that shielding those with delicate sensibilities from the details of your "homosexual life-style" only makes it easier for heterosexists to discriminate blatantly! Instead of empowering us, our "self-control" very often only empowers those who exploit, maltreat, and despise us.

Given that that's the case, very often at least, sometimes you wonder: Why try to be responsible? What's the point? I can't succeed at this Classical Liberal political game; I can't assert and act upon my status as a rational mind negotiating for maximal control over my interests. So why try to exercise any self-control at all? Whenever I do, I just collude with the systems that oppress me. They tell you you're a mind in control of a body, but then they exploit every facet of your bodily being, and the more discipline you can exert, the more there is to exploit. To take responsibility or not to take responsibility, to exercise self-control or not, that was the political (and ethical) question I found myself faced with over and over in my young life. Should this mind make this body obey the dictates of civility and rationality, or should this mind abdicate responsibility and by doing so at least expose the workings of power that caught me in their grip?

It is early morning. I know this not because I can see sunlight but because the day nurses are on duty and the psych techs are rousing ambulatory patients on the adult unit, getting them in line, handing them their paper cups of meds. I stand just inside the always open door of my semiprivate room, hanging on the steel doorjamb, leaning out. My eyes are on the water fountain adjacent to the nurses' station. We all look there every morning, because above the fountain is where they post the list of patients who don't get breakfast. There are only two reasons why you might not get breakfast: Either they're going to draw your blood, or they're going to give you shock. I can't read the list from where I stand, and I can't go closer to get a look because when the adults are in the common area we adolescents are not allowed to enter it; patients on different units are permitted absolutely no contact with one another, not even a friendly wave. Contact with unauthorized persons impedes therapy. Contact, even attempted contact, with an adult means lockup.

I'm not afraid my name is on the list. They drew my blood a couple of weeks ago, and they don't shock minors at this facility. What I'm waiting to see is whether Johnny's mom is on the list. They've shocked her several times before. The shock room door is right next to the water fountain, so we've all seen her wheeled in and wheeled out. Every time it happens, Johnny screams and cries and begs them to let him talk to her. They usually lock him up or put him in wrist restraints. Sometimes if it's bad enough they revoke all our privileges.

I see Johnny's mom in line for meds. She'll check the list pretty soon. I see Johnny too, the back of his greasy, curly head as he leans out from his room on the boys' side of the unit. We know it's coming.

She sees the list, and at the same time a psych tech sees her see it. She takes a step back, stumbles over a thorazine zombie tied in a wheelchair, starts to cry out. The tech reaches her and pulls her up, calls for assistance. She's really screaming now, words that don't make any sense, syllables that aren't even words, gulps of sound along with the sounds of banging limbs and tearing hospital cloth. Johnny springs out of his room, runs toward the nurses' station, yelling in his breaking half-man voice, "Mama!" That's enough for lockup, I think. The nurses fly from behind the station desk calling for tech backup.

Two male techs meet Johnny halfway down the corridor. "Take it easy," they say as they each grab an arm. "Don't make it hard on yourself." But Johnny keeps screaming, "Mama! Mama!" as the techs push him and pin him against a wall. I can see his face now. Tears are streaming down it. Tall and lanky as he is, he looks little in the grip of the two burly techs, and the tears look like baby tears. He's bawling now and spewing snot and screaming as loud as he can, "NO!" And the techs keep throwing his shoulders against the wall and saying the doctor knows what's best. John, they call him. John. Because the doctor said in group last week that Johnny is a childish name, mama's boy name, fag name. "John," they say, "buddy, get hold of yourself, man. You're out of control." And he's crying, loud sobs, like a little child.

Then he pushes back, hard as he can, and just starts flailing. Long, skinny arms and legs, oversized hands and feet, zigzagging through space with no plan, moving like crazy. His head makes hard contact with a psych tech's jaw. Now there's blood coming from the tech's mouth, and the other tech is screaming they've got a situation here. More staff appear in split seconds. Johnny kicks, slaps, butts, screams, hisses, bites, jabs, scratches, his body in constant motion for motion's sake, his nose streaming with blood. He spits in a tech's face, tears at the guy's shirt. There are four techs on him now, pinning him to the floor, but he's still kicking like he's having some kind of seizure. It's a long time before he's still, except for the shaking and the sobs.

"You had your chance, John," the bleeding tech says. "If you won't control yourself, you're just asking us to do it for you." They drag him off to lockup, where they'll strip him naked in the bright light and leave him until he stops resisting therapy. Maybe he'll stop right away and be back on the unit tomorrow. Maybe he'll rip up his mattress, defecate on the floor, spread shit on the two-way mirrors, throw the food they give him against the walls, and we won't see him again for a month, like time before last.

I just stand there, watching them carting him off, feeling numb and sad at the same time. And I think: he's so much braver than I am.

It is a gesture of last resort to sacrifice every ounce of control simply to prevent its being appropriated by oppressive others. But sometimes there is no *penultimate* resort. Sometimes you either refuse to control yourself at all, or you do their work for them. I was a gay kid who survived. Johnny was a gay kid who probably didn't. Johnny refused to cooperate. I stood, docilely, leaning against the doorjamb, time and time again, the oft-cited model of self-control, letting them—helping them— do what they did to us. Is that what I should have done? I don't know. I survived and Johnny didn't. I can write this book and Johnny can't. Does that justify anything? I doubt it does.

This incident—Johnny's lockup—is what Foucault calls a situation of total domination.[7] Power relations—relations between individuals struggling to influence one another's behavior—disappear the instant one individual or group gains total control and is able completely to determine the other's immediate future.[8] Such events are relatively rare. Most interactions are and remain political—that is, each person tries to influence the choices and actions of the other, because neither is completely in control; it's uncertain whose behavior will change at each moment and in exactly what respects. But, rare as it is, I've seen politics come to an end. Rare as they are, I've seen a great many situations of total domination. I've seen many people dragged off to lockup, tied to their beds, wasted on thorazine. Total domination is not as rare as it might be.

Forced to subsist in situations of near-total domination, you develop an acute sense of physical vulnerability. You can be knocked down and stripped naked in a heartbeat. You can be gagged and immobilized without a prayer of escape. You can be beaten, starved, raped if someone takes a notion, and there would be nothing you could do. Your body is their playground and their laboratory. Even your insides are theirs to manipulate, even your nerves and your brain. You know this, you feel this, and you live this knowledge every moment in every move you make. But despite the very obvious bodily dimensions of this knowledge, it is no surprise that under conditions of near-total domination, mind/body dualisms have flourished. You have to survive, so you pull back, numb yourself as much as you can, search for some place deep inside where they can't follow you, contract yourself to a zero point so they can't get a grip. You are mind, not sweating flesh; you are spirit, and you are free. Boethius in his dungeon cell partakes of the consolations of dualistic philosophy.[9] Such as they are. And so have I. I don't know how I would have survived sometimes if I had not. In the midst of such a situation, you can't change the terms.

But the terms need to change. If the terms don't change—if we can't come to some way of understanding human selfhood that doesn't treat mind and body as distinct and bodies as ahistorical, unthinking objects to be controlled—people like me will always fall victim to those in a position to advance that horrifically complacent little claim: "If you can't control yourself, we'll have to do it for you." We'll always be vulnerable; we'll always be frightened; we'll always be manipulable. Mind/body dualisms set up the situations in which that kind of domination is possible; what comfort they may offer people who suffer within those situations is precious little compensation in the long run for the trouble they cause.

I needed to be able to think about what happened—what always threatens to happen to people at the lower end of society—in some way that didn't construe every power struggle, every act of resistance, in terms of that old Lockean model of minds battling for control of bodies and material goods. I needed another way to think about politics, power, and selfhood, because without any new way to think, the next time it would be just the same. I would have to choose between collaborating and being obliterated; in the midst of the situation, I wouldn't be able to change the terms within which I had to act. Changing the terms, though, isn't a matter of just saying mind/body dualisms are illogical or politically incorrect and therefore we don't believe in them anymore. Plenty of philosophers, feminist theorists, and social critics have already done that much; they've been doing it for years. Genevieve Lloyd pointed out nearly twenty years ago that Cartesian dualism is sexist and perpetuates sexism.[10] Based on her work and others', feminists recommended that we abandon Cartesian theories. Carol Pateman has repeatedly demonstrated the ways in which Locke's assumption that the body, sex, and kinship are natural givens that preexist politics is both incoherent within his own theory and systematically oppressive of women and children. She recommends a thorough revision of political theory.[11] These days, that mind/body dualisms and ahistorical conceptions of selfhood are intellectually and ethically problematic is something that we can be said to *know*. But we know these things only as propositions we hold to be true, and holding a set of propositions is not the same as living out those propositions; asserting something is not the same as incorporating it. Too many of us—the most highly educated of us especially—assume that if we've read a few books, understood their arguments, and maybe written some words about them here and there, we therefore have undergone those books' radical critiques of the most fundamental truths of our culture. And, having survived intact (which can only mean we've convinced ourselves we never were materially implicated in those truths) we can side with those books against the dominant culture. This tendency is probably one of the most obvious vestiges of our resilient Cartesianism. We believe we can change our minds without changing our hearts, without changing our bodies, without changing our lives. Foucault strongly disagrees. In a 1978 interview he asserts, "One is not radical because one pronounces a few words; no, the essence of being radical is physical; the essence of being radical is the radicalness of existence itself" (CQP, 191). We can't simply pronounce an attack on Cartesian dualism, Lockean naturalism, or any other idea or institution or way of thinking; we have to embody that attack, and we have to embody it starting with the very bodies those ways of thinking have given us. Every aspect of a human being, including our bodies, is implicated in the powers and knowledges we want to critique. What is at stake in critique, then, is our very bodies, our very selves. These are what we have to change if we are to change the terms.

A GENEALOGY OF MY BODY, PART 3: TEMPORALITY

I arrived in my third decade of life, already a thoroughgoing dualist and naturalist. Dualistic religious traditions had shaped my experience since before I could remember, since before there was an "I" at the center of it. The routine humiliations of a difficult childhood reinforced the notion that my body was something separate from the real me, something it was my job to control. Institutional confinement in adolescence impressed upon me the importance of maintaining mental governance over my corporeal allotment. Experience had carefully taught me: All that was good, free, and creative was mental. The body was nothing; or rather, the body was just that same old something that it always was and could not help but be: a natural object essentially outside cultural or political progress, a mere resource to be exploited, a natural force to be controlled. Naturalistic conceptions of selfhood operative in American public debate constantly reinforced that view. Thus I arrived at adulthood, the wary and protective owner of a body devoid of thought.

Little wonder, then, that when Foucault proclaimed "bodies" to be a potential rallying point for radical politics, what I first understood him to say was that the body is our primary object of conquest and battleground. Little wonder that what I first understood him to assert was that the purpose of radical politics is to establish a "penultimate resort," to open up some domain of self-control that does not amount to a collusion with oppressive powers, to the usurpation of that very "self"-control. Little wonder that at first I understood him to declare that my body should be my domain to rule, my property to use and enjoy. The only wonder is that on some levels I knew quite well that wasn't what he was saying at all. Or, well, maybe it was no great wonder, for all that. After all, for a long time I'd experienced the demand that I be a mind in charge of a body as precisely that, a *demand*, not a description of a natural state of affairs, and it was a challenge I really couldn't meet. Simultaneously, as a result, I experienced myself as perpetually vulnerable to those who would "do it for me." Out of a Lockean drive for self-protection, I sought a different path. I was ripe for an alternative, less humiliating way of understanding my female, working-class, epileptic, homosexually carnal self.

I was sure Foucault offered an alternative even before I had any idea what that alternative might be. Foucault's opposition to the dualistic and naturalistic assumptions of classical liberal theory are explicit; we need only remember the passages Alcoff criticizes to realize that Foucault directly opposes a central tenet of Locke's view, namely, that both bodies and minds are natural entities that preexist political history and power. Foucault doesn't believe in any kind of naturally existing, identifiable human subject waiting in readiness to retake control of its naturally existing flesh. Foucault's genealogical analysis aims to operate entirely "without having to make reference to a subject which is either transcendental in relation to the field of events or runs in its empty sameness throughout the course of history" (TP, 117). There is no human subject originating beyond relations of power who could be construed as the "natural" or "rightful" exploiter of any particular body. Nor are there bodies, naturally existing entities originating outside networks of power, that can be identified and distributed as exploitable resources either justly or unjustly. On the contrary, "[t]he body is the inscribed surface of events (traced by language and dissolved by ideas), the locus of a dissociated Self (adopting the illusion of a substantial unity), and a volume in perpetual disintegration" (NGH, 148). On Foucault's view, then, politics can't be a struggle that erupts only when mind-selves begin to contest existing distributions of material, bodily resources. If we want to imagine a Foucault-inspired or at least a Foucault-compatible politics, the whole Cartesian, Lockean universe will have to be turned inside out.

There are people who say politics—liberatory or progressive politics at least—can't survive this inversion. Some say if we construe minds or selves or personal identities as historical formations rather than givens, then there won't be anybody left with enough freedom to take a stand against the status quo. We'll all just be products of the communities we hale from, so we won't have any means of criticizing their values or their claims to knowledge and legitimate power. Likewise, some say, if we construe our bodies not as natural givens but as products of arrangements of discursive power, then we won't have any basis upon which to demand that our bodies be liberated from the arrangements of power that we find ourselves in. David Michael Levin, for instance, asserts that Foucault's genealogical "conception of the body makes it impossible for us to *empower* the body with any capacity to *talk back* to history, drawing not only on its pain and suffering, but also on its depth of needs, desires, and utopian dreams, and to call for an end to the history of domination and alienation," for, "when the body is reduced to history, it has no escape from oppression."[12] I think, however, that Levin (and other critics who would say similar things) hears in Foucault's words a description of a body that is radically different from the bodies that we now inhabit and are; he thinks Foucault is telling us that we don't really have the bodies we think we do, but instead we have different bodies, foreign bodies, bodies we have yet to dream about. Foucault, however, can't be making that kind of a claim. He has no place to stand outside of the history of these particular bodies that we have to make any observations about what our bodies "really" are. The bodies he points to are the bodies we already have. He just calls our attention to some aspects of them we often overlook or fail fully to conceptualize. While it is true that most of us most of the time conceive of our bodies as natural objects and intimate property, it is also true that there are other characteristics we readily conceive those same bodies to have. The most important one for Foucault is the fact that our bodies are functioning organisms that are essentially temporal and developmental in nature. To get from dualistic naturalism to some other way of being, we have to start with the bodies we have, and Foucault's work indicates that our temporality is a good place to start.

Neither Descartes nor Locke conceived of their bodies as organisms in quite the way that we do now. Descartes certainly did not, since he thought of bodies as machines. Even Locke, who did think of bodies as natural entities existing and functioning in the natural world prior to the origination of politics and government, did not think of bodies as temporally developing organisms; for him, bodies were givens whose processes and cycles were dictated by factors external to them. The idea that bodies are inherently developmental in nature, while certainly a central component of my self-understanding, did not form a part of anyone's conception of the human body in the seventeenth century. Descartes' body and Locke's body are ancestors of my body, but they are different from my body. And in that difference lies the potential for a radical revision of both corporeality and politics. To get at that difference that could make such a difference, it will be necessary to delve into Foucault's 1975 text *Discipline and Punish,* where he offers his most extended discussion of bodies. The crucial point is his description of the way in which Descartes' notion that the body is a machine dropped out of our bodies' lineage and was replaced by the notion that bodies are organisms. He focuses on events that occurred in the last quarter of the eighteenth century, on the emergence of what he calls "normalization."

Through most of the eighteenth century, Foucault holds, most thinkers and administrators conceived of bodies as machines—matter in motion, as Descartes said in the seventeenth century. Bodies were assemblages of parts that could be made to operate in relation to one another more or less effectively. Efficiency of movement was the issue in disciplinary practices in the military, in schools, in factories, and wherever large groups of people had to be managed to produce results. Experts analyzed these body-machines, divided the necessary movements into steps, and devised drills for training bodies to accomplish these sequences of movement quickly, with no waste of time or energy. These "mechanical" disciplinarians had inherited from monastic communities the notion of the time-table and the practice of breaking routines into temporally quantifiable units so as to describe disciplined gestures and to set out steps for accomplishing work. But they transformed the idea of the time-table by employing it for new purposes. Before the mechanical disciplinarians took it up, Foucault writes, "the principle that underlay the time-table in its traditional form was essentially negative; it was the principle of non-idleness: it was forbidden to waste time, which was counted by God and paid for by men; the time-table was to eliminate the danger of wasting it—a moral offense and an economic dishonesty" (DP, 154; SP, 155). Disciplinarians in the seventeenth and eighteenth centuries were not concerned about the proper use of time and the negative goal of not wasting it, though; their new goal was a positive one: "exhaustion rather than use" (DP, 154; SP, 155). For them, the question was how to get the most out of time; it was a question "of extracting, from time, ever more available moments and, from each moment, ever more useful forces" (DP, 154; SP 155–56). Mechanical disciplinarians hoped to maximize efficiency by specifying down to the smallest detail the order, duration, and direction of each move the body had to make. They broke gestures into precise stages, and divided the gesturing body, accordingly, into the parts and mechanisms by which these regulated gestures were to be executed. Mechanical disciplinary power thus "constitutes a body-weapon, body-tool, body-machine complex" (DP, 153; SP, 155).

But in the last decades of the eighteenth century, Foucault says, this picture of the body as a machine made of contiguous parts began to be replaced by a new picture of the body as an organism, a series of temporal processes. This shift marks the beginning of a move toward "normalization." The best way to understand the significance that Foucault attributes to this shift is to attend to the contrast Foucault draws between the "mechanical body" and the "normalized body," a contrast that appears most starkly in Foucault's discussion of a 1772 text from the military disciplinarian J. A. de Guibert.

Guibert, according to Foucault, was a zealous but realistic disciplinarian. He wanted to make the best possible soldier out of each and every raw recruit. But he observed that, while the drills in use effectively trained *most* men to be soldiers, there were always a few bunglers or at least some who took much longer to train. Guibert asks himself why this should be. What is it about some people that makes them less susceptible to training than others? He observes, further, that some of the movements that soldiers are being trained to make don't coincide with what he takes to be the "natural" bearing of the soldierly body. He criticizes disciplinarians who use such over-stylized drills and suggests that training needs to follow more closely what is "natural" for the body. Only so can training be made most effective and efficient. Guibert is looking at resistance—particularly unwilled, purely bodily resistance—and coupling it with what he calls "nature." Putting the two together, he is suggesting that there is something inherent in bodies that resists training.

Now, if the body is nothing but a machine, then there is nothing inherent in it that can resist anything. It obeys only those laws of nature that are external or heterogeneous to it, such as the laws of physics; the body does not give itself the laws it obeys. After hours of diligent practice, if a soldier still can't execute a certain move, that must be because the laws of physics constrain him in some way. Perhaps he is too fat to move quickly enough or too short to strike a certain pose with a rifle that is too long for him. In other words, the body-machine parts in question are the wrong size or shape relative to one another. But if there is something in the body itself, some force that is internal to it, then the body is no longer purely a machine.

Guibert, then, is moving away from a conception of the body as a machine. He is positing that there is some force other than the laws of physics that governs the disposition of bodies, some force internal to the body itself. Thus his analysis prefigures a concept of the body that casts it as a seat of natural force (rather than as a set of naturally existing parts), particularly as a seat of force that seeks to operate and develop in its own peculiar ways, ways that may be contrary to some forms of discipline. This force must be reckoned with, but, being bodily, it cannot be reasoned with. It is natural, and like nature itself it can be harnessed and used, but it can never be blatantly defied. Disciplinarians must observe bodily forces of resistance until they learn how to manage them, how to bring them under their control.

Although Guibert's project—disciplining soldiers—is nothing new by 1772, his emerging conception of the soldierly body is new. Thus, Foucault asserts, "Through this technique of [disciplinary] subjection a new object was being formed; slowly, it superseded the mechanical body—the body composed of solids and assigned movements, the image of which had for so long haunted those who dreamt of disciplinary perfection. This new object is the natural body, the bearer of forces and the seat of duration; it is the body susceptible to specific operations, which have their order, their stages, their internal conditions, their constituent elements" (DP, 155; SP, 157). Through Guibert's and others' works, a new conception of the body, which Foucault calls the natural body, emerges. Disciplinarians gradually come to view the bodies in their charge not as a machines, collections of movable parts related in space, but rather as organisms, perfectly unified wholes that are most essentially characterized by temporal processes, forces that constitute their "functioning" through time. These natural bodies may resist military discipline, for example, simply because the processes most natural to them are contrary to the process of the drill. To train an organism requires that the drills used be compatible with—though of course not identical to—the natural processes that organism would undergo or initiate if it were left completely untrained. At each stage of training, it is important to note, the natural body's capacities and proclivities change. If the body has received training to a certain degree and is then left alone, the processes it will undergo on its own may differ from those it would have undergone if it had never been trained at all. Thus it is possible for successive stages of training to depart more and more from the "original" condition of the body without violating its "natural" condition. The point of normalized training is to augment and channel, not to impose, but the result should far exceed anything pure imposition could produce.

As this new conception of the trainable body caught on, it grew more sophisticated. Bodies came to be understood not just as functioning organisms but as thoroughly temporal beings that always operate according to a describable set of functional norms. In fact, we might say, this emerging concept of "the natural" simply consists of these sets of norms; the natural just is the normal, the developmental patterns still supposedly discernible beneath the layered impositions of mechanistic regimens, patterns that can be "re"-constituted by observing how the body resists the regimens overzealous disciplinarians seek to impose. Thus, normalizing power/knowledge grids construct this seemingly unconstructed natural body even as they claim to discover its recalcitrant existence beneath the distorting inscriptions of disciplinary history.

Normalized discipline, while radically different from mechanical discipline, grew out of it directly. As disciplinary techniques evolved over the next two centuries, the drive to maximize bodily efficiency itself generated this new conception of its own body-target, "the natural body," which Foucault says is "discovered" by Guibert. This body differs from the mechanical body in that it has functional systems rather than interrelated parts. The mechanical body's parts were related to one another spatially; its capacities and limitations were produced by various volumes and configurations. The organic body's regions and tissues, however, stand primarily in temporal relations with one another. The mouth is not related to the stomach simply by the fact that it occupies a space seventeen inches above it; the mouth is primarily related to the stomach in that it occupies a position temporally prior to the stomach in the process of digestion. The organic body is a functioning body; it is what it is because of the processes it undergoes to maintain itself. Processes are essentially temporal. Thus the organic body, unlike the mechanical body, is not simply traversed by time; it is the very incarnation of time.

Readers of Foucault's earlier work, *The Order of Things,* will recognize that this shift that Foucault describes in military, pedagogical, and industrial organization and their theories of the body coincides with very similar shifts in discourses of wealth, natural history, and general grammar. As Foucault points out, after the work of Adam Smith, "the time of economics was no longer to be the cyclical time of alternating impoverishment and wealth; nor the linear increase achieved by astute policies . . . ; it was to be the interior time of an organic structure which grows in accordance with its own necessity and develops in accordance with autochthonous laws—the time of capital and production" (OT, 226; MC, 238). At the same time, language, with the new study of inflectional systems, is seen to be ordered by the processes of its own internal historicity (OT, 232–36; MC, 245–49). And in the discourse of natural history, classification of beings on the basis of visible structure begins to give way, in the work of Cuvier and others, to a new understanding of living beings as temporally functional units (OT, 226–32, 263–79; MC, 238–45, 275–92). With the birth of the new biological sciences at the turn of the nineteenth century, the organic is clearly separated from the inorganic. Temporally organized function supersedes the spatial arrangements of structures studied in the discourses of natural history. By the end of the nineteenth century, Foucault claims, this concept of the natural body was fully articulated and ensconced within normalizing discourses, practices, and institutions.

Normalization, according to Foucault, is a new form of disciplinary power, and it is quite different from the mechanistic discipline from which it emerges. Once bodies are conceived as temporally unfolding sets of functions, it becomes possible to study those processes and learn not only how to influence them but also, and far more importantly, how to draw on their own inherent energy and power to do so. A machine must be set in motion, but an organism is always already in motion and needs only to be directed. If we can learn about and plot out the direction the organism's development will take without our intervention, then we can decide when intervention is likely to be most effective and what sort of technique is most likely to work. This sort of plotting is a mathematical undertaking. (More specifically, it is a statistical undertaking and therefore was not possible before the invention of calculus.) We observe large numbers of similar individuals. Based on what we observe, we calculate the likelihood of any individual reaching a particular point in development or a particular level of achievement given a certain length of time. Then, based on that calculation, we can establish developmental norms and measured degrees of deviation from them. Measuring tools now firmly in hand, we can begin experimenting with different methods of intervention in the process we are studying to determine whether any one type of intervention produces significant deviations from the norms in ways we like.

To use a latter day example, if we want someone to be bilingual, it helps to know a lot about the normal course of language-acquisition. How does language-use naturally develop in the course of a human life? How long does it take before one learns the use of pronouns, for example? At what stages of language-acquisition are more complicated aspects of grammar or vocabulary most readily assimilated? If we know the answers to such questions, we are more likely to be able to intervene in a person's life in such a way that she will become bilingual. How do we learn the answers to those sorts of questions? Obviously, we observe large numbers of children as they acquire language skills. We conceive of their language-learning as a temporally unfolding series of events, as a kind of natural development. From our observations we can generate developmental norms and create tests to determine, in relation to those norms, where any given child is in the process of language-acquisition at any given time. That way, not only can we construct theories about when children in general are best able to acquire the elements of a second language, but we can also determine when any given child is ready to be taught any particular element of any language. In other words, we can "normalize" language-acquisition and the individuals engaged in it.

As this example demonstrates, by "normalization" Foucault names a mode of observation, ordering, intervention, and control that simultaneously homogenizes and individualizes its target population. Careful observation of the members of that target population enables technicians to generate norms. Norms homogenize the group by enabling all differences among its members to be understood as deviations from a norm and therefore as essentially related to it. No one stands outside of normalization; everyone can be located with regard to the norms. There is no pure difference, only measurable deviance. At the same time, norms individualize each member of the group by enabling a precise characterization of that person (animal, etc.) as a case history of particular, measurable degrees of deviation from the set of norms. Normalization has proven to be a very powerful means of ordering groups of people (and other organisms) for the purpose of acquiring knowledge about processes and for the purpose of intervening in and reshaping those processes and, therefore, the future individuals that those processes construct. Its use is now so widespread that it hardly seems innovative and only occasionally threatening. It just seems . . . normal. Yet it is less than two centuries old, and it could never have become a part of our world at all had it not been for the invention, at the end of the eighteenth century, of that now taken-for-granted entity, the temporally unfolding natural body.[13] An essentially temporal body is the only type of body that could become a target of normalizing power. Normalization is rooted in the notion of temporal process—norms have to do with stages of growth, stages of moral development, stages of civilization, etc. The natural body—the organic body that consumes and excretes, grows and deteriorates, reproduces and dies—is a body that is essentially developmental, perpetually self-transformative. Disciplinary discourses and practices, whose basic purpose is transformation, found in the organic body far more potential for exploitation than the mechanical body could possibly have provided. The transformation of mechanical discipline into normalizing discipline would have been unthinkable without the concurrent transformation of the machine-body into the natural body. Furthermore, because normalizing power can present itself as a benign power that merely helps the natural body realize its own hidden potential, the techniques and technicians of normalization are permitted to penetrate deeper into and range further across the lives it orders than other forms of power might. Normalizing power and the natural body arise together historically because they require one another.

It has become popular of late for thinkers to explore "the question of the body." But for the genealogist, "the body" doesn't exist; therefore, "the question" can never be: What is the body? The genealogical question is: What are our bodies now, and what is the history of those bodies? One answer is that our bodies now are normalized natural bodies, temporally unfolding, organic developmental trajectories more or less deviant from collections of functional norms, and they are so in part because of techniques developed over the past two hundred years to manage large groups of materially productive individuals efficiently. This natural body with its cultivated capacities and its hidden potentials is constituted in history, in networks of power and knowledge. Such is "the body" of Michel Foucault, the "bodies" that are to serve as rallying points for counterattacks against sexual oppression. They are not foreign bodies. They are perfectly recognizable bodies. One of them is in fact mine. But, familiar and natural though they are, these bodies are not entities originating outside of power and outside of history. They are historically constructed tools and targets of normalizing power.[14] In particular, my body is a product of the normalizing discourses of sexuality. It is a sexual body and a homosexual body. My body, unlike Descartes' body and Locke's body, has Guibert in its lineage. My body may be a natural entity and a brute thing, but it is also a natural brute with "a mind of its own," or at least with a developmental course and power all its own. And that changes things.

US DEVIANTS

So that's what I am, time incarnate, a functioning organism, an evolutionary outcome, a metabolizing, mitosizing, luteinizing locus of biotic interface. Or, well, that's what my body is. And, likewise, my neurological functions, including my ability to process information, manipulate symbols, and reproduce patterns in response to appropriate stimuli. All of these processes are normed, and my body's performance against those norms reveals my specificity as this individual body that I am/have.

In the midst of all this bionormative activity, I can almost lose sight of what it is that mind is and is supposed to do. The mind is no longer the sovereign over what would otherwise be chaos, no longer that which gives the law to a materiality that can be ordered only by forces external to it. The body is autonomous; it lives by its own laws; it has no need of a mind to tell it what to do. Moreover, the mind itself is subject to forces within itself over which it has no conscious control. Learning, for example, is a developmental process, much like sexual maturation.

The mind participates in the process, undergoes the process, but does not control it. According to some psychologists, moral reasoning is a developmental process as well; there is no need to posit free will to explain moral choice, since growth patterns can account for most of the variations in choice we observe. The mind, like the body, develops. It too is essentially temporal in nature.

Tied thus to time, the mind is also tied to the body more tightly than ever before. The mind's beginning in time, its developmental starting point is roughly the same moment as the body's. All along the way, its stages of development are correlated to development of the body. My friend Beth, a child development specialist and former elementary school teacher, tells me that the rule of thumb for determining whether a child is ready to start school is to have the child raise her hand palm outward, bend her elbow, and see whether her forearm rests horizontally on her head. If so, she is ready for school; if not—if her arm is too short for her elbow to reach the top of her head—she is not ready for school. In other words, the development of a child's body is at least a very good clue to the level of development of the child's mind. It is not simply, as Locke would have it, that it takes time for a mind to acquire enough experience to reason effectively and so a child of five might not be ready to read whereas a child of six is; it is, rather, that the mind's development and the body's development are interlocked, so that regardless of how long the child has lived, if for whatever reason the body hasn't developed sufficiently, the mind will not have done so either.

Even if we maintain a strict dualism of mind and body, if the mind requires time to mature and if its starting point is birth or shortly before, the bare fact of the body's temporality, if nothing more, will dictate the mind's progress and its ultimate level of achievement. Locke himself acknowledges this and thus insists that children—actually, male children—pass a certain number of years on earth before they are granted full citizenship, and this idea is still very much a part of our legal system today. But more and more often nowadays we assume not just that it takes a few years for someone to acquire enough experience to make good decisions—that is, that it takes time to gather enough information to know your options and be able to make good predictions—but rather that it takes awhile for any person to acquire the *capacity* to make good decisions. The capacity for good decision-making is more than just a familiarity with options and consequences. An illustration may make the distinction clear. A three-year-old child, presented with two glasses of juice, will choose the glass in which the liquid stands higher. This is the case even if the glass in which the liquid stands higher is a thin highball glass, and the glass in which the liquid stands lower is a squat tumbler. The child spontaneously registers greater verticality as "more." In a few months, the same child will be able to tell that the tumbler with a lower level of liquid actually has more in it than the highball glass, because he will have learned, again spontaneously, that volume is a measure distinct from height. The three-year-old has all the information that the four-year-old has; he also has the same goal. He simply does not "process information" in the same way. Furthermore, when he becomes able to see that the tumbler contains more liquid, his "realization" will not be the result of teaching or experimentation; he will simply "see." This new ability that he has at four, this new "way of seeing," seems not to be the result so much of what Locke would call "experience"—quantity of input—but rather of some kind of mental development. In short, the mind itself seems to be essentially developmental; and, therefore, the mind itself seems to function in relation to developmental norms.

This notion that everything, including the mind, is developmental in nature, that everything is in process and functions in relation to norms, makes it even harder for the poor Cartesian mind to do its job. It is very hard for the mind to maintain its careful and strict control over the body if the body has a "mind of its own," if the body embodies its own developmental force with a preestablished developmental trajectory. The mind's job is not just to shape what would otherwise be something very near to material chaos but to work against what would otherwise be something more like material counterorder. Further, the mind must accomplish this difficult feat while contending with its own developmental limitations and alterations, all of which lie outside its control. The Cartesian mind may well be the most beleaguered member of the modern conceptual workforce. Under these circumstances, its task, which in the history of philosophy has seemed to be its *raison d'être* as well, seems virtually impossible. Increasingly, then, the mind is coming to be defined in ways that render it an unlikely candidate for the job of controlling the body, or even itself. Likewise its position in modern philosophical discourse has become increasingly tenuous. Nevertheless, the mind lingers on, fictive though it may in some ways be; it still names for many of us the locus of our sense of self, and it still marks whatever there is of us that doesn't coincide completely with pure physical presence. And of course it still functions as the bearer of rights and civic responsibility; it is the classical liberal political subject, the only form of political subjectivity that most of us can imagine.

Each of us, accordingly, lives in the cleavage between these two concepts of mentality, concepts that come out of two different discourses that did not arise together and have not grown old together gracefully. Each of us is both a responsible, autonomous, fully formed and present citizen subject and a thoroughly developmental organism whose full being can never be given in a specific present moment. But of course these two ways of being can't coexist peacefully since to some extent they contradict each other. All around us, it seems to me, people are giving up or losing the ability to be fully formed and present political subjects at all as the discourses of psycho-physical development extend ever further into our lives. Most Americans no longer think of themselves as citizens; they no longer have a civic identity. Nineteenth- and twentieth-century practices of normalization have made seventeenth- and eighteenth-century citizenship obsolete, but no new civic discourses have come to take its place.

When we try to hold the discourses of citizenship—discourses in which the mind is conceived of as the true citizen and owner of the body—together with the newer discourses of psycho-physical development, the job of the mind becomes not to rule the body as a sovereign but to govern the body as a supervisor or manager. Instead of a king, the mind is now more like a CEO. It oversees processes, the goals of which are given, not a matter of deliberation or debate. The body does what it does according to natural dictates; its sovereign is nature itself. The mind simply looks ahead, removes obstacles, tries to anticipate and shape conditions under which the mind-body developmental complex's potential can unfold. Obviously, this way of conceiving of mentality leaves us very little in the way of liberty, traditionally conceived. The mind rarely chooses its own ends, and it acts more as a servant of the natural body than as its master. Equally obviously, since the mind has little control over itself as a bundle of developmental processes, it typically ends up subject to the direction of others; it must look to experts to anticipate what lies ahead in the stages of development through which it has not yet progressed. The child is subject to the adult not because she lacks information but because she is incompetent to judge regardless of the amount of information she has; her judgments are simply not credible. Those whose development is retarded are in the same position. No matter how much information the mentally retarded man has, he still is subject to those more competent than he to guide him through each stage of his training. Similarly, those deemed deviant on any developmental scale are rightfully subject to others who are not deviant and who have the expertise to redirect development to bring it back into accord with the ideal norm. And we are all deviants in one respect or another.

In light of all these considerations, the realm within which I can truly exercise my freedom looks pretty small. My inclination is to resist its being constricted any further. I think I share that inclination with many people, which is, I think, one reason why so many people read Foucault's descriptions of normalization as descriptions of horrifically insidious mechanisms for mind-control. Our history has led us to believe that the way to resist what appears to be this growing usurpation of the mind's sovereignty is to retreat to a pre-normalizational mind, to return to the Lockean or even the Cartesian conception of the body in order to give the mind something over which to reign. No, we want to say, our bodies really are our property and we will fight to retain our rights of ownership, rights we believe we once exercised freely in some time before insidious normalization crept into our lives. And we will tend to read anyone else's attempt to enlarge the realm of freedom as just such a return to the pre-normalizational body as well. But Foucault's point, I think, is that the idea that we can reclaim a Cartesian or Lockean dualistic past is illusory, and if it's freedom we want, we'll have to embrace rather than reject the developmental, normalized bodies that we have become. How can we do that, though? How can I get beyond Cartesian and Lockean dualism—that lived insistence on my body's estrangement from my mind—not just in my philosophical thinking but in my daily life? How can I practice this knowing of myself as a minded body? How can this normalized organism think itself?

Earlier in this chapter I described some of the ways in which I became a mind in charge of a body-object, some of the social practices and beliefs that fostered that development and some of the networks of power that enforced it. Along the way, however, I also noted some of the phenomena that had to be ignored or downplayed in order for the notion that minds and bodies are different entities to be maintained. I mentioned piano-playing and softball as well as the dark foreboding I frequently felt that my body had a mind of its own. These are the sorts of memories we need to pay attention to and learn from. These are the sorts of phenomena and events that we need to cultivate, live and relive, *practice*, if we want to embrace the normalized bodies that Foucault sees as a potential rallying point for counterattack against regimes of sexuality. In the next two chapters, I'll explore some of the possible ways in which normalized bodies and their pleasures might serve as rallying points for counterattack. For the rest of this chapter, I simply want to describe two practices I have engaged in—two practices that I happened upon in adulthood—that have intensified the movement away from mind/body dualism. These practices are examples, only; they are not prescriptions. My hope is simply that descriptions of my experiences will evoke memories ("counter-memories," to use Foucault's term) that can serve as starting points for others.

EXAMPLE #1: BECOMING DIRT

Several years ago I became completely disgusted with grocery store tomatoes. I wanted tomatoes that had actually turned red on the vine without the aid of chemical supplements. But it seemed the only way to get tomatoes like that anymore was to grow them yourself or drive somewhere distant and pay through the nose. I had never gardened before or even actually seen anyone garden. In my family, gardening wasn't done. The word *gardening* was not even part of my parents' vocabulary. Having moved off the farm and into town in 1953, my mother and father vowed never again to coax a seed to planthood and to have no animal taller than knee-high. All plant cultivation was "farming," and they hated the very thought. But I hated grocery store tomatoes even more than they hated digging in the dirt.

The year was 1989. I lived in northeast Missouri, in a town where for months the only movie playing starred Sylvester Stallone, and so there was nothing really to look at but the ugly ground and the vast sky. Mostly I paid attention to the sky, but the more I thought about good vine-ripened tomatoes the more I stared at that ugly ground. I wanted vine-ripened tomatoes, and I didn't want to pay through the nose. Thus began my venture into gardening.

I had no intention, then, of renting a rototiller or buying fertilizer and insecticide. I wanted something for nothing, or as next to nothing as possible, so I took my shovel out back and turned a square of earth six by six. I bought four little tomato plants already in progress, and while I was at it I picked up a couple of packages of bean and basil seeds. After the frost-free date, I stuck all those little suckers in the turned ground and waited to see what would happen. I had no idea what the seedlings would look like, of course, having never been intimately tied to a garden before. Every day I would take my first cup of coffee out back and squat in the furrows and look to see what, if anything, was up. I let everything that came up stay up, since everything was edible for all I knew. Every morning I sat there with my coffee and gazed at the dirt and at whatever little green tendrils had pushed their way through it the night before.

One day I was squatting in the furrows gazing at the young leaves of what I was finally sure was a green bean bush, and I happened to glance across the alley at my neighbor Bob's catalpa tree. Catalpas are not as common in north Missouri as they are in Alabama. Back home there are catalpas everywhere. I can hardly imagine childhood without groves of catalpa trees. Their smooth bark makes them excellent for climbing, and they provide room and board for black and yellow horned caterpillars that eat their leaves and menace barefoot kids. Through summer and fall they produce long, hard bean pods that can be dried and smoked like cigars. Bob's tree stood over forty feet high and a good two feet in diameter, almost majestic against the Missouri sky, fully leafed out, its bean pods shining green and already over a foot in length. It was a big proud tree, several decades old. Pushing up into the glassy blue sky, it looked like the proverbial bean stalk. I glanced back down at my little bean bush barely one foot tall, at its spade-shaped leaves on bright green twigs of stems. Suddenly it occurred to me that I was looking at cousins, close cousins even. For all their obvious differences, differences of scale mainly, they were very much alike—the same leaves, same flowers, same fruits. Twenty-nine years on the planet and all that time climbing trees and feeding on beans and never once before had it occurred to me that catalpa trees are great big bean plants and bean plants are little catalpa trees.

But they're not exactly the same. There's a crucial difference: Bark. It's bark that makes it possible for the catalpa to survive a winter and live through another set of seasons, whereas the uninsulated bush bean plant takes frostbite and dies. All the differences of scale follow from that one evolutionary innovation. Millions of years ago one little proto-bean plant stem here and another there thickened and hardened in response to the cold. And then at some point some of them thickened and hardened enough that they were able to regenerate in the spring. That was the birthday of trees.

I suppose it was a deviation in development at first, the appearance of woody stalks. Given the way the world was then, there was no call for wood. And there was no reason why living through a winter was better than dying in the fall. As long as seeds could be produced in one growing season, survival through winter did not give an evolutionary advantage to a species or to any particular gene. Perennial bean plants were not superior to annual bean plants; they were no more "fit" to survive. Looking at it from the perspective of the individual plant (as humans tend to do), the catalpa is "fittest," because one plant will live longer and produce many more seeds than an annual bush bean plant possibly can and so its genes will likely outnumber competitors' in the gene pool (unless its own large size eventually precludes its progeny's flourishing). Looking at it from the perspective of the species, though, annuals' seasonal death means more space, food, water, and light for more plants next year, which means greater ability of the species to respond to changes in the environment. There are advantages and disadvantages to both genetic dispositions. In short, neither annual nor perennial is superior to the other; the two are just different. So when the woody stems first appeared, they were deviations merely, not improvements. They were abnormalities, freaks. In those days, though, there was no one around to propose therapeutic intervention. So they remained.

It is neither good nor bad that there are trees, although I like trees and can't imagine what the world would be like if they didn't exist. (I write these words while sitting on a wooden deck nine feet off the ground looking down a slope covered with towering Virginia pines waving like ships' masts in the spring breeze.) What is good, it seems to me, is that there was the possibility for trees. What is good is that accidents can happen and new things can emerge. It was deviation in development that produced this grove, this landscape, this living planet. What is good is that the world remain ever open to deviation.

These were the sorts of thoughts I began to have as I squatted with my coffee every morning in the furrows. The plants came up and grew steadily, and I watched each one. At first I watched to see if they would take on any recognizable shape, since I didn't know which were crops and which were weeds. Then I watched because they fascinated me. I began to be able to detect the most minute changes in each one. I could tell they were wilting before they drooped. I learned which species liked cool weather and which liked more sun not by reading seed packages but by watching each plant's response to light and shade. I could tell something about what was happening in the roots by looking at the height of the plant or its leaves. I learned to watch other things too—rabbits, the path of the sun as the summer wore on, ants and moths and endless varieties of bugs I couldn't name. Then I began watching other people's gardens, began wandering up and down alleys and side streets, leaning over back fences to catch a glimpse of an onion patch or a row of Swiss chard. Before long I found myself striking up conversations over those fences, talking about cutworms and blossom end rot and recipes for beets. I could feel myself coalescing, becoming a part of a network of endeavor, spreading out, putting down roots. A world was opening toward me, and I was starting to belong.

Some new people bought the house next door and started growing tomato plants with chemical fertilizer. Soon their plants were twice as tall as mine and lush green. I looked upon those plants with offended righteousness. Indirectly, those tomatoes would be paid for through the nose. But I also looked upon them with growing alarm. They were so big! They were monsters! Next to them my plants seemed to be struggling, like skinny country kids had looked in school standing next to the strapping offspring of those scientists NASA brought down to build solid rocket boosters in the middle of our cotton fields. The message was clear: The plants have got to be fed.

I refused to buy fertilizer. Instead, I started reading about compost. I wanted a long-term, sustainable solution to the plant food crisis. I did not want monstrous leggy tomato plants that produced more stem than fruit. The more I read, and watched, the clearer it became to me that my new neighbors had it all wrong. They were feeding their plants. But you don't feed plants. What you do is feed the dirt.

It sounds simple, but it is an amazing shift from the ordinary way of thinking. Most people treat dirt as nothing more than the place where plants happen to be, like a kind of platform that plants stand on, or in. It has to be there, of course, to support the plant, but beyond that dirt is irrelevant in most people's minds. What matters is what they call "inputs"—sunlight, water, nutrients—and defenses like insecticides and herbicides. These are considered the important ingredients in a good crop. Dirt is inactive, inert. Nobody pays much attention to dirt.

In a magazine I found a description of a composting method that sounded easier than most. It was called "bastard trenching" and was said to be used by British gardeners with small plots.[15] You dig a trench six to twelve inches deep. Day by day you toss in your table scraps and whatever else you have and cover it up. That's all there is to it. Of course you can't plant near the trenches too soon, because the scraps beneath the surface will "go through heat," just like above ground compost will. If plants are too near the trench while the bacteria that convert the scraps to soil are active, their roots will be burned.[16] Once the organic material is converted to compost underground and the soil temperature has returned to normal levels, you can plant directly over it. Plants will grow well, just as volunteers in compost heaps do. This process, like almost all composting methods, takes a full season. Unlike some methods, though, it requires that you pay attention directly to the dirt. You aren't adding organic material to your garden, as you would be in spring when you shovel compost from a heap into a planting bed. You are feeding the dirt you'll plant in next year. So you can't make the mistake of thinking the dirt is just where your plants happen to stand. The dirt must be treated as a living thing that is cultivated and cared for, just like a plant.

The more I learned about dirt the more I realized it was far from just some sort of inert platform. Not only did it shelter the bacteria that converted kitchen scraps into useable nutrients and the fungi that live symbiotically on plant roots and enable them to gain access to those nutrients, it also supplied many of the nutrients itself. Plants actually consume dirt; they eat it. This passage is illustrative: "Soil is the source of thirteen of the sixteen elements essential for plant growth. Twelve of the thirteen elements originated in the parent rock from which the soil developed."[17] Furthermore, organic matter makes up very little of most fertile soil, only about five percent of it, in fact.[18] Most dirt is just dirt, not "input." But dirt itself is a highly complex phenomenon with an intricate functional structure that can suffer damage and can also repair itself if damage isn't too severe.

Most people don't think of dirt as having a structure or performing functions probably because they don't think of dirt as being anything in particular. After all, dirt doesn't naturally come in units like plants do. I can count the number of trees in my yard, but I can't count the number of dirts. Nor is there just one dirt. Whenever I come in from the yard I have dirt on my knees, under my nails, in the treads of my shoes. Dirt blows around in dry weather and washes down the hill when it rains. When there are storms in the mountains the James River is a soup of it. Dirt circulates; it never stays put or settles down. That's the trouble with dirt: Dirt has no integrity.

Dirt isn't a particular, identifiable thing. And yet it acts. It aggregates, and depending upon how it aggregates in a particular place, how it arranges itself around various sizes of empty space, it creates a complex water and air filtration system the rhythms of which both help to create more dirt from exposed stone and also to support the microscopic life necessary for turning dead organic matter back into dirt. Dirt perpetuates itself.

People have known this for a long time. Everything comes from dirt and eventually everything becomes dirt again; ashes to ashes, dust to dust. Plato was very upset about that. He didn't care for the countryside, great expanses of fields and furrows, vast tracts of nothing but dirt—what the Greeks called *chora*. So he made up a story about Chora, a primordial feminine being that resists rational formalization and drives all created things to eventual dissolution and destruction. It is Chora, Plato suggests, that men must overcome if they are to achieve true wisdom. He put this story in his dialogue *The Timaeus*, and dirt has had a bad name ever since.

But let's think about it from dirt's point of view. Dirt goes about its business, setting up the conditions under which there will be ever more dirt. In the process, conditions are set for all sorts of other events—like life cycles of bacteria and fungi, like the establishment of conditions under which plant life can evolve. It's not that some external force (like Plato's demiurge) comes on the scene and subdues dirt temporarily and carves life-forms out of it, only to have dirt reassert itself and drag the beautiful forms back down. It's that the dirt's activity gives occasion for the play of beautiful things. Life never surpasses dirt, because life rides on dirt's coattails. Life has no vehicle of its own. Whatever discreteness, integrity, and identity living things may have, it all comes from the activity of that undifferentiated, much maligned stuff we call dirt. There wouldn't be individually integrated, identifiable things were it not for that unindividuated volume in perpetual disintegration.

I began to have a high regard for dirt. One Sunday afternoon I was finishing a bag of Doritos. As I pulled the last two chips out of the bag, I pondered whether to toss the crumbs in a bastard trench. I read through the list of ingredients on the bag: partially hydrogenated oil, monosodium glutamate, disodium phosphate, yellow 6, red 40, disodium inosinate, disodium guanylate. . . . "Nope," I thought, "can't feed that crap to my dirt." I threw the bag of crumbs in the trash and reached for that one last chip. It was halfway to my mouth before I was struck by what I'd just said. I looked out the kitchen window at my garden, my trenches, my dirt, and then my gaze turned downward toward my Dorito-stained hand. Dirt, and flesh. Suddenly it occurred to me that, for all their differences, these two things I was looking at were cousins— not close cousins, but cousins, several deviations now removed. I haven't purchased a bag of Doritos since.

EXAMPLE #2: BECOMING WHITE

In 1992 I left the rural Midwest and moved to the sprawling metropolis of Richmond, Virginia. Dirt was much less in evidence there.

I considered farming the North Davis Avenue median strip in front of my apartment building, but since it lay so near the Jeff Davis Memorial and historic Monument Avenue, the city came and beautified it periodically. So I moved indoors. I tried to make compost for my house plants. I put table scraps in a bucket on my tiny third-floor balcony. But the bucket was too small; everything stayed wet inside it; and soon the whole thing was writhing with maggots. I had to throw it out.

Not much dirt to look at. Not much sky either. My eyes turned to eye-level things. I decided it was time to meet some girls.

Meeting girls is not what I do best. There were plenty of them in the bar on Friday nights—Babe's it's called, and there were some babes as well as some women and men and individuals at various transitional points in between. But nobody talked to me. Virginia is a very conservative place; people are reserved, even in gay bars. Maybe especially in gay bars. You never know who you're talking to, and it doesn't pay to trust.

The first night I ever went to Babe's the management hustled us all out at 2:00 A.M. sharp for reasons I didn't fully appreciate until I saw what awaited us on the street. There were five police cruisers, two cops in each, parading slowly past, ready to close down the bar at the slightest hint of illegality. I was scared. In a new town, I had no friends to help me and a new job to lose. I looked through a windshield into the face of a policewoman who looked grimly back. She edged the cruiser after me, following just a few feet behind, as I walked toward a parking lot. I dared not get into a car with her on my back, though, so I ducked into an alley, disturbed some teenaged dope-smokers, and squatted behind a dumpster for twenty minutes until the police got bored and left.

You have to go to a lot of trouble to meet girls in Richmond. But the law was not the main obstacle to courtship. My clumsiness was.

I always gravitated to the pool tables, because somewhere along the line I had learned how to slap down coins and win a table. But that didn't win me friends, nor did I generally elect to pursue intimacy with the kind of girl you typically find hunched over a pool cue. When it wasn't my turn I'd rest my chin on my hands and gaze out at all the good-looking women on the dance floor—and sigh. There was no getting around it: The pretty girls go for a dyke who can dance.

I had never danced—well, except for a few anomalous interludes like doing the Hokey-Pokey at the Decatur rollercade in 1967, but nothing serious. I had been out on dance floors; I had balled my fists, rolled my shoulders, and shifted my weight regularly from foot to foot; I had listened to countless lovers and friends say over and over to me, "just let yourself go, just move to the music"; and I had felt the music all right, heavy rhythms moving through me like April thunder—*kuh-thunk, kuh-thunk*—inspiring me to do nothing at all. I hated to dance. But there I was living at eye-level in a reserved and cliquish town. It was time for a bold, brash, innovative strategy. Eventually, one suggested itself to me.

At a pride festival I chanced to see a line dance demonstration. I'd seen line dancing once before, at a gay bar in Joplin, Missouri. It had delighted me then in a quiet sort of way, four lanky men in cowboy hats moving calmly in unison, each one distinct yet joined to the others in the wholeness of their line. The Richmond group was much larger, about twelve people, and they danced, hatless, in a sort of matrix or array. Their dancing was more intricate and faster than the cowboys' was. But the effect on me was much the same. "I bet I could do that," I thought. "That looks like something a person could *learn*." Enquiry quickly revealed that the group leader, Carol, gave line dance lessons weekly at a bar on North Boulevard. A few weeks later I got up my nerve and went. There was an odd collection of people there when I walked in. Particularly notable were several young men doing The Time Warp from "The Rocky Horror Picture Show." Halloween decorations hung from the ceiling, and knots of people talked and laughed half hidden in streams of crepe paper. Soon, though, Carol appeared and wrought order out of chaos. Where there had been knots of people, there were neat rows, and we solitary strays were herded into place among them. She proceeded to teach a dance called The Copperhead. I proceeded to be a good student, to be serious, to buckle down and learn.

Combinations of steps, I was surprised to find, have names. There are grapevines, ball changes, box steps, hitches, pivots, slides, scoots, shuffle steps, strolls, scuffs, buttermilks, and of course stomps. Step combinations form the basic units of each dance. Becoming a line dancer means first of all becoming technically proficient at these units. Almost all of line dancing is done with the feet. The only exceptions are pelvic rolls and thrusts (sometimes called "gettie-ups") and the occasional clap. Shoulders, arms, head, and torso simply follow the lead of the legs—and they do follow, with hardly any planning or thought at all. After awhile, the whole enterprise starts to feel not like something the dancer does but more like something gravity does, like the self-expression of gravity come conscious, like the earth's own force has come to life and is exploring itself.

At the end of the lesson Carol proposed a contest. From a large bag she took several dozen surgical gloves—remnants, she said, from a recent safer sex seminar—blown up like balloons. Contestants were to hold these balloons between their thighs while doing a dance called The Down 'N' Dirty. When your balloon hit the floor, you were disqualified. Last dancer left won forty dollars.

I was too embarrassed to participate. The Down 'N' Dirty, never mind the inflated sex aids, was too risqué for me. There was nothing on earth, I thought, that could persuade me to do a "gettie-up" with the lights on. The other bar patrons didn't seem embarrassed at all, though. Most danced. Some cheered from the sidelines and laughed as the floor became a sea of bouncing latex and failed contestants grinning sheepishly. In the end someone named Dayle won the forty-dollar prize and everyone hugged her. I found myself smiling my congratulations at her too.

I kept working on the basic steps—in the privacy of my own home—

and going to Carol's lessons at the bar. Technical proficiency was what I concentrated on. I tried not to think about the people at the edge of the dance floor who might be watching me. In a month or so I had some of the steps pretty well down and was ready to make a real commitment to the project of learning to dance. It was time to invest in a pair of boots.

At Myrna's Boots 'N' Bits I learned that cowboy boots are ageless and genderless things. There are two whole walls of boots from tiny to huge, but there are size increments only, no divisive categories like "boys" or "women." At the small end there are more pairs of red and lavender, but otherwise boots are boots. I chose a pair in basic black that seemed like nice starter boots.

The boots improved my dancing considerably in two ways. First and most obviously, they made it much easier to slide and scuff, two essential ingredients in most line dances; the dances are conceived for feet in smooth, leather-soled footwear and are hardly doable in anything else. Second, though, was that they made me feel like showing off. They looked good, and they made me look good, adding a good two inches to my height, all in the leg. I began to worry a little less that people might actually be watching me.

I started going to Babe's on country night. I still didn't know many of the dances, but if I could talk my friend Pat into going so I'd have someone to sit with, I went. Pat, a native Richmonder with two grown sons and forty-six years of upright respectability behind her when she finally plunged into "the life," is usually game for just about anything. So most Tuesday nights we were at the bar. If we knew a dance, we'd get up and join in. Between dances we knew, I would sit and study the feet of the best people on the floor, trying to work out the grammar of the dance, trying to analyze it. Gradually I came to feel I knew a few dances very well. I relaxed when I did them. I no longer looked at my feet or tried hard not to look at the dancers around me. In fact I stopped looking at all. I was just an experiment of gravity. I eased down into myself and went along for the ride.

I took my project very seriously. At home, alone and music-less, I went over and over different steps and practiced dances all the way through, to all four walls. But that didn't seem like enough. I convinced Pat to take lessons with me at the Metropolitan Community Church where Carol taught once a week to raise money for a new church basement floor. We enrolled in an eight-week course. Carol made us practice tapes and gave out written step sheets. I did my homework faithfully. The muscles in my legs filled out and hardened. I found I could kick higher than my own chin with ease. My sense of balance improved markedly. "I know where I am," I thought. "At any given instant I feel myself exactly where I *am*." I was in space, spread out through space, and I was *aware of that fact*. I don't know if I had ever felt spread out in space before.

One night at Babe's when there was a particularly large and enthusiastic crowd and I had already sweated my way through three Diet Cokes, something wonderful happened. I have forgotten which song Stacy was playing, whether it was Garth Brooks' "Ain't Going Down" or Travis Tritt's "Trouble," but it was something fast, and the dancers had launched into Slap Leather. Slap Leather is a popular old standard; it's in fact what most people think of when they think of line dancing. Its signature step is a quick series of slaps across the side of the right boot during a full-body quarter turn to the left. Here are Carol's written instructions for the dance:

> RT heel, together, LF heel, together, REPEAT, RT heel 2X, RT toe in back 2X, RT heel in front, RT toe side, RT foot behind LF knee and slap it with LF hand, back to RT toe side, RT foot in front of LF knee and slap it with LF hand, flip foot over while swinging 1/4 turn to LF, slap with RT hand, RT vine stomp CLAP, LF vine stomp CLAP, Back 2–3–4, LF foot step slide/step stomp. Start Over. 4 wall dance. Counter clockwise.[19]

It's fairly complicated when you spell it all out.

I am not a good mimic. Doing what other people do has never come easy to me. Furthermore, prior to that night I had never been shown how to do Slap Leather and had never attempted to do it before. Something about the situation, though, compelled me. I slipped into line and began the dance, at first keeping one eye on my neighbor's feet but then ceasing altogether to keep my eyes on anything. The dance just flowed through me. I had it. I knew it. And it wasn't a matter of knowing how the dance was supposed to look. I could feel the dance from the inside. What I knew was what it felt like to *be* that dance. It was absolutely exhilarating.

Afterwards people smiled at me and clapped me on the back and shook my hand. I smiled back at them, some of them strangers, and I could feel my eyes shine.

From that time on, I went to Babe's even on the Tuesday nights when Pat couldn't go. I didn't worry about looking out of place hanging around the sidelines. From that time on, I was at home. Whether I knew anyone, whether there was anyone to talk to or not, didn't matter anymore. I had a place there and a connection to other people that didn't depend on knowing names or facts.

People who say "just let go and feel the music" are complete idiots. Dance, of whatever kind, is a disciplined activity. It requires knowledge and practice and musculature of a sort that nobody's born possessing. Virtually all human bodies have the potential to dance just as virtually all human bodies have the potential to speak a language. But five years ago I could no more have walked out on the floor and "felt" Slap Leather than an infant can speak sonnets. The freedom, the release, and the power I felt on that dance floor that night were the result of discipline, the result of psycho-physical development carefully nurtured over a period of time. Freedom is the expanse of possibility; as such, it is not opposed to discipline at all.

I began to enjoy dancing more than anything else I did. There is a pleasure in dancing that is all its own, unlike the pleasure I'd ever taken in anything else. For me, it was a new kind of pleasure, and my capacity for it grew, developed, and intensified as I practiced and learned. I began to love existing as a self-reflective, disciplined, and developmental organism spread out in space, thinking itself. Dancing was sheer joy.

But there was also a dark side. At the same time that I was breaking in my new boots and learning to revel in the fact that I could occupy space, I also came to be troubled about the . . . well . . . the *whiteness* of what I was doing. Almost every Tuesday night as I would pull on those boots I would suddenly feel awfully, sometimes painfully, white. It wasn't that only white people would be at the bar. Though whites predominate at Babe's on country night there are a few regulars of both African and Asian descent. And there have always been black voices in country music and the Southern subcultures that spawned it. One of the first country music artists ever recorded, Jimmie Rodgers, sang songs he first heard the black railroad workers sing when he was a water boy in Mississippi in the 1910s. In spite of Jim Crow racism, black musicians sang and played with whites in the studios and radio stations that stretched across north Alabama and Mississippi up to Memphis all through the 20s, 30s, and 40s, and blacks were major forces in the development of the rockabilly that eventually gave way to rock 'n' roll. Neither country music nor country dancing are exclusively white phenomena. Yet I felt white. Excruciatingly white. Embarrassingly white. For a long time, I pondered that. I don't fully understand that feeling still. But I have a couple of ideas about it.

The first is that it just makes sense that one of the first things anybody moving away from Cartesian, Lockean dualism would come up against is race. I am a "raced" body in a world where race matters. Under other historical circumstances the color of my skin and the texture of my hair might not mean anything at all, but in these historical circumstances they do. I am white just as surely and just as unalterably as I am female. Dualism invites me to ignore both those facts. But as dualism diminishes in power, that ignorance can no longer be maintained. It wasn't just the dancing, then. No matter what discipline I had engaged in to move away from dualism, race would have become an issue for me. Eventually I would have had to find a way to live out my being white consciously and reflectively. But I think there is a deeper reason why race became such an important issue when and how it did. It was tied directly to the boots. The body that I was coming home to, coming to be, is a body that fits very comfortably into those boots and therefore very neatly, very comfortably, into a position, a social location that is constructed in great part by racial division. Boots are standard issue redneck-wear. When I pulled on those boots—those comfortable, wonderful, sexy and beautiful boots—there was no hiding from the fact that I was a redneck. And a redneck is inescapably white.

Strictly speaking, I'm always white, of course, not just when I wear the boots. Ethnically speaking, I'm also always a redneck. I am an American of Scotch-Irish descent, and I look the part. Prolonged exposure to sunlight turns my skin ruddy, and with my hair cut short the first skin to turn is on the back of my neck. My relatives never called themselves rednecks. They always referred to our summertime epidermal bitonality as "a farmer's tan." *Redneck* is an ethnic and socioeconomic slur. Its close relatives are *cracker, hayseed, hillbilly, bubba,* and *rube.* It refers to white, rural, often poorly educated people who spend their lives doing hard manual labor usually associated with agriculture. But the term connotes more—not merely ignorance, but stupidity; not merely poverty, but degeneracy; not merely cultural deprivation, but a lack of civility, a love of cruelty, a tendency toward brutality, and an irrational fear of anything and anybody different from oneself. Quintessentially, a redneck is a racist and very often a violent one. When I put on those boots, I put on that history and those social significations as well. And when the boots felt good and sexy and right around my feet, I was scared by the possibility that those characterizations were somehow fitting too. After all, some of them obviously were.

I know people who fit the entire description. I was raised among them—klansmen, gay-bashers, wife-beaters, and child-rapists with a penchant for incest, as well as moonshiners, cardplayers, snake-handlers, and revival preachers. Some are relatives by blood. All are relatives by water, air, and dirt. Our bodies are made up of elements from the same piece of ground. Through endless cycles that dirt perpetuates itself. We arise from it and return, and it circulates through these permeable membranes that individuate us temporarily and to some small degree. It won't do to claim that I have no part in the ugliness that that version of historically constructed whiteness entails. That would be a lie.

It is ugly, though, too ugly not to take some active notice of. So I had to do something. But what? I could pretend the boots don't actually mean all those things, just the ones I want them to mean. But we all know better than that. Non-rednecks who see me in those boots and hear me speak in my native dialect will assume those meanings, all of them, no matter what else I do. They'll assume that because I participate in one aspect of redneck culture, rather than join them in condemnation and ridicule of it all, I am condoning and even promoting it in all of its aspects. Of course I want to condemn and oppose some parts of the culture I was born into and shaped by, so there is a great deal of pressure to condemn it in its entirety. What should I do? I could give in to the vast majority who equate rednecks with ignorant, violent bigots and who devalue all aspects of rural Southern culture, including its music and art forms. In order to fit the mold of the well-educated, sophisticated, enlightened and unprejudiced college professor, I could distance myself from my heritage. I could act as if I didn't *come from there*. I could stop dancing and put the boots away. But I love them far too much. So I've chosen to keep dancing, keep working on the discipline and expanding myself into the freeing spaces that dancing gives to me. I just have to accept and live with and through the reality of race as part of the practice of overcoming dualism. I believe that it's the living, not the avoiding or denying, that will teach me what to do.

In the meantime, though, I realize that it makes me very angry that there is so little room in our society for the notion of a well-educated, decent, peace-loving redneck. It makes me angry, because I know why that's the case. Rednecks serve a distinct and very valuable function for well-educated, sophisticated, overtly nonviolent white people: Rednecks bear the stigma of white-ness, the ugly part of white-ness, so that middle class people with college degrees don't have to. If I take off the boots and speak in standard English, none of my white, well-educated associates believes I might harbor any racial prejudice or be guilty of doing any harm to nonwhite students or employees in my charge. I'm assumed to be fair and upright and free of unenlightened attitudes or assumptions about any racial group. But if I put the boots back on—in other words, if I claim my own specific embodiment— suddenly I'm available to be held responsible for all the racism that lurks in this country. Not by black people—most of whom, I've found, are on to this ruse—but by educated white people, people who want to have someone to point a finger at so that they never have to examine the institutionalized forms of racism that their actions reinforce on the job and the street every day, so that they never have to question or work against a system that rewards them for who they are.

What this makes me realize is that mind/body dualisms are functional parts of current social practices. They're reinforced by the social punishments lined up for those of us who make some effort to live our raced and sexed bodies reflectively in all their specificity. And both these practices and the sanctions that exist for people who refuse them are embedded not just in the obvious places like traditional religion but in the seemingly most unlikely of places, like the progressive academy. That way of punishing, that way of blaming somebody else and refusing to look at your own place in an unjust social system, is also in my academized head—isn't it?—which could be why I felt so uneasy about wearing the boots in the first place; I knew I'd be giving up my protection and making myself liable for blame. That's the price of the dance. To me the gift the dance offers is worth that price. I also suspect that the act of paying the price may turn out to be part of the gift in the end as well.

SUMMATION

[Increasingly, our society is organized in such a way that the old concept of mentality isn't operative anymore and bodies are neither conceptualized nor treated as static objects or personal property. The major institutions in our society (schools, hospitals, prisons, psychological treatment centers, governmental social services) treat us as normalized organisms, and those in our society who are most subject to those institutions probably experience themselves as normalized organisms far more often than they experience themselves as autonomous citizens. But, as I hope my own examples have helped show, even those of us who are in positions that allow us to maintain a broad sense of personal autonomy engage in activities and have thoughts and experiences that defy and undermine the notion that we are minds distinct from the bodies we inhabit and supposedly control. Dualism is dying.]

Foucault pushes us to notice this impending death. He presses us to realize that we are not the bodies or the minds that our post-Cartesian, post-Lockean ancestors were; we are post-Guibertians. Foucault insists that we take notice of and begin to think through the bodies we are now, that we find ways to live ourselves as developmental organisms. For if we intend to resist and oppose the *dispositif de sexualité*, these bodies— these normalized developmental bodies—are the ones that will launch the counterattack.

6

Self-Overcoming through Ascetic Pleasures

why we shouldn't focus on desire

The rallying point for the counterattack against the regimes of sexuality must not be sexual desire but rather bodies and pleasures. In chapter 4 I tried to explain why Foucault warns us away from desire as a ground for our opposition to sexual oppression. Desire, I claimed, is a central category of most if not all current discourses of sexuality, even those that claim to be focused on material, biological bodies. The history of sexuality is a history of the elaboration of desire as a concept and as the basis of human identities and cultures. If we make desire central to our analyses, critiques, and political activities regarding sexual networks of power, we run the risk of simply reproducing the structures and values that hurt us and of missing opportunities to create new possibilities for ourselves. In chapter 5 I argued that the bodies Foucault points us toward are not futuristic postmodern bodies that we have not yet created or acquired; they are our own bodies, our natural, historical, normalized bodies, the very bodies that we have and are right now. Once we begin to understand ourselves as normalized bodies and let go of the old seventeenth-century discourses of dualism and the classical liberal and enlightenment rhetoric that cover over so many of the unpleasant realities of normalizing power, new possibilities for resistance and political action may come into view. It remains here, then, to examine pleasures, the pleasures specific to these normalized body-selves that are to serve as our rallying points. What are they? And what role does Foucault expect them to play in an attack on sexual normalization?

Foucault wrote a lot on the subject of pleasure. In *The History of Sexuality, Volume 1,* he described the pleasure that comes with exercising power, especially the powers attendant to surveillance. He suggested that those who observe others take great pleasure in doing so, but even those who suffer observation find pleasure in being pursued. *The History of Sexuality, Volume 2* was all about pleasure, about the "use of pleasure" in ancient Greece. In interviews conducted during the time that he was working on that volume, he always listed pleasure, along with desire and action, as fundamental elements in his analyses of sexuality's genealogy. In his later works, he listed pleasure among the basic components of ancient ethics; pleasure, at least in ancient Greece and Rome, held an important place in accounts of the good life. And its place was not that of a mere by-product of vitality and goodness; pleasure was a force in the production of a good life, not simply a consequence of its achievement.

Pleasure figures prominently, then, in Foucault's understanding of power as normalization, but it also figures prominently in his excursions into discourses and practices having to do with shaping an ethos, with leading a good or beautiful life. Pleasure, on Foucault's view, is not just a state of the body and/or mind that occurs following some particular accomplishment or stimulus. Pleasure is not just an outcome. Pleasure, like power, is creative. As this chapter will show, Foucault advocates the use of pleasure and the expansion of our capacities for pleasure as a means of resisting sexual normalization and creating different lives for ourselves.

Most philosophers have ignored Foucault's comments on pleasure,[1] perhaps because most of us just aren't used to thinking of pleasure as anything but an outcome, as an effect that has very little effect of its own. As a result of this philosophical neglect, Foucault's claims about and explorations of various forms of pleasure-production and enhancement—what I will call his *askeses* of pleasure—have been left to the biographers to investigate; consequently, they have been individualized and psychologized until they seem to be nothing more than items in the profile of Michel Foucault as a "case." Mention of Foucault's interest in hallucinogenic drugs and kinky forms of sex is an occasion for a smirk. Pleasure is dismissed as a strange personal and probably neurotic preoccupation of Foucault's or a bizarre adjunct to his study of sexuality rather than a central issue in his philosophy. There have been no serious attempts to understand the role that pleasure plays in Foucault's conception of counterattack against sexuality, much less its role in his broader and more positive conception of ethics. The purpose of this chapter and to some extent the next is to make such an attempt and, I hope, to open discussion that will lead to a full analysis of Foucault's work as a philosophy of pleasure.

THE USE OF PLEASURE

We most often think of pleasure as we think of pain—as a function of the body, entirely dependent upon the body's physical condition. As such, pleasure is held to be ephemeral, relative, ahistorical, and private. It is ephemeral because the body itself is changeable and vulnerable to its environment. It is relative because different bodies may have idiosyncratic reactions to the same stimulus. It is ahistorical because the body itself is held to be ahistorical, and the ability to experience pleasure and pain are held to be among its most fundamental capacities. And it is private because it inheres within individuated bodies; we can experience pleasure together, simultaneously and through each other's activity, but we cannot experience each other's pleasures. Pleasure itself is incommunicable.

Hence, pleasure per se is rarely a topic for serious conversation. Likewise, it has not made much of an appearance in philosophical literature, although its counterpart pain has been examined in some detail. "The body in pain" has been found to be worthy of phenomenological inquiry,[2] but "the body in pleasure" doesn't even make good grammatical sense. Epicurus and Bentham considered pleasure, but only as a naturalized phenomenon, as a counterpart to pain within our ethical deliberations, and in the final analysis Epicurus thought avoidance of pain was a much stronger drive than acquisition of pleasure was.

Pain has, by contrast, had quite a big role to play in philosophical discussions. Wittgenstein used it as the prime example of an event taken to be private, the property of a solipsistic self. His discussion of pain is central in his analysis of language, selfhood, and society in *Philosophical Investigations*. But he was certainly not the first to take up the subject of pain as a crucial philosophical pressure point. For virtually all the liberal political theorists, pain is essential to the creation of the social world as we know it, since it is pain that drives us from the state of nature into the rightful condition of civil society; for thinkers as seemingly different as Kant and Marx, it is pain (in the form of social conflict and material want) that pushes us to develop ever more advanced modes of civil interaction, means of economic production, and technological capability; for Freud and his followers, it is pain that stimulates the construction of the ego out of the energy of the frustrated id. Pleasure, by contrast, seems to do nothing for us at all either philosophically, politically, psychologically, or socially. It is just an intermittent given, a speechless moment, a sort of nonevent that occurs when no great forces clash. "Pleasure," Foucault once said laughing, "nobody knows what it is."

If pleasures can be said to belong to the body—as is usually assumed—then to ask about the nature or being of pleasure with Foucault is to ask what pleasures belong to an essentially developmental body, an organism whose "essence" is constant change. To raise the question of pleasure in relation to such a body is to raise a very different question from the ones that might have been raised by Locke, Kant, Marx, or even Freud. For nothing about such a body is simply given. If developmental bodies have pleasures, those pleasures must be developmental as well. In other words, in relation to normalized bodies, pleasure and pain are not fundamental categories that name basic physiological or psychological states that simply oscillate but do not change their own natures with time; pleasure and pain must be inherently changeable too, subject to diminishment, intensification, and qualitative variation through time and with cultivation or exercise.

When we think with the categories of normalization rather than with the categories associated with seventeenth-century conceptions of human being, we know this potential for development is true of pain. In fact, we count on it. The toddler might not understand anything— respond to any painful stimulus, that is—other than a slap on the butt. But the older child, properly socialized, can be shamed. The pain of the adolescent's humiliated sense of self is not only more intense than the pain of the toddler's smarting fanny; it is qualitatively different. The adolescent has a capacity for a *kind of pain* that the toddler doesn't share and thus she is apt to be compliant and docile in situations where a toddler would resist. Pain is a tool that is used extensively in virtually all normalizing disciplines.

Pain and the threat of pain usually bring compliance with the dictates of a disciplinary regime; they render the subject obedient, docile. The greater and more varied the subject's capacity for pain, the wider the range of disciplinary techniques that can be used on her, and, thus, the greater her potential for directed development. Normalizing discipline uses pain, often carefully measured and graduated, as a tool for increasing the subject's productive capacities while rendering her passive and controllable; furthermore, it not only uses pain but it also develops the capacity for new kinds of pain in the subject, thus multiplying the means for maintaining the subject in near complete docility. Power, using pain and our capacities for pain, produces new capacities for pain just as it produces new capacities for productivity.

This coupling of increased productive capacity and increased docility makes it very difficult for us to imagine a normalized organic body exercising freedom. Normalizing disciplinary practices may tremendously enhance a person's ability to perform certain kinds of functions or accomplish certain kinds of task, but they decrease the number of different ways a person might be able to respond in a given situation; they narrow behavioral options. With that picture of the normalized body in front of us—that picture of a highly productive and cultivated individual who is at the same time meek and conformist, unable to imagine alternatives and act in innovative ways—we may feel little hope for a new politics on the ground of normalized bodies and pleasures. This is, I believe, why so many readers have characterized Foucault's works as evocative of nothing but despair.

It is true, historically, that disciplinary practices have led to increased docility just as surely as they have led to increased productivity. Their very reason for being in the modern world has been to serve as techniques for managing large groups of people efficiently—and, in some cases at least, even more significant than the sizes of the groups these techniques are designed to manage are the tasks the individuals in these groups are being trained to perform. According to Foucault, disciplinary normalization was first used on soldiers, people who were being trained to use deadly weaponry. If you want to train a soldier to use a lethal weapon, you want to be sure that he can and will use it effectively, but you also want to be equally sure that he will use it *as you tell him to.* His obedience, his docility, is not an incidental outcome; it is essential to the task you have set for yourself. Unless the training makes the soldier docile at the same time that it makes him proficient, he will not be a good soldier and the training will have failed. And a failure of that sort might be costly, if not fatal, for the trainer. Docility is a major objective of most successful normalized disciplinary practices.

If we want to oppose the regimes of normalization that constitute sexuality, one possibility is to try—within normalizing practices—to break the link between increased capacity (progression along a developmental scale) and increased docility (the narrowing of behavioral possibility). This is Foucault's gambit: "What is at stake, then, is this: how can the growth of capabilities (*capacités*) be disconnected from the intensification of power relations?" (WE, 317). How can we normalized beings keep ourselves open to ever more development and yet not make ourselves vulnerable at the same time to the narrowing forces of regimes like the *dispositif de sexualité*? How can we remain within the movements of development in such a way that they remain movements of change, difference, becoming, and self-overcoming—ever open to newness, unconstrained by some predetermined developmental trajectory? For me, a part of this question is: How can I affirm the "truth" of my normalized (homo)sexual "identity" while at the same time I refuse the cancellation of freedom and the foreclosure of becoming that sexual identities have produced? How can I move through sexuality, at the same time letting it be and letting it go? How can freedom here be intensified?

Counterattack against sexual normalization in general and sexual identities in particular, based on normalized bodies as a rallying point, depends upon affirming development without affirming docility, depends upon affirming the free, open playfulness of human possibility even within regimes of sexuality without getting stuck in or succumbing to any one sexual discourse or formation. We need to find ways to continue to grow in capability, even in sexual capability, ways to be strengthened and enabled, that don't make us more docile, more disabled at the same time. Growth, development, change must be fostered, but it must not lead to a narrowing of behavioral possibilities. In short, instead of rejecting disciplinary practices altogether—which we could not in any case do—what we need are disciplinary practices that we might engage in carefully, deliberately, but with modifications that militate against standardized outcomes. Instead of refusing normalization outright, we need to learn ways to use the power of its disciplines to propel us in new directions, which might (or might not) eventually establish something outside normalizing power networks.

In this project, we cannot know where we are going. To know where we are going would be to have mapped out a developmental program that could and would be subject to normalization. To know where we are going would be, at the outset, to have already failed. This is a project of which neither we nor anybody else can be in charge. But these facts— both the impossibility of any normalized subject projecting a particular final outcome and the implicit affirmation within this undertaking that freedom (the open play of possibilities) exceeds all subjectivity—do not preclude our knowing how to take a first step and our being in charge of deciding to do so.

The first step is to pay attention to how standard disciplinary practices, ones that *do* increase docility, do their work. Ascetic discipline as traditionally practiced has two very obvious characteristics. First, as I've noted, it involves the use of pain. Pain is a very important tool in virtually all normalizing disciplines, and some normalizing disciplines have as their object the creation of new capacities for pain. Another characteristic of ascetic discipline is that it has an extra-disciplinary telos. Asceticism is never taken to be its own end. At least implicitly, asceticism always draws a distinction between means and end, process and product, pathway and goal.

It might be possible to begin breaking the link between increased capacity and docility by refusing or subverting these two characteristics—pain and the distinction between practice and result. What if we deliberately refused to separate practice from result and simply engaged in graduated disciplinary practices for their own sake—for the pleasures they bring—rather than for some goal beyond them? What if we used our capacities for temporal development not for preparation for some task beyond that development but for the purpose of development itself, including the development of our capacities for pleasure? What if we used pleasure rather than pain as our primary disciplinary tool?

In one sense, the very proposal is paradoxical: We set as a goal the disruption of normalization, and then we engage in disciplinary practices without a goal in order to effect that disruption. So it seems that we have a goal after all. Upon close examination, however, the paradox dissolves. The "goal" is the expansion of behavioral options. That means that the "goal" we aim at is simply that of being able to continue to change, to engage in new behaviors, to try new things, to let new things happen without our sovereign determination laid down in advance. The "goal" of such practices is just the continuation and proliferation of such practices. The "goal" is freedom, and freedom only exists in and as events, practices, or exercises.

Normalized bodies, developmental bodies, are both inherently resistant to disciplines and also inherently changeable. These characteristics make us vulnerable to insidiously manipulative regimes of power and truth; the "natural forces" of our bodies, their functional momentum and developmental thrust, are what disciplinary regimes harness and direct. But these very same characteristics also make us open to other possibilities of bodily development—even up to and including the possibility that our bodies might resist the entire notion that bodies must be controlled by something nonbodily and might begin to develop their power, as bodies, to develop themselves. Change is possible, even fundamental change, because we are essentially developmental creatures—an "essence" which is also, ultimately, subject to the possibility of change. We have been shaped by our history into inherently self-overcoming beings. It is a history that we can use against some of its own most deleterious effects.

Instead of an increase in docility, then, we might seek out, create, and cultivate disciplinary practices that produce an expansion of behavioral repertoires, practices that increase the range within which we exercise our freedom and within which freedom plays itself out beyond who we currently are. Most likely, those practices will in themselves be intensely pleasurable and will also increase our capacity for pleasures of new sorts.

I have already described two of my own pleasurable and pleasure-developing disciplinary practices—gardening and dancing—which I hope serve as illustrations for the claims I'm making here. Foucault also explored at least three pleasurable and pleasure-cultivating self-overcoming disciplinary practices. These are drug use, sadomasochistic sex, and philosophical writing.[3] Biographers have made much of these pursuits, at least the first two, as if they somehow explain Foucault's work at a psychological level but are not philosophical undertakings in their own right. Some people have ridiculed or condemned Foucault's interest in drugs and sadomasochism and see his involvement with these things as detrimental to his philosophical projects. But I don't think any of his critics have really considered these interests and activities in the context of Foucault's project of countering normalizing power and developing counter-*askeses*. I will spend most of the rest of this chapter examining Foucault's notion that philosophy itself is an *askesis*. Before I do that, however, I would like to consider drugs and sex as centerpieces in pleasurable practices of self-overcoming discipline that Foucault considered and undertook either as oppositions to or, more likely, as means of departure from sexual normalization.

DRUGS AND SEX

Our society tends to conceptualize and problematize both drugs and sex primarily in relation to desire. We are expected to regulate our practices regarding them in accordance with discourses of desiring subjectivity—that is, we are expected to make ourselves subjects of drug- and sex-desire and to take responsibility for managing those desires in socially approved ways. In relation to drug use, the problem set before us is how to control ourselves and others in the face of highly desirable substances that are ever before us and yet are not to be circulated or consumed—officially, at least. Once desire is awakened, we are enjoined to examine our desires or the desires of others to see whether they are addictions, cravings out of control and, if so, to take steps to reestablish the control that has been lost—steps such as checking ourselves into rehabilitative institutions or generating court orders to confine those in our charge in such institutions. But the desire itself is never to be eradicated; instead it is to be managed throughout our lives. The case is similar with sex. We—particularly those of us who are young, female, or gay—are warned that sex is dangerous, unhealthy, and evil. Yet no one contests the notion that everyone—absolutely everyone—desires sex. If you don't think you desire sex, then you are in denial and need therapy. Your desire must be reawakened in order for you to establish control.

If one aspect of Foucault's strategy is to disrupt discourses of desire—as I suggested in chapter 4—then we might expect him to launch part of his counterattack just at the sites where desire is most vocal and alternative discourses seem most difficult to conceive—drugs and sex. And, indeed, he points out that there is another highly cultivatable dimension to both drug use and sex: the dimension of pleasure. In an interview in 1981 Foucault asserts: "What we must work on, it seems to me, is not so much to liberate our desires but to make ourselves infinitely more susceptible to pleasure" (FWL, 137). And again in an interview in 1984 he repeats, "Pleasure must also be a part of our culture. It is very interesting to note, for instance, that for centuries people generally, as well as doctors, psychiatrists, and even liberation movements, have always spoken about desire, and never about pleasure. 'We have to liberate our desire,' they say. *No!* We have to create new pleasure. And then maybe desire will follow" (SPPI, 28). Clearly for Foucault pleasure is not just an alternative to desire as a central category or to pain as a disciplinary tool, though it is both those things. Pleasure, and our capacities for pleasure, are cultural and political resources in the struggle against sexual normalization.[4] Pleasure, well used, might counter the power of discourses of desire where they draw most of their potency.

Like desire, pleasure is temporal and developmental (in the sense that our capacity for experiencing pleasures can be developed). But normalizing discourses have not colonized pleasure as they have colonized desire. Despite pleasure's temporal dimensions and cultivatable potential, attempts to quantify pleasure and measure it, to capture it in terms of statistically manipulable developmental norms, have not met with much success. Therefore, it might still be possible to work out *askeses* of pleasure that draw on our current ascetic skills but that don't keep us confined within and defined by our relation to norms. In other words, by using and cultivating pleasure at the site of discourses and practices relating to drugs and sex, it might be possible to develop disciplines that increase our capacities but that don't increase our docility.

Drugs can and should be a part of cultural and political experimentation, Foucault insists. "We have to study drugs. We have to experience drugs. We have to do *good* drugs—which can produce very intense pleasure" (SPPI, 28) and pleasures of new kinds. Foucault believed that a measured, studious, *ascetic* approach to drugs could bring about intensifications of physical experience that could make important and freeing differences in human individuals and society. He did not advocate the wanton abuse of drugs that wastes so many lives around us. He certainly did not advocate abandoning intellectual, cultural, and relational projects to lose ourselves in drug-ridden oblivion. What he hoped for was a new, pleasure-affirming exercise of freedom. He had more faith in drug companies and street suppliers than I do; I'm leery of the risks involved in the process of separating the "good" drugs from the "bad." But I agree with his basic point: We've got to find ways to live our bodies as who we are, to intensify our experiences of bodiliness and to think from our bodies, if we are going to push back against the narrow confines of the normalizing powers that constrict our freedom. Some practices of drug use might be able to help some of us do that.

Foucault's comments about sadomasochistic sex are similar to those he makes about drugs. The issue is the intensification of bodily experience and the use of pleasure to open new possibilities both for new pleasures and for new ways of being. Sadomasochism as practiced in many gay (and straight) communities and as described in books like *Leatherfolk* and *Coming to Power*[5] originates in sexual practices, but it stretches the notion of "sex" far beyond the usual understanding of the term. Sadomasochism, says Foucault, is "the real creation of new possibilities of pleasure, which people had no idea about previously" (SPPI, 27). Once sexual intercourse becomes easily attainable (as it was for urban American gay men in the 1970s when Foucault was thinking about these issues), it can also become boring. Sadomasochism is, perhaps at first and in part, a response to that threatened boredom. It involves carefully planned "scenes," decided upon in advance by both (or all) participants, and the techniques used for producing pleasure require a high degree of skill. These techniques often focus on parts of the body or on contact between parts of bodies that are not usually held to be erotic. A prime example is "fist-fucking," insertion of one person's hand into the rectum or vagina of another. This process is very slow— it can take hours—and involves a great deal of caressing and gentleness while the insertee relaxes sufficiently to allow penetration. A tremendous amount of mutual trust and alertness to the other is required for the success of this practice, which may but usually does not involve orgasm.

Many people, from denizens of the religious right to radical lesbian-feminists, have condemned sadomasochistic behavior. Feminists have done so primarily because they believe it entails endorsement of violence and cruelty.[6] Foucault vehemently disagrees. "The idea that S/M is related to deep violence, that S/M practice is a way of liberating this violence, this aggression, is stupid. We know very well that what all these people are doing is not aggressive; they are inventing new possi-

bilities of pleasure with strange parts of their body—through the eroti-
cization of the body" (SPPI, 27). This process, Foucault believes, eventually turns sexuality against itself, because it draws on sexual contexts,
energy, and imagery to create forms of behavior that are not recognizably sexual at all. "I think it's a kind of creation," Foucault asserts, "a
creative enterprise, which has as one of its features what I call the
desexualization of pleasure" (SPPI, 27).[7] Foucault was convinced that at
least some of the gay and lesbian subcultural activity that he witnessed
in San Francisco and Los Angeles in the late 1970s and 1980s was
involved in the project of producing, through ascetic practices modeled
on programs of developmental normalization, new corporeal possibilities that would exceed the normalized, natural bodies of their practitioners, the bodies formed through the last three hundred years of the
exercise of disciplinary power.

Foucault did not believe that drug experimentation or sadomasochism were the only avenues to the disruption of sexual normalization,
and he was aware that any practice might be circumvented and co-
opted. His practical suggestions and interests are not paradigmatic;
they are situational. His main point stands, however, regardless of
which disciplinary practices we undertake or find ourselves engaging
in. Sexual normalization can be opposed, but not directly, because we
don't yet have any alternative network of power/knowledge relations
from which to launch an attack. Sexual normalization gives us ourselves; it creates us as we are. We have to start with the bodies and
knowledges that we have and use the techniques we already know how
to employ in order to work toward expanding our capacities without
increasing our docility. In these endeavors, pleasures will be essential,
both as the means for self-overcoming and development and as those
processes' implicit goal. The ascetic use of pleasure is an integral part of
the practice of freedom.

PLEASURE AS A WAY OF LIFE

In the introduction to the second volume of the *History of Sexuality*
series Foucault defines the philosophical essay as "an 'ascesis,' *askesis,*
an exercise of oneself in the activity of thought." He goes on to say that
the book's "object was to learn to what extent the effort to think one's
own history can free thought from what it silently thinks, and so enable
it to think differently" (HS2, 9; UP, 15). The purpose of philosophical
exercise, then, is not to establish a set of truths, not to produce a report
on a project already complete. Instead, writing is simply a vigorous

practice of freedom, an exercise through which thinking engenders more thinking, through which it becomes possible to continue to think. Foucault asks:

> After all, what would be the value of the passion for knowledge if it resulted only in a certain amount of knowledgeableness and not, in one way or another and to the extent possible, in the knower's straying afield of himself? There are times in life when the question of knowing if one can think differently than one thinks, and perceive differently than one sees, is absolutely necessary if one is to go on looking and reflecting at all. (HS2, 8; UP, 14)

The purpose of the exercise of thinking is to perpetuate the practice of thinking, which involves changing the knower him- or herself. For Foucault, writing is a process of becoming, but unlike other processes of becoming such as becoming a good soldier or a proficient pupil, the goal of writing is simply the affirmation and intensification of the process of philosophical becoming. There is no end in sight. Writing is not the process of becoming a recognized authority, a knower; writing is the process of becoming a thinker, which means the knower must continually overcome him- or herself in this movement of affirmation of philosophical thought. Writing, as a process of self-development, originates in ascetic practices and even in normalizing disciplinary practices, but it betrays and strays from its origin; it attempts to create an asceticism that does not and cannot normalize because it has no telos, no end point, no extra-disciplinary goal.

For many ascetic beginnings, there are clear goals. When I first started gardening, I had a goal: eating fresh vegetables. When I first started dancing, I had a goal: meeting hot women. But in both cases, the disciplines I undertook changed me to the extent that the goal I started with became relatively unimportant. I disciplined myself to the dirt, and I became something new. I disciplined myself to the dance, and I became something I never imagined I could become. I strayed afield of myself. And in the process I discovered and cultivated immense capacities for pleasures I'd never dreamed of before. The same is true in becoming a philosopher and has been true for me in the practice of writing this book. This discipline of thinking, of remembering, of working through and reworking ideas, texts, arguments, and images has changed me in ways I didn't foresee when I started. I imagine it must be so with every book any philosopher might write, although I suspect that's one of those events or phenomena that most people don't pay enough attention to when it happens to them. Even if there is a goal at the outset, pleasurable disciplinary practices very often subvert that goal and end up perpetuating themselves outside or beyond any relation to it.

For Foucault, this practice of philosophical writing is an anti-normalizing ascetic discipline, an *askesis* of freedom. It is also, in a sense, a way of life. And so it would have to be—because once you begin to give yourself over to a discipline that is its own end and leads in directions indeterminate ahead of time, no part of your life is invulnerable to change. As his thought developed through the late 1970s and 1980s, Foucault spoke more and more often of his work in relation to ways of living, creative ethical undertakings, practices of freedom, and life itself as a work of art.

"The idea of the *bios* [life] as a material for an aesthetic piece of art is something that fascinates me," he once remarked. "[I]n our society, art has become something that is related only to objects and not to individuals or to life . . . art is something which is specialized or done by experts who are artists. But couldn't everyone's life become a work of art?" (OGE, 261). Foucault undoubtedly thought of his own life as an artistic medium, like paint or clay or sound or physical motion, and he thought of philosophical writing as an artistic practice by which he worked that medium into a beautiful form. His writing's main purpose, he says in the introduction to *The Use of Pleasure*, is to transform the writer, a process that he once described as "something rather close to the aesthetic experience" (SR, 131). The work of the philosopher is to transform the philosopher, to shape a philosophical life. That is why Foucault always valued consistency of argumentation far less than he valued innovation: He valued difference, change, much more highly than he valued sameness and stasis. For transformation, artistry, is all about change, not stasis, and anybody who celebrates artistry implicitly celebrates process, difference, becoming, and otherness.

It is no coincidence that Foucault turned his attention to pleasure, philosophical *askesis,* and the development of a philosophical life as a work of art while he traced the genealogy of sexuality. Perhaps more than any other phenomena in western society, sexual regimes militate against self-reflective artistry. They refuse difference and deny becoming. By identifying and labeling and categorizing, sexual regimes of knowledge tell us we can't be other than we are—or, if we can be other, we can only be so by progressing along a developmental path already traversed by statistically significant myriads before us. As individuals we can deviate from the norms more or less than we currently do, but none of us can ever be anybody truly new, truly different. Sexual regimes of truth deny human freedom, and sexual regimes of power and knowledge punish those of us who seek to exercise our freedom anyway. Where sexual power/knowledge networks dominate, our capacities for self-overcoming, for innovation, for developing non-normalizing and pleasure-intensifying disciplines diminish toward zero.

Foucault's interest in intense and reflective self-cultivation, in an "aesthetics of existence," is in part his means of opposing sexual regimes of knowledge and power. Insofar as he offers any suggestions for how we might live our lives against and beyond regimes of sexual truth, his last works point us in the direction of the deliberate developing of something that could be and has been called "style." Some commentators see these last works—especially *The Use of Pleasure* and *The Care of the Self*—as offering no help in confronting the decidedly political problems his earlier books sketch out, including sexual normalization, because they read these works as radical departures from his previous books' concern with power, manipulation, normalization, and domination. Many see these works as focusing on personal life as opposed to impersonal political networks, processes, and resistance. But in my view the last two books are not a departure at all. Foucault never drew a line between what might be called personal life and what might be called impersonal fields of power relations. The two are intermeshed. Georges Canguilhem, who knew Foucault's work from the very beginning, agrees: "The introduction to *L'Usage des plaisirs* as well as Michel Foucault's interview with François Ewald were judged by certain commentators at the time of the philosopher's death to be a kind of admission of his conversion to a new historical problematic. Reading the end of that introduction closely, however, it in fact appears that Foucault had not ceased to propose as the object of his historical research the 'conditions in which human beings "problematize" what they are, what they do, and the world in which they live.'"[8] Canguilhem goes on to assert that Foucault's final book, *The Care of the Self*, is a completion of the problematic that drove him since his early work in *Madness and Civilization*. "It was normal, in the properly axiological sense, that Foucault would undertake the elaboration of an ethics. In the face of normalization and against, *Le souci de soi*."[9] If Canguilhem is right, Foucault actually does advocate "style"—including ethics—as an answer to the question of how we might oppose oppressive forces; style emerges as, among other things, a means of counterattack and, at the same time, a means of cultivating freedom.

Now, many people would be tempted to sneer at this suggestion, for how can any moral or political progress ever be made if all people pay attention to are the details of daily existence, or trends in art, fashion, and good taste? What do these things have to do with the serious business of opposing domination, fighting for justice, and envisioning a better world? Style as Foucault understands it, however, is no trivial matter. It certainly may involve trends in art and fashion and it certainly does involve the cultivation of taste, but that's not the whole of it. Style involves all our practices of self-overcoming and self-transformation. It comprises all our *askeses*, our disciplined pleasures. It involves all the technologies that human beings have devised for shaping themselves and the world around them. To see how all-encompassing that is, we only have to look at Foucault's list of types of human endeavor and the types of technologies developed to aid in each kind of pursuit:

> (1) technologies of production, which permit us to produce, transform, or manipulate things; (2) technologies of sign systems, which permit us to use signs, meanings, symbols, or signification; (3) technologies of power, which determine the conduct of individuals and submit them to certain ends or domination, an objectivizing of the subject; (4) technologies of the self, which permit individuals to effect by their own means, or with the help of others, a certain number of operations on their own bodies and souls, thoughts, conduct, and way of being, so as to transform themselves in order to attain a certain state of happiness, purity, wisdom, perfection, or immortality. (TS, 224–25)

Style, the lifelong project of giving shape to human existence may involve the use of any of these types of technology, and at times it may involve the creation of new technologies of these or, possibly, other types. Style is the form that human existence takes, and it is the process of forming that existence. The work of style is the artistry with which we live our lives. We can't just say no to sexual regimes; if we want to undermine the regimes of power and knowledge that oppress and threaten to dominate us, we have to cultivate a new way of life that stands counter to them and eventually that is just other to them. And that is a matter of the deliberate cultivation of style.

It would be a mistake to think of style as a means of counterattack only, of course; Foucault is not merely a reactive thinker. Style is also a name for what we seek to enhance, nurture, or shelter even as we attack sexual regimes—which includes an openness to what is beyond the styling subjectivity's control. When I was young, what scared me most—next to physical assault, confinement, or homelessness—was the thought that, if everybody found out I was queer, nobody would ever again see me as a changing, growing, creating, *living* being. In most people's eyes, to be homosexual was to be a thing, an unchanging object. And if that was how the world treated me, I knew that in effect that was what I would become. There would be no place in the world for my gifts, my innovations, my contributions, my experiments, my emotions or point of view, because all those things would just become part of—*symptoms of*—my homosexuality. What scared me most, in other words, was the fact that the world could rob me of any chance for the kind of artistic work that Foucault calls "style." It was this, more than almost anything, that I had to defend myself against and oppose.

Opposition, as I've already said, involves a great deal more than resistance. Resistance is merely negative, a no to domination. Opposition involves something positive, a departure from dominating networks. It involves the production of a different sort of self and a different sort of community—selves and communities not bound by the dictates of sexual identification. But, much as we might like to stop there with the affirmation of creativity, this project involves even more than our most creative work. Hard as it is just to begin to build a culture and a sense of self counter to what the dominant society seeks to impose, that emerging alternative culture and that incipient sense of self will not be enough—because they will not be allowed to flourish. Counterattack against sexual regimes of power is—inevitably and obviously—*attack*. It entails more or less violent assault on sexual practices and institutions and, yes, even on the people who believe their lives depend on them—institutions like compulsory heterosexuality, the modern oedipal family, enforced sex roles and gender identification, and sex discrimination of all kinds. Those institutions and people will fight us, and the firepower is mainly on their side. We must not pretend that they will not have to be fought. And, indeed, if we succeed in destroying or dismantling or even just seriously altering the institutions that they hold dear, their injuries will be very real. Counterattack can never be innocent.

Opposition, then, is not just a matter of re-creating ourselves or of creating a counterculture; opposition will involve changing the dominant culture as well. And, therefore, opposition entails exercising power over other people to force them to allow us to do our self-transformative work. If we are going to undertake seriously to oppose the regimes that oppress us, we have to think about all these things—resistance to domination, the pleasures and disciplines of cultural and self-transformation, *and* the exercise of power over other people. All of these will have to figure into our style. In the next and final chapter, I will examine each of these.

Although Foucault gestures in the direction of style as a means of counterattack, he never proposes a "right way" to oppose sexual regimes, a program of action to abolish sexual normalization and the misery it produces. Once, when a journalist asked him to articulate his vision of gay community and politics, he replied, "I am wary of imposing my own views, or of setting down a plan, a program. I don't want to discourage invention, don't want gay people to stop feeling that it is up to them to adjust their own relationships by discovering what is appropriate in their situations" (SC, 154). The particular practices in which he chose to engage and the directions he chose for self-cultivation were his own and the community's to which he belonged. These choices cannot be universalized. All answers are situational and subject to change; they function more like hypotheses for experimentation than like solutions rooted in established truth. We must not imagine that Foucault ever meant his choices to stand as a prescription for ours. "[T]he idea of a program of proposals is dangerous. As soon as a program is presented it becomes a law, and there's a prohibition against inventing" (FWL, 139). And it is just that sort of prohibition—the prohibition upon inventing our own senses of self and our own ways of life—that we oppose and seek to overcome.

Instead of offering a program or a set of prescriptions, Foucault offers only a few tools, "instruments for polymorphic, varied, and individually modulated relationships" (FWL, 139) that may make cultural creation possible. His written works exemplify the task he once proposed to the editors of the magazine *Gai Pied*: "We have to dig deeply to show how things have been historically contingent, for such and such reason intelligible but not necessary. We must make the intelligible appear against a background of emptiness and deny its necessity. We must think what exists is far from filling all possible spaces" (FWL, 139–40). Foucault's work is designed to point out gaps, cleavage, empty spaces where new thought, new movement, new practices might emerge. It's up to each of us to do the work of invention that will foster those emergings.

The question for me (and for each of us) becomes, then: What techniques, what *askeses* shall I engage in? What pleasure-developing practices might I cultivate that will enable me to resist, oppose, and counter sexual regimes of power? What do I want to do, and what can I open myself toward? How can I free myself toward the exercise of freedom that is becoming without telos, without trajectory, without a plan? After a while, this question can become: How shall I begin to shape my self and my life? How shall I live? In other words, the question can become a question of the cultivation of an ethos, the question of ethics.

7

Counterattack
An Ethics of Style

Foucault does not propose a "right way," a proper style. But there *are* wrong—that is, ineffective—ways. Some ways of engaging in self-styling practices don't counter normalizing regimes. Stylizing practices that pursue goals beyond stylization itself, goals beyond the practice of becoming other, while implicitly affirming freedom, don't seek to affirm freedom in the end; they seek simply to achieve a static point of pure self-presence that would no longer change. For example, if in order to give style to my existence I engage in practices that aim toward reaching a Spinozistic oneness with God (an eternal, unchanging state), then my practices, which implicitly affirm freedom by drawing on the capacity for change, are in the service of a goal that is external to those practices, heterogeneous and even opposed to them. If I seek to become a being who is incapable of becoming anything new, I seek to become something other than my capacity to become. If we want to oppose normalization, we should develop disciplinary practices that don't aim at stasis. Our style of existence should be an openness to becoming—which is to say, an affirmation of freedom. If we want to oppose regimes of sexual normalization, to find ways to live lives not bound by the identities and values those regimes enforce, we have to become people who affirm our freedom in our very existence. We have to become people who dare to give ourselves over to the process of becoming new, becoming different, becoming other than what we are. That becoming is both our goal and our practice, one and the same.

In chapter 6 I cited Foucault's list of the four types of human technology (of production, of sign systems, of power, of the self). As that list implies, the "elements of style"—the kinds of self-styling practices that one might take up under any one of those four headings—are practically innumerable. And these elements can come together in many different combinations to produce many different ways of life, including both ways of life that refuse to acknowledge their own contingency and ways of life that celebrate contingency in their every facet. New elements can also be produced. There is no way, therefore, to catalog all the "elements of style." In this chapter, then, I will confine myself to exploring the possibility of a freedom-affirming, self-overcoming "style," and I will examine only three elements of such a style: (1) an ethics (a network of practices, values, and patterns of conduct) based on what Foucault calls "care of the self"; (2) counter-memory, one means by which we can expose the contingency of things, the empty background against which historical forms appear; and (3) "governmentality," the domain where ethical practices intersect with and interpenetrate practices that involve intentional exercises of power over other people. These are by no means all of the elements of freedom-affirming style,[1] but they are three that enjoy some prominence in Foucault's writings and that have been important to me as I have worked to oppose and undermine the sexual regimes that seek to render me docile by enforcing sexuality as my essential nature and deviance as my identity, and as I have worked to build a life that affirms the contingency of who I am and the possibility of being other. They are three that I offer as worthy of consideration by anybody who wants to oppose sexual regimes from a position similar to mine.

THE CARE OF THE SELF

One of the four domains of human endeavor and technical innovation, according to Foucault's list, is that of self-cultivation. Part of the work of creating a way of life—the part that springs most readily to mind when we hear the word *style*—is the work of producing patterns of personal behavior, value systems, networks of intimate relationships, and both the practices that sustain them and the rules that govern them. Foucault refers to this work as "ethics." Ethics, then, is an activity— which may or may not involve reference to any particular code. To engage in ethics is to establish patterns of conduct, routines that evince values and that create values. To engage in ethics is to create and enact a way of life.

At the level of an individual human life, ethics is probably the most important domain within which freedom is exercised. "[F]or what is ethics," Foucault asks, "if not the practice of freedom, the conscious [*réfléchie*] practice of freedom?" (ECS, 284). This is so whether the way of life one establishes avows its origin in freedom or denies it; in other words, this is so whether you acknowledge that to some extent you chose your way of life and take responsibility for it or you claim only to be following the dictates of some transcendent power. "Freedom is the ontological condition of ethics. But ethics is the considered form that freedom takes when it is informed by reflection" (ECS, 284). If we could do nothing but obey some other person, some deity, or some set of genetically programmed rules, we couldn't be ethical. Ethics has to do with actions and choices, not with mindless behavior. But freedom is not only a necessary condition for the possibility of ethics, as Kant claimed; *ethics is the form that freedom takes*. When people think about how to live, when they reflect upon their resources and options and consciously construct patterns of behavior for themselves, they are engaging in ethics and at the same time they are exercising freedom. Ethics is freedom stylized, shaped, given a form. Ethics is the work of the artist of freedom.

Obviously, the ethics (the set of practices) that we need to cultivate if we are to oppose normalizing regimes must be one that acknowledges its own contingency and affirms its origins in freedom. This kind of ethics—practices of reflective, artistic self-transformation—Foucault often refers to as "caring for the self." Care here is understood as cultivation or development of potential, capacities, talents, and strengths. But this cultivation does not take place in relation to the dictates of some ideal of "humanity" or some code of conduct imposed on us all by the gods or in relation to some essence hidden deep inside the self. Care goes beyond the mere drawing out of what was already there; in caring for yourself, you don't just coax the embryonic self to full maturity. There is no predetermined shape that maturity must take; there is no telos. Caring for ourselves is artistic work; it is self-stylization that is an affirmation of becoming *other* than we are.

But exactly how would caring for ourselves help us to oppose networks of domination, whatever they might be? How could caring for ourselves work against the discourses of sexuality? Perhaps the answer is already somewhat clear, at least in the abstract. Discourses of sexual normalization identify us (whether as normal or deviant) and define us in relation to our history of progression or regression along a series of developmental norms. Regimes of sexual normalization deny the possibility of being other, of being simply different rather than deviant, deny the possibility of any "becoming" that exceeds normalizable scales. To conceive of our lives as artistic undertakings would be to conceive of ourselves as never fully captured within any normalizing regime. To engage in *askeses* that acknowledge and invite the possibility of becoming other would be to begin to experience ourselves as other than what we have been made to be.

Foucault notes a couple of factors that work against our making care for the self a priority. One amounts to a sort of perversion of care for the self, as Foucault understands that phrase. Our society encourages not so much care for the self as another process, one we often hear called "self-discovery." Foucault sometimes calls the resulting phenomenon "the California cult of the self," a kind of self-absorption that attaches significance to the minutiae of personal life—like what kind of coffee you drink or what the brand name on your jeans is.[2] "Cult" members, Foucault explains, tend to think that "if they do what they do, if they live as they live, the reason is that they know the truth about desire, life, nature, body, and so on" (OGE, 262) or that the truth lives within them and expresses itself through these displays. This kind of self-absorption is in effect a refusal of creative processes. Unfortunately, this condition is not peculiar to Californians.

The second factor that often works against our making care of the self a central concern is that for a long time now our culture has condemned such undertakings as a sin: selfishness. Foucault writes, "We find it difficult to base rigorous morality and austere principles on the precept that we should give more care to ourselves than to anything else in the world. We are more inclined to see taking care of ourselves as an immorality, as a means of escape from all possible rules" (TS, 228). This is so both because our society's religious heritage makes self-renunciation the condition for salvation and because its secular heritage makes law, and therefore obedience, the foundation for morality. Care of the self is opposed to strict and unthinking obedience to others, to moral codes, or to law, and so it sounds to most of us like the end of discipline, concern for others, and self-control.

But, while it is opposed to obedience, Foucault points out that care of the self need not be opposed to ethics. In ancient Greece, care of the self was not considered selfish; on the contrary, it was the basis for virtue and right action. Self-renunciation would have been unthinkable for a free man of good character. To be virtuous required that one make one's own decisions and choose one's own values and goals. As this example shows, care of the self need not be antisocial. It is even possible that putting care for one's self above all else might mean developing the competence and the self-confidence that make true generosity possible, the peace of mind that makes real sharing possible, and the desire for community that makes honesty, patience, and cooperation paramount. Putting care for one's self above all else could be the founding moment of an intensely ethical life.

But "could" is not the same as "would." If we made care of the self central in our lives, if we affirmed contingency and freedom in our ethics, would we conduct ourselves in ways that would create and sustain communities and cultures, or would we withdraw from communal and cultural pursuits, as some of Foucault's critics have implied? Do Foucault's ideas lead us to quietism, as so many claim, or to vigilance and creative activism, as Foucault himself claims?

There are no guarantees. But I see reasons to believe that caring for one's self would lead, often, to caring for others and for one's community and world. For one thing, no one engages in any sort of ethical practice—no one establishes routines, values, systems of meaning—alone. Self-transformation and creation (as well as self-destruction) occur in contexts, in networks of power and knowledge already in place. Just as a tree can't grow in the absence of sunlight, water, and soil, a person can't transform what she doesn't have or make herself into something her culture and physical surroundings can't possibly support. My ethics—the processes of self-overcoming and transformation that I undertake—must grow out of who I am, who I have been made to be by the culture I was born into and the culture and subcultures I've moved through over the past thirty-some-odd years. And my ethics has got to be sustainable within those subcultures to which I remain tied. Therefore, even though my ethical work must be my own, I need the work of other people. So I'll be inclined to pay some attention to others and to care about and even foster at least some of their work. Furthermore, just as self-creation depends upon culture, cultural creation depends upon the activities of selves. Cultures can't come into existence and can't continue to exist without these transformational processes anymore than plants can live without metabolic processes. Communities and cultures depend upon the ethical work of individual people.

Queer cultures are a good example—although certainly not the only current example—of both these processes. As Foucault puts it, "To be 'gay,' I think, is not to identify with the psychological traits and the visible masks of the homosexual but to try to define and develop a way of life" (FWL, 207). As homosexual people gradually came together and built cultural forms, more people were enabled to "become gay," to live gay lives as opposed to remaining in and trying to fit into the interstices of a heterosexual society. Individual homosexual people coming together and reflecting on their lives made these cultures possible, and now these cultures make possible individuals' coming together and reflecting upon their lives.

Within contemporary queer communities, there is a great deal of awareness that our cultural forms, our traditions, and our codes of conduct are fairly recent inventions and are in need of constant revision. Most of us do not rest assured, as our heterosexual siblings might, that we are following the guidelines laid down definitively by our distant forebears and tested by time. In the absence of long and well-developed traditions for living good queer lives, we have to be concerned about ethics (in Foucault's sense of the term). The question is only whether each of us will be able to develop an ethics, a way of life or style of existence, that values the conditions that make possible continued self-overcoming through experimentation and questioning, that incorporates practices of reflection upon past decisions and actions, that empowers us to fight discourses and regimes that diminish our own and our community's capacity for self-transformation. Will I be able to develop an ethics that affirms itself as a practice of freedom and that does not hide behind illusions of stasis or transcendentality? Will the communities and cultures that sustain me be able to support such an ethical practitioner? Within my community and my culture, will I be able to care for myself?

I don't know the answers to those questions yet. Only time, experimentation, and plenty of reflection will tell. Right now, I just try to examine my decisions, my conduct, my priorities, my beliefs, and the judgments I make about and comments I make to other people always in light of these questions: (1) Does what I'm doing support the idea that there is no transcendental code to which I and those around me ought to be obedient? (2) Does it imply a firm rejection of the notion that the course of a human life is fully determined by the past? (3) Does it risk anything, or does it just repeat a standard formula that I've learned is usually safe? Looking at the things I do and say in light of these questions and thinking hard about the answers I give myself is the best general description of my current ethical practice that I know how to give. And it is on the basis of some of my answers to these questions that I have begun to develop some of the ethical practices I will describe in the section of this chapter on "governmentality."

But that kind of questioning is only a critical tool, a way of appraising what has already occurred. Artistic work, by contrast, is not first of all critical; it is first of all experimental. I've got to try new things, think new thoughts, work on new ways of seeing things before I can ask myself how I'm doing with them. For me, ethical work and the work of self-stylization more generally requires constant exploration of things other than my own behavior or motivations. My ethics first of all turns me outward. The first and most crucial part of my ethical practice involves being open to other people's lives and ideas, reading other people's works, listening to other people's accounts of themselves and of the world around us from their point of view. In particular it seems important much of the time for me to try to listen to people whose lives have been very different from mine or whose current social positions are different from the one(s) I hold. Furthermore, whenever I listen to people who speak from positions of authority, I need to try to hear what they omit, to find the "emptinesses" that might surround official accounts of things. It is by doing this kind of work that I become able, as Foucault puts it, "to know how and to what extent it might be possible to think differently, instead of legitimating what is already known . . . to explore what might be changed" (HS2, 9; UP, 15). This is the starting point for my ethics, my philosophical work, my project of creating a way of life.

THE PRACTICE OF COUNTER-MEMORY: READING *HERCULINE BARBIN*

The creative part of caring for oneself is often the most difficult. It isn't easy to make ourselves aware of what official interpretations of the world leave out, to find where the gaps lie and where, therefore, the potential lies for thinking and living differently. Sometimes we can remember events in our own lives that reveal alternatives or at least indicate places where official knowledge doesn't quite cover its slips. My own memories of being forced to take on a homosexual identity can work that way; they can reveal to me the fact that sexual identities are not natural occurrences. Similarly, sometimes historical events, recounted by those whose voices were almost suppressed rather than by those whose interpretations won out, can help us see the contingency of many of our beliefs. Foucault calls these sorts of occurrences "counter-memories" and the practice of finding and collecting them together "counter-remembering." I see counter-remembering as possibly the most important ethical practice in my current stylistic work. This book is a work of counter-remembering.

Counter-memory is an important element of style—an important ethical practice—first of all because it helps us escape from the cage of official truth and start thinking again and second because it is the very stuff of alternative matrices of knowledge and power, because it can function as the building material of alternative systems of meaning. Counter-memory is particularly important in opposing domination, because by enabling the construction of alternative networks of meaning, it helps provide a "place" from which to analyze oppressive forces and to think through strategies to oppose them. Counter-remembering is also self-transformative; in producing new networks of meaning and new alliances of power, it may well produce new capacities and ways of living. Therefore, counter-remembering is a practice that can be an ongoing part of a way of life.

One way to see how counter-memory figures into style is to examine an instance of it. A year after Foucault published *The History of Sexuality*, he published a book called *Herculine Barbin: Being the Recently Discovered Memoirs of a Nineteenth Century French Hermaphrodite*. That book, I will argue in what follows, embodies one of Foucault's most interesting and least studied counter-memorial attempts to oppose regimes of sexual normalization.

My reading of *Herculine Barbin* finds little resonance in secondary literature on Foucault. Far from viewing it as an elaboration on the political assertions in *The History of Sexuality*, most commentators consider *Herculine Barbin* to be a minor work. Some treatises on Foucault's *oeuvre* don't even mention it at all.[3] One reason for this neglect may be that the volume is a casebook, not a sustained philosophical essay. Foucault actually wrote very little of it, only a few paragraphs. The book consists mainly of a set of official documents, some newspaper reports, a personal memoir, and a novella. But a more important reason, I think, is that most readers take Foucault to be offering *Herculine Barbin* not as a counter-memory that can contribute to counterattack or even as a textual counterattack itself but, rather, as a description *of* a counterattack that occurred in history. Read in that way, the book is very discouraging, since despite his/her heroism, the hermaphrodite Barbin just ends up dead. And if that were all that Foucault had to offer us by way of political advice, his most vigorous critics would surely be right to warn us away.

In the analysis that follows, I want to make two major points. The first is that there is an important difference between resistance—which is amply exemplified by the life of Herculine Barbin—and counterattack—which Barbin's life does not exemplify. While Barbin resists sexual regimes of power, he/she doesn't manage to launch any kind of effective assault on them or to move beyond them to something new. Barbin's resistance to sexual labeling is no more successful than my own youthful resistance was; he/she still gets labeled male according to the standards of the day, and I still get labeled homosexual. My second point is that Foucault isn't holding Barbin up as an example of a good political or ethical practice or strategy. The book must not be read as a work of monumental history but as a work of counter-history. Only so can it help to open a space for alternative ways of living and thinking. Foucault's text *Herculine Barbin* (in contrast to the life of Herculine Barbin) is a step toward that kind of countering and creative work. Foucault's compilation is not a book *about* a counterattack; it is a component *of* a counterattack.

Herculine Barbin is divided into three sections, the first of which contains only one document, Barbin's memoir. Born in 1838, Barbin, then called Alexina (confusingly enough), was believed to be a girl. Soon her father died, leaving her mother and herself in poverty and necessitating her going to work. She was a bright child, though, and so eventually was able to get a convent education and become a teacher. Although she remained thin, didn't menstruate, and didn't develop the breasts and hips of a maturing adolescent girl, no one thought there was anything wrong. She was respected by the members of the convent.

Throughout her adolescence she had special feelings for certain other girls and longed for intimate physical contact with them. Around the age of twenty she became very attached to another teacher, Sara, and her feelings were reciprocated. The two often slept together, and at some point they began engaging in genital sexual activity. Barbin was well-read and sophisticated enough to know by that time that her body was in fact atypical and might be categorizable as the body of a man. She was in love with Sara. She was unsure what to do. The situation erupted into a crisis when she began having severe abdominal pain. A local physician was called in, and the secret of her hermaphroditic body was no longer hers and Sara's alone. At the age of twenty-one, then, Herculine Barbin made a formal request for a legal change of sex.[4]

In July of 1860, after two medical examinations and two hearings, the request for legal change of sex was granted. Herculine Barbin became Abel Barbin. But Barbin's problems were far from solved. Despite Abel's new status, Sara's family refused to permit him to marry her or even to have any more contact with her. Furthermore, Abel could no longer live and work in the convent. Because of his small stature, ill health, and lack of training in anything but the female professions of convent teacher and lady's maid, Abel was unable to earn enough money to support himself. He moved to Paris, leaving his mother and all his acquaintances behind, but even in the city work was hard to find. Without sufficient food or warm shelter, his physical condition worsened. At this point the memoir breaks off. We know from other documents in Foucault's casebook that Abel Barbin committed suicide in February of 1868.

The second section of the book consists of three medical reports, including the autopsy report, which describes the state of Abel's body when he was found dead in his Parisian room. There are also newspaper articles on the change of status, letters documenting young Herculine/ Alexina's educational progress, and an amended birth certificate. The third section of the casebook is Oscar Panizza's novella *Scandal in the*

Convent, which was based on Barbin's memoir and was composed about fifteen years after Barbin's death. Panizza changes very few of the details of Barbin's early life, but the tone of the story he tells is quite different from the tone of the memoir. In the novella, there is nothing sexually ambiguous about the central character; he is very clearly a boy who has been mistaken for a girl. The picture Panizza paints makes those around young Barbin seem blind and foolish and Barbin's youthful sexual adventures seem deliciously defiant while yet cloaked in natural innocence. The contrast between Panizza's story and Barbin's own autobiographical account reveals a lot about the ways Barbin's life was manipulated to fit the categories of nineteenth-century sexual discourses. It is likely that this contrast and what it demonstrates is what most interested Foucault, a point we will return to later on.

The most obvious thing about the story that unfolds in *Herculine Barbin*, whether narrated by Herculine/Abel her/himself or by physicians, lawyers, or journalists, is that it is a story about a body. Throughout the documents in the casebook, the status and significance of this body is the central issue. Given Foucault's claim that bodies and pleasures are to be the site of counterattack's inception, this fact is unmistakably important. But important in what way? What significance does Foucault attach to the body of Herculine Barbin? What counter to sexual power is this body supposed to enable or release?

The seemingly most obvious answer is the wrong answer. Barbin's body is not important because, in its uncategorizable condition, it resists sexual identification. Morphology is not the most significant component of Barbin's resistance to normalizing power. To see why, we have only to remember Foucault's account of the rise of the natural body in *Discipline and Punish*. In his discussion of Guibert, Foucault describes a shift in the ways that human bodies are both understood and experienced. This move that Guibert's musings herald—from a view of bodies as movable parts to a view of bodies as inherently temporal, as beings-in-process—becomes a widespread phenomenon in European sciences by the end of the eighteenth century, and it is this new way of thinking about living beings that is seen in full force in the medical discourses concerning Herculine Barbin's body nearly a century later. Barbin's seemingly anomalous body can be explained rather easily as a developmental aberration of a quite specific and statistically predictable sort. Although her/his body surprises and even shocks the country doctor first brought in to treat Herculine/Alexina's abdominal pain, this body does not present itself as an enigma to the more sophisticated anatomists who examine and discuss it. Published treatments of Barbin's case make very clear that all those professionally involved agreed on the true sex of this individual: Herculine Barbin was male. He had one fully formed testicle, one malformed testicle, and a small prostate. He was able to ejaculate semen from ducts that opened on each side of his unsutured (labia-like) scrotum. Possibly he was capable of fathering a child. Goujon, who conducted the autopsy, insists—even uses Barbin's case to prove—that "hermaphroditism does not exist in man and the higher animals" (HB, 139). He then expounds on the normal course of development of the genital organs in human fetuses and explains how arrests at certain points in that development can cause the genitals to look like those of the other sex; nevertheless, all human genitals are either male or female, regardless of how they might appear. The exact shape and placement of the organs do not matter; what really counts, according to Goujon, is how they function.

If Barbin's body resists medical and sexological discourses, it doesn't do that simply by displaying what is allegedly "natural" to it, i.e., its atypical genital structure. Its morphology does not defy categorization as male or female. On the contrary. The physicians who take an anatomical interest in this case do so not because Barbin is anomalous—not because a given body defies the laws of anatomical development—but precisely because his deviations from the norm enable them to document, understand, and perhaps influence normal development more readily. Deviant individuals help rather than hinder normalization's spread, even if they themselves aren't ever brought into conformity with the ideal, because they help disciplinary technicians learn how development works and how to intervene in it. For normalizing disciplinarians, natural bodies are a living resource that, theoretically at least, can be endlessly remade, but like nature itself, natural bodies are encountered first in their essential stubbornness, their resistance to the projects of civilized man. Nature's resistance doesn't frighten normalizing theoreticians; quite the reverse. Resistance is exactly what excites and attracts them, because they seek to use the power that expresses itself in that stubbornness. Their conception of the body thus coheres nicely with older discursive constructions of the body as, for example, the site of the irrational and the source of error; but it is not the same as those previous constructions, for this body's resistance is not deemed a liability but rather the indication of a great strength that, if one knows how, can be tapped, mobilized, and redirected. Like all the "monstrosities" studied by the teratologists of the day, then, Barbin was a source of knowledge and potential bio-technological power. We should not fail to note that Goujon extols the virtues of the latest surgical techniques to remedy these "malformations" (HB, 139). And, as a bonus to the medical profession, Barbin's senseless suffering and death, which resulted from his misidentification at birth, can be used as an argument for the presence of professional physicians (presumably rather than ignorant midwives) at the birthing bed—an argument the physician-sexologist Auguste Tardieu does not hesitate to make (HB, 123). In short, Herculine Barbin's body, resistant though it may be, is fully explicable and exploitable by the power/knowledge discourses of his day. To those medical specialists, there is no violation of nature to be seen in the deviant Herculine Barbin.

If we assume, as some critics have, that Barbin's resistance amounts only to an anatomical deviation coupled with psychological dysfunction leading to a refusal to acknowledge his/her status as male, Foucault's interest in this long-dead hermaphrodite will be impossible to grasp. In fact, Barbin does not simply fail to instantiate a masculine physiological and psychological ideal—a normal male body and a normal male sense of self. *Barbin actually resists nineteenth-century sexual normalization per se*—that is, he/she actively and reflectively resists being classified according to standards of normality and deviance. He/she is not a deviant male; he/she is not really a male at all, nor is he/she really a female. Barbin doesn't just resist becoming normal; he/she resists normalizing discourses and categories, normalization itself. But it is not possible to see this if all one does is pay attention to the brute body or the disembodied mind, or—more precisely—if one insists on treating Barbin as a Cartesian doublet.

If Barbin's body resists sexual normalization, if it resists the entire classification system that attempts to locate it in measurable relation to ideal norms, it does so not because of what it is (structurally) or because of how it functions (physiologically) but because of what it does. Maintaining a strict Cartesian dualism as we read, however, will prevent us from seeing that the body does anything at all. A Cartesian reading, construing Barbin's body as a brute, mute thing distinct from Barbin's mind, will attribute the possibility of action to the mind alone. The body, on this view, can neither choose nor act, because it cannot think and decide. All it can do by itself is behave according to unthinking physiological dictates. Any action Barbin undertakes, then, will have to have originated outside the materiality of the body. Thus, on a dualistic reading, if Barbin's body does not resist by its structure or its function, it does not resist at all. To see Barbin's bodily resistance and to understand Foucault's use of these texts, we must put Herculine back together again; we must read his/her memoir as a product of a material body both generating and pervaded by thought. If we can manage to do that, the whole picture will begin to look very different.

In spite of what the documents from the authorities say, this is a body that does not experience itself and will not speak of itself as definitively male. In a journal written over a span of more than four years it oscillates between male and female, sometimes refusing one or the other, sometimes fusing or refusing both of them. At points it rails against "you, degraded men" (HB, 100); at points it speaks of the women in Barbin's life as clearly other to its own masculinity. And on some occasions it locates itself in between. "As the result of an exceptional situation, on which I do not pride myself, I, who am called a man, have been granted the intimate, deep understanding of all the facets, all the secrets, of a woman's character. I can read her heart like an open book. I could count every beat of it" (HB, 106–7). Thus it speaks as a body caught between two identities, neither of which it can relinquish and neither of which is adequate.

Now, if we insist upon a mind/body dualism, we can assign one identity to each half of the binary. We can say Barbin's body was male, though abnormal in its development (in terms of its adult genital structure), and we can say Barbin's mind was female (as a result of socialization), though abnormal in its development (in terms of its sexual object choice). Identities are just the end point of developmental processes, and in this case the body and mind arrived at different end points. Then we can say that the problem here is that Barbin was truly a male-to-female transsexual lesbian, and have done with it. Our dualistic categories may be stretched somewhat and troubled, but they can remain intact.

The problem, of course, is that Barbin him/herself refuses dualism. He/she is both mind and body, both feminine and masculine, simultaneously. In the narrative this he/she constructs, Barbin presents one single history of his/her physical *and* emotional development, but that development is both male and female. Barbin presents in one unified narrative a record of his/her deviations from two distinct sets of developmental norms, norms that constitute full, ideal adult identities that are supposedly related only by the principle of mutual exclusion. The body that is Herculine Barbin thus occupies a space that is, while imaginable, absolutely impossible within mid-nineteenth-century sexual discourses. One can think the category man/woman, but one knows that the category names and must name an empty set. Herculine Barbin's resistance was to live and speak from that alleged emptiness, to inhabit the non-place of that impermeable boundary—if only in the end to die there.

Let me reiterate. Herculine Barbin resisted nineteenth-century discursive regimes not by the brute fact of an anomalous body, nor by rejecting normalizing discursive practices outright, but by the years' long daily struggle to speak in relation to two opposing sets of developmental norms and to speak as one who deviates equally from both.

Barbin maintained a voice at a point of deviance equidistant from both masculine and feminine identity. Had he/she simply refused both sexual identities, refused any relation to the identities constituted by the norms of sexual development—an impossibility in any case—he/she would not have been audible or even visible as an object in sexual regimes at all. But by appearing as deviant in relation to both identities, he/she was and is able to appear and be heard but is also able to evade, at least for a while, the finality of categorization. This is accomplished not by stepping outside of normalizing power networks and detaching from any and all developmental sexual norms, but by pitting two supposedly mutually exclusive developmental norms against each other. And that is only possible based on Barbin's refusal to live within a dualistic conception of body and mind.

The result of this struggle for Herculine Barbin was not victory over the *dispositif de sexualité*; it was loneliness and suicide. Resistance alone, no matter how passionate and sustained, is not enough to weaken networks of power that tend toward total domination. Resistance in itself is not subversive; it does not amount to counterattack. When Abel Barbin's memoir began to circulate among medical authorities, a little work had to be done to neutralize its criticisms. But most of those who wrote commentaries on the Barbin case found no difficulty in passing over in silence Abel's indictments of the medical, legal, and religious establishments that led to his/her suffering. In their minds, Herculine Barbin was a man, and if life had been hard for him, it was because he hadn't received the socialization, education, and training a man needed to have. That was all. Oscar Panizza's novella *Scandal in the Convent*, reprinted as the final section of Foucault's *Herculine Barbin*, shows this interpretation of Barbin's life in action.

Panizza does to Barbin what Barbin always refused to do: He splits Barbin into a Cartesian doublet, a body and a mind. Fifteen years after Barbin's memoir was found at the scene of his/her death, Panizza retells the story. This time, the central character, the sexual deviant who is mistaken at birth for a normal female, is a naive but irrepressible adolescent male in a world full of innocently sensual young girls. Barbin's structurally ambiguous body is retained, but his/her angry and sexually ambiguous voice is replaced by a voice that is decidedly masculine. In other words, to speak from a Cartesian framework, Panizza provides Barbin's body with a different mind. Thus the hermaphrodite in Panizza's story is masculine in both body and mind, but is simply ignorant of the fact. And thus Panizza erases all the ugly tensions that made Abel Barbin's life after 1860 a raging nightmare.

Placed alongside Barbin's memoir, Panizza's novella is revealed for what it is: a deliberate enforcement of binary sexual categories. The

Cartesian body in its recalcitrant materiality is something Panizza is perfectly comfortable with; the post-Cartesian minded-body in its bitter denunciation of sexual categorization and its defiant refusal to name itself is what cannot be accounted for and, therefore, what will not be tolerated. Split into a dualistic body/mind, Barbin's resistance can be neutralized. But that requires that his/her embodied voice not be listened to and that no one notice the effort that goes into its erasure.

It is when we counter-remember, when we notice the effort toward erasure, that something new may come into play. For resistance to surpass itself and become something more than just one pole in a relation of power, the energy of resistance must reorient itself; it must join forces with other nodes of resistance and create a counter-network of power. Once a counter-network is begun, resisters have a base from which to launch criticisms and to which to retreat when they are attacked; the counter-network can expand and strengthen itself. If we notice that what parades under the banner of "the given" or "ahistorical nature" in fact has to make some effort to enforce its own acceptance or pervasiveness, we may have the beginning of a network of power that exceeds resistance and can constitute an alternative way of thinking and living.

Such an alternative power/knowledge network can emerge in many different ways. When women's groups of the late 1960s and early 1970s in the U.S. began to use discussion techniques that came to be called "consciousness raising," they were in effect assembling multiple nodes of resistance to masculinist networks of power to create a counter-network of meaning. Creation of this counter-network involved personal commitment to the group, but even more importantly it involved developing the interpretive analyses that together those nodes of resistance gave rise to. What happened was that a new understanding of the world, and with it a new "place" came into existence, a place where people could situate themselves while thinking through issues and working for political and social change. The resistances already existed, but until they were linked together, the alternative interpretations and alternative forms of behavior possible within that new network of forces did not exist. Often when counter-networks of power form, they do so because people have come together, physically, to share some aspect of their lives. But it isn't necessary for individual people to join together in physical space and commit themselves to each other personally. New ways of understanding the world and of living can emerge regardless of anyone's intentions and sometimes without establishment of any new personal alliances at all. They can form from the linkage of events scattered through a lifetime or through history. Counter-memories collected together, even from the distant past, can serve to illuminate and reinforce acts of resistance in the present as people struggle to establish new networks of power to counter whatever network now oppresses them.

Foucault's textual resurrection of the embittered and defiant body of Herculine Barbin constitutes one such counter-memory. Although any one piece of documentation in the casebook alone would not be enough to expose the operations of sexual power, when we see them all together, we realize that Herculine Barbin's sexuality was in no way simply the politically neutral natural object of medical and legal inquiry. Abel's "true" masculinity is revealed in the texts of *Herculine Barbin* as a product of normalizing power rather than as the politically neutral reality normalizing discourses assert it to be. Regardless of how the authors of these documents understood their work, Foucault's juxtaposition of their texts allows us to see the tremendous effort that had to be made in order for nineteenth-century sexual discourses to enforce their binary model of human sexual development—allows us, in other words, to see sexual identity as contingent upon exercises of power. And in so doing, it allows us to link that past with our own experiences of sexual identity as an oppressive political construct, even as it seems to be a central fact of our existence. Thus *Herculine Barbin* constitutes a move from mere resistance toward the possibility of counterattack. The text, therefore, is more than just a depiction of resistance; it is an intentional effort to link together forces that might oppose a network of power that Foucault (along with many of the rest of us) finds oppressive.

Counter-memory, then, can move us a step beyond resistance. Counter-remembering keeps power relations in play, keeps things unstable enough that the moment of total domination recedes. If we can remember Herculine Barbin—*counter*-remember Herculine Barbin—as an injured and enraged minded-and-bodied man/woman who resisted sexual identification to the bitter end, we will have pushed the moment of sexual normalization's total domination of our lives back just a little bit, because we will have come upon one of that discourse's limits and upon one of the points at which its denuded power shows in all its ugliness. And we will not believe in it so easily when it tries to tell us who we definitively are, especially if it evokes personal counter-memories of our own. If I can remember—*counter*-remember—my adolescent self undergoing sexual identification not as an enlightening revelation but as a kind of branding, a searing of minded-flesh, and if I can link that counter-memory with others, then I will have pushed back the moment when sexual normalization can declare itself victorious over me and claim total domination over my en-sexuated self. The present book is a counter-memory of how my lesbian identity came to be, one act in the process of producing a counter-memorial network of knowledge. The disciplined interlacing of one counter-memory with another is a way of beginning to produce a network of power and knowledge counter to the dominant discourses of sexuality.

Linked together, counter-memories can provide matrices for self-cultivation and development, which eventually may give birth to very different kinds of selves. The point of counter-remembering is not to discover something already present. The point is to develop sources of strength that will make possible the emergence of something that wasn't there before, to cultivate the potential for self-cultivation, to create the matrices of meaning that will foster self-creation. Counter-remembering is a practice of self-overcoming. As such, it is an important element of freedom-affirming style.

THROUGH ETHICS TO POLITICS: GOVERNMENTALITY

There are people who don't want me to engage in counter-remembering or to develop ethical practices that affirm freedom and contingency. There are people who want to maintain their ability or the ability of the institutions they serve to determine my conduct and to impose upon me a static identity to which they assign a low value while they measure me in terms of deviations from their norms, people who want to prevent the existence of any community or subculture that might support me in developing the values and terms and of my own existence. Therefore, if I am going to care for my self, it isn't enough to dismantle historical and symbolic formations; I have to find ways to restrain these other people. And chances are good that simply offering them a reasoned argument or handing them back a few of their pet categories deconstructed is just not going to do the trick. It will be necessary in many cases to force them to allow me to exceed the categories they want to impose on me. If the deliberate attempt to exercise power over others can be called "engagement in politics," then I have to engage in politics—or possibly cease to be an ethical person at all.

In January of 1984, an interviewer put this question to Foucault: "Could the problematic of the care of the self be at the heart of a new way of thinking about politics, of a form of politics different from what we know today?" (ECS, 294). Foucault hesitates. "I admit," he replies, "that I have not got very far in this direction, and I would very much like to come back to more contemporary questions to try to see what can be made of all this in the context of the current political problematic. But I have the impression that in the political thought of the nineteenth century—and perhaps one should go back even further, to Rousseau and Hobbes—the political subject was conceived of essentially as a subject of law, whether natural or positive" (ECS, 294). The theoretical frameworks our tradition offers are inadequate for thinking about ethical practice and political practice together, except insofar as we mean by both "obedience to law," which rules out any ethics based on care for the self. In addition to conceiving of the political subject as nothing more than a juridical subject, liberal theories tend to maintain an implicit commitment to mind/body dualism and to the conception of bodies as property, thereby enforcing a conception of the body as a natural. Thus they tend to preclude a conception of the self as bodily, a preclusion that has at least two serious consequences: (1) It blinds us to the power of normalization, which operates on a body that is not a piece of static property, and (2) by blinding us to the contingency of our current bodily comportments and dispositions, it prevents us from engaging in deliberate self-transformative practices at the site of the bodily. We can't resist or oppose normalization if we can't see it; likewise, we can't exercise our freedom to become, bodily, something other than what we are if we can't see that becoming other is actually possible (which does not mean, of course, that such events cannot occur at all, only that we cannot intend them or work self-reflectively to bring them about). Marxist theories are hardly better than liberal ones. Though they view politics as class struggle, not just obedience or disobedience to law and the state, the goal of that struggle is to bring an end to politics, not to produce new politico-ethical selves. Politics, like the state, supposedly withers away upon the return of both bodies and bodily products to those whose property they naturally are. The ultimate outcome is an end to historical conflict; neither political analysis nor politics has a place beyond the end of history. Therefore, neither marxism nor liberalism offers us any way to conceive of caring for our selves—our normalized, bodily selves—as part of or at least as consonant with our ongoing engagement in power relations.

Theories have not improved much since the nineteenth century. "[C]ontemporary political thought allows very little room for the question of the ethical subject" (ECS, 294). Meanwhile, the forces of normalization extend themselves and continue to structure our lives, closing off possibilities as they establish developmental trajectories. One important result, as I suggested in chapter 5, is that most of us no longer have a civic identity; politically we've become little more than our voting behavior or our disobedient delinquent deviations, certainly not free subjects engaging in self-transformative ethical disciplines. If the care of the self is going to lead to political engagement, it is going to have to include what Foucault's interviewer calls "a new way of thinking about politics, of a form of politics different from what we know today."

For the most part, Foucault doesn't use the term "politics." Instead, he introduces the term "governmentality" as a name for what occurs when the technologies of power (that is, techniques for influencing or determining the conduct of others) and technologies of the self (ethical *askeses*) are practiced together, and it is this domain of intersection that is of most interest to him. For if there is any possibility for the development of new political subjectivities compatible with post-Guibertian, self-overcoming ethical subjectivities, that possibility will occur within the region marked out by this new term. Likewise, if counterattack against regimes of sexuality is possible, it is in this domain that it will most likely occur—because dismantling sexuality will require both overcoming ourselves as identified sexual subjects through our ethical work and also influencing and changing the conduct of those around us through deployment of technologies of power.

Despite his reluctance in the 1984 interview, Foucault goes on to discuss governmentality at length. He insists that it is possible to engage in exercises of power that at least partially determine the conduct of others as a means of opposing domination. His linking of practices that aim to influence the conduct of others with practices whose purpose is cultivation of the self clearly indicates that he believes it is possible to exercise power over others ethically, to exercise power over others as a part of self-overcoming, as an element of "style." If his belief is reasonable, the door is open to the possibility of a political subjectivity, one that surpasses the Lockean self-interested property owner and the marxian liberator, one that is capable of effecting transformations in society as it works on transforming itself.

Governmentality, then, is the use of strategies for influencing others while (and as a part of the practice of) caring for one's self. It includes any practice that seeks to shape the lives of others as well as the self, for it involves both "a relationship of the self to itself" and "the whole range of practices that constitute, define, organize, and instrumentalize the strategies that individuals in their freedom can use in dealing with each other" (ECS, 300). If we begin to use this concept as we think about politics, Foucault believes we will be able to come to a clearer understanding of what possibilities exist in our society for political subjectivity and for an interrelation between political and ethical life. "I believe that the concept of governmentality makes it possible to bring out the freedom of the subject and its relationship to others—which constitutes the very stuff [*matière*] of ethics" (ECS, 300).[5] Without some such concept, we won't be able to think about political subjectivity differently from the ways it gets thought about in the political theories we've inherited from the nineteenth century. Says Foucault, "[I]f you try to analyze power not on the basis of freedom, strategies, and governmentality, but on the basis of the political institution, you can only conceive of the subject as a subject of law" (ECS, 300)—which leaves us stuck in an illusory Cartesian liberal individualism while the world around us turns us into docile, normalized bodies with very little freedom at all. Ethics—freedom formed into art—will be lost in any such analysis, and counterattack against sexual regimes of power/knowledge will be inconceivable.

Before delving any further into Foucault's work on politics and governmentality, it is necessary to dispel a misconception that some readers of Foucault seem to hold about his analytics of power. It is true, as I have discussed in previous chapters, that Foucault insists that the subject, the agent, is not prior to power; human subjectivities arise within networks of power, not vice versa. In *The History of Sexuality,* for example, Foucault describes power as productive and intentional but nonsubjective. He suggests that events simply occur and nobody is ever really in charge. So what sense does it make to talk about politics at all, some readers have asked, if what we mean to name with that word is an intentional project, conceived by a human subject, to change someone else's conduct? Isn't it impossible for a human subject to engage in intentional exercises of power?

Obviously if the answer to the above question were yes, it would not make much sense to analyze the ways in which subjects undertake to wield or develop technologies of power, and thus the concept of governmentality would be, at bottom, nonsense. To avoid this confusion, then, it is important to note that when we begin to speak about governmentality, we have shifted analytic levels. Power is not the same as technologies of power. When we begin to examine the deployment of technologies of power, we are no longer focusing our attention only on vast fields of power relations wherein subjects emerge; we are focusing our attention on the relations of power that exist between subjects who have already been constituted historically. These subjects can change and new ones can emerge because of the deployment of technologies of power, but at this level of analysis, forms of human agency do already exist (even though they do not have the stability that classical liberal theorists, for example, would attribute to them). Unlike "power," then, technologies of power can be possessed (although they need not be) and can be employed by individual subjects. It is perfectly possible, while remaining within a Foucaultian analytic framework, to speak of one person exercising power over another intentionally. Exercises of power are always relational and always involve resistance, but one subject in the relation can certainly be said to deploy a technology of power while the other can be said to undergo it. Foucault's claim that the subject is not prior to and in control of all exercises of power is not the same as the claim that no subject is ever prior to and in control of any exercise of power. Foucault never makes the second claim, although some commentators have attributed it to him. On the contrary, for Foucault, governmentality is the development and deployment, by historically constituted, subjectified ethical agents, of technologies of power. There is no contradiction in positing a particular historical subjectivity who is prior to a particular technological deployment.

It is possible, then, for me as a particular historically constituted subject to formulate strategies and engage in projects whose aim is to attack certain social institutions and practices and to alter the conduct of people who currently take their identities from those institutions and practices. Not only is it possible, but if I want to attack sexual regimes of power, it is absolutely necessary that I cultivate my ability to exercise power over the conduct of other people, my capacity for the deployment of technologies of power.

For many of us—especially many women and queer people—doing this kind of work will not be easy. Any person who has been forced to live for long under conditions of near total domination learns how dangerous it is to oppose others overtly, which means we almost never learn how to exercise power over others (that is, to work effectively to influence their conduct) in any but the most covert or passive—and often least efficacious—of ways. But passive resistance is not counterattack; counterattack involves pressure, coercion, and destruction along with creativity and the liberation of resistant forces. If we are going to attack sexual regimes of power successfully, other people (and some aspects of ourselves) will have to be bent to the force of this new will, and some will undoubtedly be broken.

A major shortcoming of pre-Foucaultian conceptions of power is that power's relational aspect is unexamined—which leads to the idea that power is something some people have and others lack entirely. This kind of conception is especially detrimental to those of us who need to deploy technologies of power to change the networks of forces that govern our lives. Many of us are used to viewing ourselves as powerless, and to thinking of powerless beings as innocent in contrast to the guilt of those more free to choose and act. We comfort ourselves in the face of oppressive forces with the saccharine assurance that we bear no responsibility for the mess that we are in. But (regardless of whether that proposition is true or false) this kind of thinking can be a hindrance. In order to deploy technologies of power, we must think of power relationally, think of ourselves as implicated in it as it currently is configured, and let go of the tendency to characterize the exercise of power over the conduct of others in terms of guilt. We must learn to deploy technologies of power without fear or shame. For those of us who've seen ourselves as powerless, learning to use technologies of power means changing some pretty basic aspects of ourselves, which means that learning to use technologies of power can be an ethical *askesis*. It can also, therefore, be an *askesis* of governmentality.

Unfortunately, many gay people refuse these undertakings. They try to avoid the conclusion that caring for our selves involves taking political action to force changes in the conduct of other people and assert instead that the only thing necessary for the world to change for the better is for all gay people to come out. We don't have to do anything to force anybody to treat us with respect, they say; all we have to do is to stand before our families, neighbors, and coworkers and tell "the truth" that we are homosexual. Then everything will be okay. Adherents to this strategy commonly cite an unnamed study that allegedly shows that most people who profess to hate homosexuals profess never to have met any. Thus, so the reasoning goes, if they did meet one, they'd stop hating us all. Then we'd be able to take our "place at the table" and participate in business and civic affairs alongside our straight brothers. The reason gays are oppressed, so this line of so-called wisdom goes, is that gays are in hiding.

While coming out is extremely important for many of us queer folk, unless it amounts to more than just self-naming according to the existing categories, it does nothing but play into existing networks of sexual power. Labeling myself doesn't change anything if the people who hear the label just assimilate me to the concepts of "the homosexual" that our society already includes (even if not all those concepts are totally negative). In that case, labeling myself is just making myself available as an anchor point and target for power—and very possibly for some of the most brutal expressions of power our species has invented. (There are no gay-bashers who claim never to have met a gay person.) But even if I don't end up unemployed and homeless or the victim of violence, even if the people around me are good liberals who would never treat me as if I were queer, my coming out doesn't alter regimes of sexual power. Self-identification is still sexual identification. Significant though it may be, coming out is not counterattack, and refusing to face that fact will prevent us from dismantling the networks of sexual power that oppress us. We have to attack sexual normalization itself. And to do that we have to learn how to use at least some of the technologies of power that are available to us.

There are, of course, many technologies of power, many strategies for shaping other people's conduct and many arenas in which to attempt to do so. A person has to choose which technologies to learn to use, and that choice has to depend upon the specific situation you find yourself in and what opportunities lie within your reach. You also have to decide which technologies mesh with the technologies of self you want to practice simultaneously—with your ethics, in other words. There is no general rule and no choice that is universally or unquestionably right.

For my own part, I want to learn to use technologies of power that are likely to be effective at changing people's behavior but are not likely to constrain people any more than absolutely necessary. (This is my own preference. I think it is likely to enable me to do as little damage as possible as I experiment, to acknowledge the contingency of my own positions, and to affirm the freedom of everybody involved. And I value those things.) I want to develop my skill at reducing the power of regimes that tend toward domination without tipping the balance toward domination by some other regime. (This requires me to cultivate my ability to tolerate differences of opinion, conflict, and variant practices—abilities consonant with my ethical commitment to listen to others.) I also want to cultivate my ability to use many different technologies of power rather than concentrating on one that precludes the use of others, because sexual regimes are multiple and various themselves. (This choice may rule out very violent technologies of power, because a person who uses overt violence to change people's conduct usually loses his or her ability to affect people in any other way.) Preliminarily, then—and I stress that this is preliminary; it is my personal choice for right now—I've decided to work most on my skill at using technologies of power associated with traditional American electoral politics. (These technologies have to do with consensus- and coalition-building, media use and visibility, negotiation, and formulating endorsement and voting strategy. They involve a lot of talking, listening, reading, meeting people, raising money, and showing up on time in designated places carrying the right literature.)

This choice of practice is not something I embrace as a definitive solution to anything. Clearly, any political practice that focuses only on state bureaucracy or legislative processes and that defines political subjectivity only in relation to them is likely to be ineffective at explaining or intervening in many of the power relations that do most to shape our world. Still, it seems to me that learning to use the technologies of power available through apparatuses of state and local government is particularly appropriate for me and, indeed, for many of us. For one thing, it's *possible*. You don't need a lot of money or a stockpile of weapons, and you can start with the basic communication skills you learned in public school. For another, some of the techniques can be applied in other political realms—like at work or in social or religious or service organizations. After all, legislative and bureaucratic institutions are *institutions*, and as such they have a lot in common with many of the other institutions we normalized deviants find ourselves in. But the main reason right now for me as a queer American to focus my ethical and political attention on government and legality is that my ethical activity—my power to exercise technologies of self, to shape my life, to form myself as an ethical subject, to create a beautiful existence for myself and to recreate my community as I do so, *my ability to do anything at all*—is severely threatened by current state policies. To a great extent, our laws and our governmental bureaucracies still treat queer people the way I saw homosexuals treated when I was a teenager—as nonhuman surfaces with no interior, as puppets with no puppeteers other than their sex drives, as cold, dense neutron stars collapsed upon themselves. And, while we need laws and social order if we are to flourish, that kind of legal treatment severely restricts what can become of our lives. If queer people want to do anything, create anything, move in any direction, have any sort of decent life, we have to try to remove the juridical barriers to communal association, to experimentation, and to self-transformation that have already been put in place, and we have to fight against all those factions that would add to the barriers that currently exist. We have to insist that the law and public policies take account of homosexuals as human beings with possibilities and points of view instead of relegating us to the status of an ever-present "danger" from which real citizens must be protected.

The legal threat to us must not be underestimated. As I've noted repeatedly, in Virginia (as in eighteen other states) the law defines homosexuals as delinquents, as criminals; it makes us fair game for state intervention.[6] Consequently, police harass queer people continually in some localities, and resistance brings nothing but arrest. But even if we are not charged with a crime, judges use anti-sodomy laws and other such laws to label us unfit parents; corporations, agencies, and school systems use such laws to fire us from our jobs; municipalities use them to deny us access to public facilities and harass us when we try to run or patronize businesses; state government uses such laws to justify a multitude of other anti-gay policies and laws. And the Supreme Court has upheld such laws, laws that make the business of ordinary life frequently difficult and sometimes impossible. It is highly unlikely that queer people can launch any kind of very effective political movement with a broadened agenda (as queer theorists who live in safer locations often exhort us to do) if we can be incarcerated in prisons or mental institutions or lose our families and means of livelihood simply by acknowledging that we are queer. And make no mistake about it—in places like Virginia, that is the situation that prevails. At times, the law creates conditions for queer human beings that come dangerously close to total domination.

In the course of daily life, however, the law often seems far away. After all, it isn't every day you lose your job or custody of your kids. So the realization that I had to fight to change the law came to me slowly and only after I given myself over to the project of "becoming gay." It came to me when these sorts of questions began to occur: On a daily basis, what could I do, how could I live as a queer person, that wouldn't have dire consequences? Was it safe for me to be out? Would I lose my job? How could I be queer and still manage to support myself? In fact, given Virginia law, how could I be queer and stay out of police custody, much less win friends and earn my colleagues' respect? At first I just decided to do—cautiously but consciously and deliberately—one clearly defined "gay" thing per week and to see what happened as a result. That was my first *askesis*. For a long stretch of time all I dared to do was engage in a solitary activity, like reading *The Washington Blade*. But, just as the right-wingers fear, one gay thing led to another. Eventually I was a reflective, consciously gay person for as many as several hours per week. During those several hours a week, I began to reflect more and more often on how hard it was to be a reflective, consciously gay person for more hours a week than I was. Oh, I could be homosexual all the time; I could hold my homosexuality tightly to me and wrap myself around it to protect it twenty-four hours a day. But to stand in some conscious, deliberate relation to myself as a gay person while I interacted with other people seemed next to impossible most of the time. Outside of exclusively queer spaces, it was tiring, exhausting even. I wanted and needed a place in a community, a sense of belonging with my neighbors and colleagues at work. But to have that, I needed people's recognition and respect not in spite of my homosexuality but *as a gay person*. Gaining that acknowledgement and that respect was crucial in my activity of shaping a gay way of life. How to gain it was a crucial ethical question for me. It was also a question of technologies of power, because it required me to find ways to change the conduct of the people around me, in some cases to force their respectful recognition of me. After all, treating someone with respect is a matter of *conduct;* respecting someone means *acting* respectfully, which straight people often refuse to do unless you purge your queerness from the interaction first. I had to find ways to make straight people conduct themselves with respect for me in the face of my gay life.

But how was I supposed to demand respectful behavior from anybody under the circumstances? I couldn't demand respect at work or in relation to anybody associated with my job, because to come out might mean to lose it. In this state, a lesbian can lose her job for doing nothing more than carrying a copy of *The Advocate* into a coffee shop on a Saturday afternoon or holding another woman's hand while walking down a public throughway. All it takes is for one person from work to guess that she's queer; a lesbian can lose her job just for being a lesbian. But if I couldn't appear to be a lesbian anyplace where somebody from work might see me, then I couldn't work on creating a gay way of life anywhere except for inside my own home with the windows shut. I could never have a real place in a community. Job protection isn't just about the right to earn a living and keep some health insurance. Like all civil rights, it's about having a place and being respected by one's fellow citizens.

Since freedom, on Foucault's view, exists only in its exercise, since it is not a quality or state of being, changing a few laws is not going to insure that freedom is "achieved." Nothing will do that. And certainly I am not so naive as to think laws give the world its full shape. If these various anti-homosexual laws were to change, people wouldn't automatically stop discriminating against me. It's clear that people haven't stopped discriminating against African-Americans, disabled people, and straight white women just because it's illegal to do so. Even if discrimination in a legal sense came to an end, there would still be people who hate me, people who would beat me up, firebomb my home and businesses I frequent, and burn our churches and community centers. But if the laws were to change, some bigots would be afraid to commit some of the acts they now commit with impunity; there would be some reduction in discrimination and some recourse when it occurred. Life could be different, and the laws could help us make that difference. Sure, America still suffers from racism too, but Bull Connor's Birmingham doesn't exist anymore, in great part because the laws changed. And that is a marked improvement in the world.

Given the lack of civil rights and legal protections for gay people, I was at constant risk anyway, and I was tired of being demoralized. I came to the conclusion that there was nothing for me to do but just go ahead and throw myself into political activity. If I lose my job, I thought, let it be because I stood up and challenged the law rather than because some sneak outted me to the authorities. I remembered my father, who used to say, "It's always more honorable to be thrown out at first base than to stand stupidly in the batter's box watching the strikes go by." In other words, do something, *connect*, hit the goddam ball. Then keep your eyes on the base and run like hell. Maybe you'll get there safe. Maybe you won't. But that's the difference between honor and victimization.[7]

Caring for my self, then, came to mean taking up the technologies of power available to me to change the conduct of legislators, judges, bosses, and police. Among other things, I joined a glbt civil rights organization, Virginians for Justice, and started working with others to change the law—and, even more importantly, to change myself into someone who could demand and effect change in the law, change in the behavior of people who make and live under the law.

Although a lot of my new political *askeses* were certainly a relief from the old discipline involved in closeting myself and in many respects they brought me great pleasure, my decision to engage in politics meant I had to do some things that weren't easy for me. Every winter during the General Assembly session, Virginians for Justice has its annual Lobby Day. Early in the morning, volunteers gather at the state capitol and call on their representatives, educating them about issues and asking them to support pro-gay bills and vote against anti-gay ones. Later, everyone gets back together and goes in two groups to the galleries of the Senate and the House of Delegates to observe the day's sessions. The first time I attended Lobby Day, I really dreaded calling on my representatives. Most members of the General Assembly do not support queer people; most would probably be glad if we all moved to Delaware—or, better yet, Moscow. I have no doubt that there are some who would disinherit their own children if they discovered they were queer and some who are happy when they read statistics showing a rise in anti-queer violence. I dreaded facing what I assumed would be their wordless condemnation, their moralistic snobbery, that kind of irreproachably polite disdain that only Southerners really know how to affect. And a little part of me, somewhere in the region of my gallbladder I think, was just a little bit afraid. I don't know what of. Being scolded and spanked with a hairbrush? Being handed a pocketknife and sent out to cut my own switch? Being told to my face that my civil rights are absolutely unimportant and my participation in the democratic process is unwelcome and meaningless? Just being looked at with disappointed eyes? I don't know. None of those things happened to me though.[8] I didn't even get to see either of my representatives, just their aides, two nice women who didn't scold me at all. But that was hard enough; it was the first time I'd ever looked a straight person in the face and asserted that people like me deserve civil rights and police protection and that consensual sodomy should not be a crime. Saying those words to those two nice women took all the moral courage I had. I left them little green sheets of paper bearing information regarding the state's sodomy laws, stepped outside, leaned against a wall, closed my eyes, and took several long, deep breaths.

Later I followed the other volunteers toward the House of Delegates' chamber. As we gathered in the hallway, I was glad (again, right down to my gallbladder) to be back in the midst of queer people—even though most of them were wearing business suits and looking remarkably like representatives in the General Assembly. We filed into the gallery and sat eight or ten across in three or four rows. I sat on the front row and flicked the snow off my overcoat.

One might wonder why I would do something as unpleasant as spend a day at the General Assembly, subject myself to the possibility of ill-treatment at the hands of a group of people who are notoriously anti-queer, and sit through a boring and pompous legislative gathering, all in order to leave a little green piece of paper that probably won't ever get read on somebody's desk. Did I think it would convince my delegates to repeal the sodomy law? Did I think it would move them to enact legislation to protect my job? Did I think it would make them understand that my intimate sexual relationship does not threaten their marriages and family ties? No. I had absolutely no illusion that my presence there would do any of that. Why was I there then?

Because I had to be. I had to be there in order to care for my self. The act, the exercise, the practice of behaving as if I, a queer person, am a full and equal citizen of this state and this country is the only way I will ever feel that I am a full and equal citizen of this state and this country. Voting, writing and calling my representatives, visiting their offices, *bodily*, and asking for their support for equal rights is the only way I will ever learn to feel, all the way down to my gallbladder and deep into my bones, that their support and their civic respect is something I deserve. Oh, I thought I believed those things, especially as I stuffed envelopes and wrote pamphlets, but the dread with which I approached my representatives' offices that first Lobby Day made it very clear to me that some parts of me did not believe I could or should demand my civil rights. And that was something that needed to change—something about *me* that needed to change. I had to stand in close physical proximity to a straight person in a position of authority and state my case before I began to believe it, to truly live it, myself. It's not a piece of abstraction. It's a bodily thing.

Maybe what I have had to do, the practices I have had to cultivate, will not work for others. There are no universal prescriptions. But those of us who want to oppose sexual normalization need to engage in whatever practices we can in order to become the sort of people who are able to demand the social conditions necessary for the exercise of freedom, for cultivation of disciplines of self-transformation, for experimentation, for the emergence of new directions in thinking and living. For many queer Americans, then, involvement in traditional political processes might be an ethical practice, a practice of self-overcoming and self-formation. At the very least, I think it's something we all need to think about.

Some people will say I'm reverting to a very un-Foucaultian liberalism and advocating nothing but minor reform. (Of course I am advocating reform—some minor, some major. But legal reform is far from the only point.) Such objections are misplaced. For one thing, participating in electoral politics doesn't preclude getting involved in other kinds of political activity and pushing way beyond basic changes like repeal of sodomy laws. (Whoever said you can't dress as a respectable citizen and visit your representatives on Monday and then dress as a hoodlum and ride with the Lesbian Avengers on Tuesday? Whoever said you can't be a Log Cabin Republican and a Radical Faery or a serious Leatherman? Leave it to the bureaucrats to keep our identity papers in order.) For another, our participation doesn't necessarily mean we endorse "the system," whatever that is. My involvement in electoral politics is a set of practices that teach me how to use certain technologies of power and that transform me and my future in the process, regardless of whether the laws get changed or not. My involvement in electoral politics is an *askesis*, and it is an *askesis* that occurs at the intersection of technologies of power and technologies of the self. It is an *askesis* of governmentality, part of the effort of stylization that forms my ethical life. But it is just the beginning. I don't know where it will take me or where anything will end.

I remember sitting quietly in the legislative gallery that January morning as the speaker of the house brought the assembly to order and called on various delegates to introduce and welcome the visitors of the day. (It's customary for all visiting groups to be introduced on the floor of the House. Everyone in the visiting group stands, and the members of the House applaud. They do this because they are Virginians and doing so is a tradition; in other words, their conservativism drives them to it.) The Catholic lobby was introduced, as were representatives from a Norfolk military base. After each introduction, the entire assembly smiled and clapped. Then we were introduced, Virginians for Justice. We stood up. My overcoat dropped to the floor. The delegate announcing our presence didn't bother (or didn't have the nerve) to explain who we were seeking justice for, but our pink triangles were visible. I looked down into the sea of faces below, some of them faces of men I knew wouldn't lift a finger to stop a gay-basher, men who thirty years ago would have been the first to defend segregation and anti-miscegenation laws and in private probably do so today, men who would rather see a girl child bleed to death in a back alley than allow her a legal abortion, men who have never known hunger or homelessness or what it means to have to *earn* a place in the world. The world runs for the most part by their rules, by their traditions, by their leave. But that day, despite whatever disdain or even hatred they may have felt, they smiled and clapped for me—me, pink triangle and all. Me.

It's not their approval I wanted, and it's not their approval I got. What I got was the realization, standing there with my overcoat at my feet, that these men don't have complete power over anything. It's not a system of total domination I live under. For in that moment the rules worked against them. They had to do something they really didn't want to do, something that probably really galled them, in fact: They had to be polite to a bunch of fags; they had to acknowledge the citizenship of a group of people whose rights they'd prefer to ignore and whose political activities they'd prefer to subvert. We didn't change the law that day, and we haven't yet. But we did get the satisfaction of causing a room full of homophobic old boys look into our queer faces, to share space with our queer bodies, and to greet us like fellow citizens. And that's no small thing.

Neither is it a big thing, of course, but it is thrilling—thrilling beyond description. Virginians for Justice's lobbyist David Perry says he's thrilled every time it happens, even though he's been attending Lobby Day for years. It's thrilling because it's an exercise of power, because it's a deliberate deployment of a technology of power—and because that is an experience queer people *as openly queer people* only very seldom have. I didn't expect to be thrilled. It never occurred to me that I would feel such pleasure in forcing another person to behave toward me with respect. But it's a pleasure that I want to cultivate.

Pleasurable though it may be, I don't have any illusions that participation in traditional politics per se is the road to freedom. But queer people, limited and trapped as we often are by the legal system and the policies it spawns, need to develop our capacities for exercising power if we are to go on developing our capacities, cultivating our selves, at all. Many of us desperately need to learn to exercise power in relation to state legislatures, bureaucracies, and legal processes. Such experiments with exercising power constitute one of the directions the project of becoming gay in the present day is apt to lead us (although I think the prospect still scares so many of us that we'd rather withdraw into the relative safety of our own homes and commit our victimless felonies with as little talk as possible). Such experiments in the exercise of power constitute one of the ways we can transform ourselves from homosexuals to queer subjectivities engaged in self-overcoming. No, exercising technologies of power in this way is not the road to freedom, but that's mostly because freedom isn't a place, an achievement, or a state of being, at all. Freedom exists only in its practice. Gay or queer self-overcoming and self-creation *is* freedom, therefore.

What I'm engaged in, then, is not just an attempt at "liberation," not just an attempt to get free of a few legal restraints. I'm as suspicious of "liberation" as an end in itself as Foucault was. For "this practice of liberation is not in itself sufficient to define the practices of freedom that will still be needed if this people, this society, and these individuals are to be able to define admissible or acceptable forms of existence or political society. This is why I emphasize practices of freedom over processes of liberation . . ." (ECS, 282–83). But Foucault is also careful to state that getting rid of some legal restraints is an essential part of practices of freedom. "When an individual or social group succeeds in blocking a field of power relations, immobilizing them and preventing any reversibility of movement by economic, political, or military means, one is faced with what may be called a state of domination. In such a state, it is certain that practices of freedom do not exist or exist only unilaterally or are extremely constrained and limited. Thus, . . . liberation is sometimes the political or historical condition for a practice of freedom" (ECS, 283). Queer people, at least those of us who live in places like Virginia, need to exercise some traditional political power, need to learn to use political technologies to counter the tendency toward domination that exists in our homophobic and heterosexist legal and governmental institutions, if we are going to continue the projects of self-cultivation and cultural creation that we have begun. For us, at the present time, liberation from those institutions is a necessary part of the practice of freedom.

I have focused here on practices of "becoming gay," but the legal and social changes I've discussed are important for everybody, not just for those of us who are gay, lesbian, transgendered, bisexual, or queer. An end to heterosexism in governmental policy and the law is vital for the ethical practice of all people. No matter what your sexual orientation, no matter how you define yourself currently, unless you are free to develop yourself in directions not dictated by strict heterosexual norms, unless such development is materially possible, you are still subject to sexual regimes of power. Sexual normalization, operating through the state apparatus (as well as other institutions) subjects us all. Nobody in our society has much latitude to experiment with forms of pleasure, household structures, types of relationship, or concepts of self-identity without paying a terrifically heavy price in terms of public disenfranchisement, poverty, violence, physical confinement, and medical intervention. All people who work to develop and practice their ethics in freedom-affirming ways have a stake in abolishing anti-homosexual policies and laws, even if they will never commit what civil or military law defines as a "homosexual act." The institution of hetero-sexuality and its concommitant promotion of homophobia are among the most powerful forces now supporting the sexual regimes that seek to define us all. One important place to begin sexual deinstitutional-ization is with the law.

So, against the predictions of Foucault's critics, this reader has become politically engaged—and not just in some broad, postmodern sense, although that too; but also in the narrowest imaginable sense. I would not say that reading Foucault's books all these years has *caused* that political engagement. But I would say that Foucault's work has served as one of the richest resources and strongest supports I've had as I've struggled to overcome what I have been made to be, struggled to become other, struggled to live a life that affirms freedom—which has involved a good bit of political activity. Caring for my self in a Foucaultian sense has not led me to conservatism, to fearful practices of self-maintenance, to protective immobility and self-concealment. Car-ing for my self has led me almost always to risk myself, to explore, to attempt, to suffer, to expand, to grow. The critics are obviously wrong, therefore; Foucault's work doesn't lead to complacency or political despair. I'm a living testament to its power to support political action and to foster courage and openness.[9]

Much more important, however, than the question of whether Foucault's readers will turn their attention to politics and become involved in political activity under any particular current description is the question of politics itself and of the kinds of subjects who can engage in political struggle within and in opposition to current networks of power. It seems to me that Foucault's work opens toward a radically new conception of politics, as his interlocutor suggested in the 1984 interview. It moves us toward a reconceptualization of politics because it engages the liberal dualistic political subject in movements of self-overcoming, because as it destabilizes the classical liberal subject it brings into the realm of consideration the possibility of new kinds of political subjectivity (even as it refuses to dictate the contours of those subjectivities' existence), and because it both generates and encourages minded-bodily *askeses* that transform the selves—including the citizen-selves—that we have been and have taken ourselves to be. What is happening within Foucault's discourse, within the textual enfoldings of reader and work, is that the traditional political subject (just like the traditional subjects of sexuality and of knowledge) is rethinking itself, reworking itself, and re-politicizing itself.

SUMMATION

In this chapter I've tried to describe three "elements of style," three types or domains of *askesis* that a person might cultivate as part of a larger project of opposing sexual normalization. First, I've discussed the possibility of disciplining oneself to think of and to live one's life as material for a work of art and of developing practices that enable one to shape an ethos. Second, I've suggested that the practice of counter-remembering may well be crucial to the effort to find new resources and new directions for ethical movements of self-overcoming. Third, I've argued that opposition to sexual normalization will take us into the domain of governmentality—by which I mean that, for those of us most severely oppressed by sexual regimes, the work of anti-normalizing ethical self-transformation cannot be fully separated in practice from the work of cultural and institutional challenge and dismantling. If we are to engage in the use of technologies of the self, we will also have to engage in the use of technologies of power, which is something many of us will have to learn and which will change us as we do so. One of the probable results of some of those processes of transformation—given the power matrices within which they will occur—is likely to be the gradual formation of new kinds of and new understandings of political subjectivity. These new political subjectivities will differ radically from the citizen-subject that was imagined by classical liberals such as Hobbes, Kant, and Locke and that was informed by the dualistic conception of human being put forth in the works of Descartes. What those political subjectivities will be like we cannot yet clearly imagine. But our first steps toward their births will most probably include conceptualizations of our own existence as normalized, developmental body-minds and experiments and exercises, *askeses*, that help us begin to live that existence self-reflectively. I don't think it is completely off the mark, therefore, to suggest that a first step toward creation of a new political subjectivity might, for me, involve line dancing and might, for others, involve sadomasochistic sex. These are the practices that transform who we are and who we take ourselves to be. Thus, today's *askeses* of pleasure may well give birth to tomorrow's citizens.[10] Foucault advocates the ascetic use of pleasure as a tool for inventing a new political world.

At no point have I intended to suggest that the three elements of style that I have discussed here are representative of all stylistic possibilities—no more than my examples of *askeses* of pleasure in chapter 6 were intended to be exhaustive. Nor have I intended to establish these three as somehow superior to the many others that could be named and described. For me, given my particular history and placement in the world, these three have been extremely important, which leads me to believe that they might be equally important for other people who are similarly situated. But others will have to make that determination for themselves.

My main goal throughout this chapter has been to present and explore Foucault's idea that life can be a work of art, that personal existence can be conceived of as a kind of material that can be stylized, and to demonstrate that Foucault's work offers us descriptions of some elements of style. Now, at the end of the chapter, I find myself worrying a bit that, despite all my caveats and the care with which I've constructed my assertions, everything I have said could very easily be misconstrued and that Foucault's use of artistic practice as a figure for philosophy and ethics might very easily be misunderstood. So I want to end this chapter with a reminder that is also a warning.

People who spend a lot of time gazing at paintings in art museums are used to a certain atmosphere—orderliness, silence, a sense of reverence for accomplishment, the purity of polished marble and the precision of modern climate controls. For such people, art itself may begin to take on that atmosphere, may come to seem orderly, accomplished, pure, and precise. If so, the work that I have done and, even more, the work that I have described and advocated in this chapter as an aesthetics of existence by contrast may seem messy, incomplete, and unevenly impassioned. After all, it's hard to imagine the efforts I've described in these pages ever producing a "museum quality" life.

When Foucault spoke of making our lives into works of art, however, I don't think he had the paintings in art museums in mind. In fact, I'm willing to bet that he, like me, had his most intense encounters with art outside quiet, well-guarded museums; I bet he had his most intense encounters with art, as I have, in the company of raucous and irreverent friends, backstage or in messy studios or claustraphobic rehearsal booths or evil-smelling darkrooms, in the midst of nothing that was yet complete. And that's what we need to recall when we read his musings about making life into art. Art, in its living and working out, is not about accomplishment. It is about energy and time and discipline and self-criticism and pursuit and letting go. Art is not about being. It is about becoming. So too, life . . . and philosophy . . . and ethics. . . and politics . . . and . . . who we are.

Inconclusion

I started this book by pointing out that most philosophers in the English-speaking world in the 1980s claimed that Foucault's work would lead us only to conservatism and political resignation, if not to outright nihilism. I have tried to respond to that charge in two ways: directly, both by examining some of the major arguments for it and attempting to refute them, and by offering interpretations of some of Foucault's key texts that are alternative to the ones most often put forth by his political critics; and indirectly, or at least less directly, by describing my own deepening and broadening political awarenesses, interests, and undertakings as I studied Foucault's work.

As I asserted in the introduction, I believe the political impact of Foucault's work is most apparent not in his overt political claims within the pages of the texts themselves but, instead, at the site of the reader, in what happens between reader and texts. Thus I have placed myself, a reader of Foucault, inside this study, made my own work over the last fifteen years one of the subjects of this book, and attempted to pull you, my reader, into and through some of the movements of thinking and living that I have undergone. I believe my experience demonstrates that Foucault's work, particularly his genealogical texts, can be radically transformative, effect significant change, and function as an exercise of power that alters aspects of the world. And this is so not just because of what those texts say but because of the ways they draw a reader in and then force her back upon herself, force the energy of her questioning to place itself in question—because of the ways they destabilize, which is to say the ways they *mobilize.*

Under these circumstances, given this reading of reading Foucault, a conclusion to the present book seems inappropriate. How do you reach anything beyond the preliminary conclusions that have offered themselves all along the way when what you are examining is the phenomenon of a work in progress, a work that only exists and only *can* exist insofar as it is a work in progress? How do you sum things up in the end, as if you had arrived at a destination, at some definite some-where? I have no choice here but to leave things incomplete. So I will close this writing not with a conclusion proper but with the expression of a hope.

I hope this book has surprised you. I hope it has made you want to read all of Foucault's works all over again or to read some of his works for the first time to see whether the things I claim to have read in them are really and truly there. But more than that, I hope that reading this book has evoked some forgotten memory, connected with something otherwise anomalous in your experience, raised a question you can't readily answer. In other words, I hope that reading this book has left you knowing a little less than you thought you knew before you began and that it has you worrying, thinking, wondering, and reckoning a little more. Writing it has certainly had that effect on me. Conclusions are harder than ever to draw, since so many of my premises have changed, and that can make things a little uncomfortable at times. But, as Foucault said, "[I]t would probably not be worth the trouble of making books if . . . they did not lead to unforeseen places, and if they did not disperse one toward a strange and new relation with [one]self. The pain and pleasure of the book is to be an experience."[1]

Instead of
sex & desire
focus should be on
bodies & pleasure

why not desire?

NOTES

INTRODUCTION

1. One place where we might have expected Foucault's work to be examined early on is in the meetings of the Society for Phenomenology and Existential Philosophy, an international philosophical association based in North America that devotes itself to the study and dissemination of, primarily, French and German philosophy of the nineteenth and twentieth centuries. A survey of meeting programs from 1985 through 1992 is revealing. For the six years from 1985 through 1990, the Society heard a total of fourteen papers on Foucault's work (four of which were given by me). This is out of a total of about 440 papers. (Both totals exclude papers given by respondents or commentators). By comparison, there were sixteen papers on Foucault in the 1991 and 1992 meetings (only two of which were mine). I think this is a fair indication of the increased attention Foucault's work received in the 1990s as opposed to the 1980s.

2. Alan Hunt and Gary Wickham, *Foucault and Law* (London: Pluto Press, 1994), vii.

3. Foucault's work challenges Marxist theory on a number of important points. He undermines Marxism's commitment to subjectivity; he suggests that power cannot be adequately understood on a Marxist model; in *The Order of Things* he gives Ricardo's work analytic primacy over that of Marx. (For some of Foucault's comments on this latter point see "On the Ways of Writing History," in *The Essential Works of Foucault, 1954–1984, Vol. 2: Aesthetics, Method, and Epistemology*, ed. James D. Fabion [New York: New Press, 1998], 281–82.) None of this sits well with Marxist scholars. If one believes that adherence to Marxist models and theories is the only means for effecting positive social change, Foucault's attacks on various aspects of Marx's work will look like attacks on the very possibility of political progress. This fact explains some of the furor surrounding Foucault's work in the early 1980s.

4. This sort of sexual language, intended to be playful, was ubiquitous in feminist appraisals of Foucault's work in the 1980s. An early example can be found in Biddy Martin, "Feminism, Criticism, and Foucault," *New German Critique*, No. 27 (Fall, 1982): 7. A more thoroughgoing use of the imagery of seduction occurs in Toril Moi, "Power, Sex, and Subjectivity: Feminist Reflections on Foucault," *Paragraph: The Journal of the Modern Critical Theory Group*, Vol. 5 (1985): 95–102. Moi's essay begins: "What could be more seductive for feminists than a discourse which, like that of Michel Foucault in *La volonté de savoir*, focuses on the complex interaction of power and sexuality? . . . Alluring as they may seem, however, the apparent parallels between Foucault's work and feminism ought not to deceive us. Feminists ought to resist his seductive plays since, as I shall argue in this essay, the price for giving in to his powerful discourse is nothing less than the depoliticisation of feminism."

5. See Moi, 95.

6. Michael Walzer, "The Politics of Michel Foucault," *Dissent*, 30:4 (Fall, 1983): 481. This was reprinted in *Foucault: A Critical Reader*, ed. David Couzens Hoy (Oxford: Basil Blackwell, 1986), 51–68; the passage quoted appears there

on p. 51. Also in the Hoy volume, see Richard Rorty, "Foucault and Epistemology," 47. Rorty's essay was first delivered as a paper in 1979.

7. See, for example, Jeffrey Weeks, "The Uses and Abuses of Michel Foucault," first published in 1985 in *Ideas from France*, ed. Lisa Appignanesi (Institute of Contemporary Art), but now available in Jeffrey Weeks, *Against Nature: Essays on History, Sexuality and Identity* (London: Rivers Oram Press, 1991), 157–69. See also David Hiley, "Foucault and the Analysis of Power: Political Engagement Without Liberal Hope or Comfort," *Praxis International*, 4:2 (July, 1984): 192–207.

8. For some of their criticisms, see: Peter Dews, "Power and Subjectivity in Foucault," *New Left Review*, Vol. 144 (1984): 72–95; Charles Taylor, "Foucault, Freedom, and Truth," in *Philosophy and the Human Sciences, Philosophical Papers 2* (Cambridge: Cambridge University Press, 1985), 154–84; Nancy Fraser, "Michel Foucault: A 'Young Conservative'?" *Ethics*, Vol. 96 (Oct., 1985): 165–84.

9. David M. Halperin, *Saint Foucault: Towards a Gay Hagiography* (New York: Oxford University Press, 1995), 15. He writes, "What is the single most important intellectual source of political inspiration for contemporary AIDS activists—at least the more theoretically-minded or better-outfitted among them? When I conducted an admittedly unsystematic survey in 1990 of various people I happened to know who had been active in ACT UP/New York during its explosive early phase in the late 1980s, and when I put those questions to them, I received, without the slightest hesitation or a single exception, the following answer: Michel Foucault, *The History of Sexuality, Volume I*." See pp. 15–16.

10. Rarified, that is, only in the sense that, tenure-track contract in hand, one need never attend an American Philosophical Association smoker again.

11. John Ransom endorses a similar response, at least to Nancy Fraser's Habermasian critique of Foucault. See his *Foucault and Discipline: The Politics of Subjectivity* (Durham: Duke University Press, 1997), 37–38.

12. Ask anyone.

1. VIEWS FROM THE SITE OF POLITICAL OPPRESSION

1. Dean Hamer claims to have proven that homosexuality is an expression of a certain genetic structure, but I am skeptical. For more on this issue, see chapter 6 of this volume, as well as Dean Hamer and Peter Copeland, *The Science of Desire: The Search for the Gay Gene and the Biology of Behavior* (New York: Simon and Schuster, 1994).

2. That concession didn't occur all at once, of course. There was a great deal of fluctuation in my self-knowledge and no stable, subjectively lived identity for a long time.

3. There are parents who do, of course, and the existence and work of the nation-wide organization Parents and Friends of Lesbians and Gays (P-FLAG) is a testament to their courage, dedication, and love. Nevertheless, the fact that in September of 1997 the governing body of the U.S. Catholic Bishops felt it necessary to issue a letter exhorting Catholic parents to love their gay children is an indication that many parents do not and, furthermore, that institutions such as the Catholic Church have supported them in the past in their rejection and abandonment of their children.

4. For information about the Canadian study, which was conducted at the

University of Calgary, see Mike King, "Suicide Watch," *The Advocate*, No. 720 (November 12, 1996): 41–44. Full results are available at http://www. virtualcity.com/youthsuicide. For information about the Massachusetts study, see Peter Freiberg, "Study Verifies Teen Suicide Data," *The Washington Blade*, May 8, 1998, p. 1. This study was released in the May 5, 1998, issue of *Pediatrics*. For a comprehensive review of older studies of sexual minority youth suicide, see the U.S. Department of Health and Human Services *Report of the Secretary's Task Force on Youth Suicide* (1989), especially Paul Gibson, "Gay Male and Lesbian Youth Suicide," in Vol. 3: Prevention and Interventions in Youth Suicide, pp. 110–42, and Joseph Harry, "Sexual Identity Issues," Vol. 2: Risk Factors for Youth Suicide, pp. 131–42. According to Harry, "The literature clearly and consistently shows that homosexuals of both sexes attempt suicide much more often than do heterosexuals" (131). Gibson writes: "Gay and lesbian youth belong to two groups at high risk of suicide: youth and homosexuals. A majority of suicide attempts by homosexuals occur during their youth, and gay youth are 2 to 3 times more likely to attempt suicide than other young people. They may comprise up to 30 percent of completed youth suicides annually" (110), which in 1989 amounted to about 5,000 suicides per year. Attempted suicides are even higher among transsexual youth, according to Gibson.

5. See Gibson, "Gay Male and Lesbian Youth Suicide," in the U.S. Department of Health and Human Services *Report of the Secretary's Task Force on Youth Suicide* (1989), Vol. 3, p. 114. Gibson cites familial rejection as one reason why so many gay, lesbian, bisexual, and transgendered youth attempt and often succeed in committing suicide. He also notes that many who do not actually commit suicide die of either violence or disease as a result of living on the streets. The outlook for queer street kids who get picked up by family service or juvenile justice agencies is not very good either. Many foster families will not take non-heterosexual kids, and group homes and juvenile detention centers rarely offer any support services—in fact, they are often physically dangerous places for queer kids.

6. According to the National Coalition of Anti-Violence Projects, crimes committed against people because of their sexual orientation increased six percent from 1995 to 1996, a period in which violent crime in general declined nationwide. See their annual report "Anti-Lesbian, Gay, Bisexual, and Transgender Violence in 1996," March, 1997, p. 3. Copies of this report can be obtained from any agency that participates in the National Coalition and from the National Gay and Lesbian Task Force in Washington, D.C. There was a two percent increase over 1996 in 1997. See "Anti-Gay Violence Continues Unabated: Legislature's Rejection of Protections Shares Blame," *The Voice* (May-June 1998): 1. *The Voice* is the newsletter of Virginians for Justice, Richmond, VA.

7. I can't help but wonder whether what W.E.B. DuBois once said of young black students is true of working class Southerners of all races: "The price of culture is a Lie." *The Souls of Black Folk* (London: Archibald Constable & Co., Ltd., 1905), 205.

8. I explored this issue at some length in my article "Foucault's Genealogy of Homosexuality," *Bulletin de la Societé Américaine de Philosophie de Langue Française*, Vol. 6, Nos. 1/2 (Spring, 1994): 44–58.

9. There are innumerable benefits to being heterosexual in our society. One has only to look at the benefits associated with marriage, which at this writing is not legally available to homosexual couples in any state in the U.S., to see that heterosexuality brings with it all sorts of privileges denied to those in homosexual life partnerships. Law and legal precedent gives married (and some-

times also unmarried) heterosexual couples the following rights, while it denies them to homosexual couples:

a. the right to demand financial support upon dissolution of the relationship

b. the right to receive social security benefits after the death of the partner

c. the right to receive workers' compensation benefits through the partner

d. the right to receive unemployment benefits through the partner

e. the legal presumption of inheritance

f. the right to claim death benefits from the partner's employer

g. the right to take tort action for wrongful death of the partner or loss of consortium (also sometimes available to unmarried heterosexual partners)

h. preferred immigration status (also sometimes available to unmarried heterosexual partners)

i. the right to make medical decisions if the partner is incapacitated

j. the right to hospital visitation (homosexual couples can secure the latter two rights if they can find and pay an attorney to draw up the necessary documents)

In addition, the following rights granted to married (and sometimes unmarried) heterosexual couples in most if not all jurisdictions are extended to homosexual couples in only some (in most cases very few) jurisdictions:

k. the right to engage in oral and anal intercourse in private

l. the right to apply for many government housing loans

m. rights associated with parenting one's partner's children and joint custody of children

n. the right to make funeral arrangements upon the death of one's partner

o. adoption preference or even exclusive right of adoption

p. the right to custody or visitation of children jointly raised

Finally, although the law supports and in some instances mandates the granting of the following benefits to married (and sometimes unmarried) heterosexual couples, it leaves extension of them to homosexual couples to the discretion of companies and employers, which means homosexuals cannot sue if they are denied these benefits whereas heterosexuals can:

q. joint health club memberships and other such "family" commercial promotions

r. the transfer of frequent flyer mileage

s. health and dental insurance through the partner's employer

t. lower car insurance for a second car owned by a partner

u. family leave to care for a partner's sick child

The law very clearly favors heterosexual partners and very clearly discriminates against homosexual partners. If same-sex marriage were legally available, homosexual couples who wanted to get married could claim these benefits, but there would still be a legal disparity between the benefits available to unmarried heterosexual couples and unmarried homosexual couples. The law simply discriminates against homosexual people both as partners in couples and, of course, in many significant ways as individuals as well.

This information comes from Attorney Linda Woods in a Richmond Pride Weekend workshop on September 21, 1996, and from personal communication on January 30, 1997. For published discussion of some of these benefits, see

Richard D. Mohr, "The Case for Gay Marriage," *Notre Dame Journal of Law, Ethics, and Public Policy,* Vol. 9, No. 1 (1995): 215–39.

10. Straight people (nonfeminists, at least) often have trouble believing this claim, so I will supplement it. Many anthropologists hold that the foundation of culture is the incest taboo; the social organization of sexuality, in other words, marks the distinction between culture and nature. The incest taboo is a set of rules (which vary from society to society) about who can or must have sex with whom and when. Doesn't that sound like anthropologists believe that sexuality lies at the foundation of culture? Need I mention psychoanalysis here? And let's talk about classical liberalism. No sexuality at the origins of society there, you say? Take a look at Carole Pateman's argument in *The Sexual Contract* (Stanford: Stanford University Press, 1988). She maintains that the social contract is also a sexual contract—that sexuality is integral to it—from the very beginning.

I run through this list for straight people and then they invariably say, "Well, but ordinary people don't pay any attention to those things. Ordinary people's lives are not founded on sexuality." It's hard to know where to point, since all directions simultaneously seems appropriate. I could talk about the concept "manhood" in our culture and the ways in which boys are expected to prove themselves to be men. But I usually start with, "What headlines did you see on popular magazines in the grocery store check-out line last night?" Then I mention advertising—how people will buy anything from toothpaste to sports cars if they think their sex appeal might be enhanced or if they fear people will think they are queer if they don't. If I have some stamina I might point out that sexual difference is the basis for almost every social interaction we have from the first years of life, that the names we are given and the clothes we wear mark us as sexual beings of specific types long before we know what sex is, and that an awful lot of the privileges and punishments to be had in the world are distributed on the basis of (1) what sex you are and (2) whether you enact that sex properly according to the standards of your community from the day you enter preschool to the day you enter that old pine box. I also might point out that many ordinary people believe that homosexuality is destroying the family and "our way of life," so obviously they do think sexuality is at the basis of everything: Heterosexuality (which of course presupposes strictly binary sexual categories) is essential to and foundational for the world they want to live in.

11. See for example Niko Besnier, "Polynesian Gender Liminality Through Time and Space," in *Third Sex, Third Gender: Beyond Sexual Dimorphism in Culture and History,* ed. Gilbert Herdt (New York: Zone Books, 1994), 285–328.

12. Simone de Beauvoir gives a brief overview of such practices in *The Second Sex,* trans. H. M. Parshley (New York: Bantam, 1952), 141–43.

13. In the late 1980s, the American Red Cross put out training material for AIDS education insisting that educators stop talking about *groups* that were "at risk" and start talking about risky *behaviors.* One reason given was that anal intercourse, which was considered an especially risky behavior, is often practiced by heterosexuals, particularly by Catholic Hispanic teenagers prior to marriage. Personal communication, Dr. Mark Bandas, American Red Cross AIDS Educator. It is also worth noting that "sodomy" can be defined in a variety of ways and is variously defined in state law in the U.S.

14. One has only to compare the wording of state laws prohibiting rape and sodomy to get a sense of this. The variation on what is prohibited is enormous. In some states insertion of any phallus-like object into any bodily orifice against the will of the insertee is considered rape. Thus rape can include such acts as

ramming a broom handle into a victim's mouth. But in other states even forced fellatio is *not* considered rape. Sodomy is variously defined too. In many states only males can commit sodomy (though females may be charged as accessories if they consent to it), since it consists solely in penile penetration of the anus. In Virginia the law against sodomy prohibits all contact not only between penis and anus but also between mouth and genitals of all descriptions; it does not, however, prohibit mutual masturbation, tribadism, or fisting, and it is not clear that it prohibits rimming. Apparently the early state lawmakers did not know people could do these things.

15. The fact that so many are willing to do so is not an indication that society has gotten more tolerant of late. It is probably an indication that there is a large number of non-heterosexual people who are either very courageous or politically desperate and a growing number of non-heterosexual people who have managed to make ourselves financially secure enough to purchase the luxury of ceasing to live the lies. I fall into the last category. Childless and tenured, I have little more than harassment and physical assault to fear, and, being a woman in a misogynistic and rapacious society, I would have that to fear in any case. Since sodomy is a felony in Virginia, I could lose my tenure on grounds of "moral turpitude" and would not be able to sue. But Southerners don't like a stink, and taking away somebody's tenure would surely raise one. Tenure, then, may well be the only thing that stands between me and unemployment and homelessness. I'm not sure I would be writing this if there were no tenure system in American higher education. My guess is that a lot of books like this would not have been written in the absence of that or similar safeguards. I suspect that's one reason so many legislators and administrators are pushing to abolish it.

16. Some feminists have cited this example as evidence that Foucault's texts are sexist, or "androcentric," in Kate Soper's words. Soper claims that the text is successful "in shifting our attention from the reality to the rhetoric, from the fright of the child victim to the phallic discipline of the academic luminary [Foucault himself, presumably], whose vision is so dazzling on the issue of 'significance' that it all but blinds us to what may really be of most moment. At any rate, it would seem rather clear that child abuse neither preceded not [sic] gets constructed in this discourse." See Kate Soper, "Productive Contradictions," in *Up Against Foucault: Explorations of Some Tensions Between Foucault and Feminism,* ed. Caroline Ramazanoglu (New York: Routledge, 1993), 43. But what is really of most moment in this story? It is possible that the child Jouy the farmhand frightened (or whose parents he frightened) was injured. Foucault does not say she wasn't. What he points out is that a "village idiot," who was acquitted of any crime, was held in custody and interrogated for the rest of his life not just about that incident but about all aspects of his sexuality. The issue is that what would once have seemed to authorities like a perfectly ordinary, if bothersome, occurrence in a French farming village had by 1867 become a matter of intense official curiosity and activity—not because newly enlightened officials cared about the well-being of little girls but because they wanted to learn how to control and administer everybody's sexual behavior, including that of little girls. It is no coincidence that the man was a marginal member of society in the first place; he was easy prey for information-hungry proto-social scientists. Soper seems to think the authorities acted correctly in disregarding Jouy's civil rights, and that Foucault should have thought so too. For this reason, feminists like Soper frighten me far more than any of the dull-witted, horny farmhands I knew as a child.

17. The French term *dispositif* is translated by Hurley in *The History of Sexuality, Volume 1* as "deployment." Lemert and Gillan translate it as "affective mechanism"; see Charles C. Lemert and Garth Gillan, *Michel Foucault: Social Theory and Transgression* (New York: Columbia University Press, 1982), 77. Colin Gordon usually translates it "apparatus"; see Foucault, *Power/Knowledge* (New York: Pantheon Books, 1980). And Barry Cooper calls it a "device, disposition of devices, etc." in his *Michel Foucault: An Introduction to the Study of His Thought* (New York: The Edwin Mellen Press, 1981), 71. Foucault gives an account of his use of the term in CF, 194ff. Put simply, a *dispositif* is a system of relations among heterogeneous elements such as discourses, institutions, laws, architecture, etc., that serves a strategic function.

18. I'll offer examples later, but for now just consider the architecture, standard procedures, and daily routines of public schools: attendance taking, bathroom passes, locker checks, dress codes, parking permits, confiscation of contraband, guidance counseling, parent-teacher conferences, school medical files, psychological testing, truancy laws, etc. And consider what can happen if these are violated: detention, arrest, therapies including family therapy, foster care, arrest and indictment of parents, etc. You may think these things don't do much to stop drug use, violence, truancy, pre-marital sex, or homosexuality, and you're probably right. What they do is identify children who engage in these practices very early in life, label them, monitor them and their families, and construe and direct their lives in certain preestablished ways.

19. The 1973 edition of the *Dictionary of Behavioral Science*, ed. Benjamin B. Wolman (New York: Van Nostrand Reinhold), gives definitions and entries for only six of these eight terms: "mixoscopophiles"—those who reach orgasm by watching their love objects have sex with another person; "zoophiles"—those who have an excessive attraction to animals; "zooerasts"—those who have sex with animals; "gynecomasts"—those [presumably male] who have an intense desire for women; "sexoesthetic inverts"—those who assume the manners, habits, and garments of the opposite sex; and "dyspareunist women"—women who have a deficient capacity for enjoying sexual pleasure or have pain during sexual intercourse. The *Dictionary* does not provide a definition or entry for "auto-monosexuals" or "presbyophiles."

20. I suspect that someone with this teacher's proclivities just a couple of decades earlier would have used similar techniques to ferret out people of African descent trying to "pass" as white. The overlap between surveillance to discover deviant sexuality and surveillance to discover race-offenders has yet to be analyzed, but no doubt it will be a rich field for investigation.

21. I make this same point in "Foucault's Genealogy of Homosexuality," 54–55.

22. Eve Kosofsky Sedgwick, *Epistemology of the Closet* (Berkeley: University of California Press, 1990), 1.

2. GENEALOGICAL DIVERSIONS

1. That fact had been clear to me almost since I realized I was homosexual. Sometimes some of us—those who are in relatively safe positions—forget how targetable we are, though. David Halperin has written about the way in which having a homosexual identity, even if one has chosen to own it publicly, de-authorizes one: "The point of coming out, I had thought, was precisely to deprive other people of their privileged knowingness about me and my sexu-

ality; coming out had seemed to me to furnish a means of seizing the initiative from them, a means of claiming back from them a certain interpretative authority over the meaning of my words and actions. As I discovered to my cost, however, it turns out that if you are known to be lesbian or gay your very openness, far from preempting malicious gossip about your sexuality, simply exposes you to the possibility that, no matter what you actually do, people can say absolutely whatever they like about you in the well-grounded confidence that it will be credited." I am amazed at Halperin's seeming naivete ever to have thought that his coming out deprived any malicious person of any opportunity for injuring him. Fortunately, most other passages in his book seem much less oblivious as to how the world really works. See *Saint Foucault: Towards a Gay Hagiography* (New York: Oxford University Press, 1995), 13.

2. Jonathan Ned Katz, "The Invention of Heterosexuality," *Socialist Review*, Vol. 21, No. 1 (Feb., 1990): 8.

3. Jonathan Ned Katz, *The Invention of Heterosexuality* (New York: Penguin, 1995).

4. Katz, 1990, 14.

5. Ibid., 19.

6. Ibid., 10.

7. Ibid., 10.

8. Ibid., 31.

9. Ibid., 8.

10. Ibid., 8.

11. Likewise, as Carolyn Merchant's work clearly shows, a genealogical analysis of the natural scientist would quickly reveal the tools of the Inquisitor. And as Nietzsche tried to show in the Third Essay of *Toward a Genealogy of Morals*, a genealogical analysis of the modern-day disciple of truth leads us back to the vengeance of ancient ascetic priests. See Merchant, *The Death of Nature* (New York: Harper and Row, 1980).

12. Foucault was very aware of the work of American and British analytic epistemologists. In "Sexuality and Solitude," however, he admitted his limitations. ". . . I confess, with the appropriate chagrin, that I am not an analytic philosopher. Nobody's perfect." *The Essential Works of Foucault, 1954–1984, Vol. 1: Ethics, Subjectivity and Truth*, ed. Paul Rabinow (New York: New Press, 1998), 176.

13. For a clear and interesting discussion of this point, See C. G. Prado, *Starting with Foucault: An Introduction to Genealogy* (Boulder: Westview, 1995), 126ff.

14. "Crimes against Genetics," *Nature Genetics*, Vol. 11, No. 3 (Nov., 1995): 224.

15. We might be tempted to say the best standards are the ones that work best, but that kind of pragmatic response conflates epistemic and non-epistemic considerations. (It also just moves the relativism to a new location, because what works best depends on who gets to choose the goals and which goals they choose.)

16. Todd May, *Between Genealogy and Epistemology* (University Park: Pennsylvania State University Press, 1993), 98.

17. Ibid., 100.

18. Prado, 39.

19. To quote Luce Irigaray, "When Our Lips Speak Together," in *This Sex Which Is Not One*, trans. Cartherine Porter (Ithaca: Cornell University Press, 1985), 205.

20. See Charles E. Scott, *The Question of Ethics: Nietzsche, Foucault, Heidegger* (Bloomington: Indiana University Press, 1990), esp. chapter 2.

21. Georges Bataille, *A Theory of Religion,* trans. Robert Hurley (New York: Zone, 1989), 19.

22. Friedrich Nietzsche, *On the Genealogy of Morals and Ecce Homo,* trans. Walter Kaufman (New York: Vintage, 1967), 33.

23. Scott, 14.

24. The very poorest Southerners would disagree with me about this. For an alternative view of genealogy, see Dorothy Allison, *Two or Three Things I Know For Sure* (New York: Penguin, 1995), 10.

25. In NGH, Foucault implies that Nietzsche also means by *wirkliche Historie* a practice of history that refuses to seek out causes for events.

3. WHY I SHOULDN'T LIKE FOUCAULT

1. Here is the text of the Virginia state law: Section 18.2–361(a): "If any person carnally knows in any manner any brute animal, or carnally knows any male or female person by the anus or by or with the mouth, or voluntarily submits to such carnal knowledge, he or she shall be guilty of a Class 6 felony. . . ." And further, Section 18.2–10(f): "For Class 6 felonies, a term of imprisonment of not less than one year nor more than five years, or in the discretion of the jury or the court trying the case without a jury, confinement in jail for not more than twelve months and a fine of not more than $2,500, either or both." According to a long tradition of case law, married couples are exempt from this statute. Virginia has a provision for the "sanctity of the marriage bed," which apparently is not defiled by sodomy. Unmarried, and in particular homosexual, people are still prosecuted for sodomy in Virginia. Violators of the law are routinely picked up in gay cruising grounds, but the law extends much farther than rest stops and public parks. On June 25, 1997, Andrew Adamson was arrested for allegedly soliciting oral sex from a repairman in his own home in Manassas, Virginia. According to his accuser, Edward Jackson, Adamson did not expose himself or attempt to force the repairman against his will, but he did solicit oral sex. Jackson's accusation was enough to persuade Fairfax County police to charge Adamson with felonious sodomy. He was released on $2,500 bond pending a preliminary hearing in Fairfax County General District Court July 30. See Lou Chibbaro, Jr., "Fairfax County Man Charged with Violating Virginia's Sodomy Law," *The Washington Blade,* July 11, 1997, p. 5, cols. 2–4.

2. In 1993 Judge Buford Parsons of the Circuit Court of Henrico County, Virginia, ruled that Sharon Bottoms could not have custody of her young son because she is a lesbian. Custody was given to the child's grandmother. The judge's opinion reads in part, "I will tell you first that the mother's conduct is illegal. It is a Class 6 felony in the Commonwealth of Virginia. I will tell you that it is the opinion of this Court that her conduct is immoral. And it is the opinion of this Court that the conduct of Sharon Bottoms renders her an unfit parent." This decision was upheld in Virginia Supreme Court in July of 1995 and again in Circuit Court in February of 1996. Bottoms announced on August 15, 1996, that she would not appeal but would instead seek more visitation rights. In the summer of 1997 she finally won the right to have her son visit her in her home with her partner present.

3. In December of 1995 members of the Virginia Housing Development Authority voted to restrict loans for first-time low-income home-buyers to those who are either married or related by blood or adoption. They did this by

changing the word *household* to the word *family* in their regulations. In January of 1996 the General Assembly adopted a resolution that ratified the VHDA's decision. The Joint House Resolution (No. 652) reads in part: "Whereas the word 'household' may include illegal and/or immoral living arrangements; and whereas the Virginia Housing Development Authority housing subsidy was initiated to support and strengthen families who will enhance, not detract from, the moral fiber of the Commonwealth," be it resolved that the word *family* replace the word *household* in the regulations.

On July 22, 1994, Virginia Attorney General James Gilmore (who subsequently has become governor) issued a legal opinion that the Commonwealth's domestic relations law does not apply to same-sex couples. The domestic relations law established domestic relations courts, which provide a variety of sentencing options not available to judges in other courts. The law specifies that these legal and social services are available to "family and household members" and defines "household member" as "any individual who, within the previous twelve months, cohabited with the defendant." But Gilmore asserts, "If the General Assembly had intended those statutory definitions to encompass unrelated persons of the same sex, either in a homosexual relationship or merely as lodgers sharing a common dwelling, in my opinion, it would have used a broader term, such as 'resides' instead of the limiting term 'cohabits.'. . ." The ramifications of Gilmore's opinion became evident in late July of 1995 when Judge Stephen Rideout of the Alexandria Juvenile and Domestic Relations District Court dismissed the petition of a gay man who filed for a restraining order against his former lover. The man, Ellis Early, filed in domestic relations court rather than in general district court because he did not want to charge his former lover with assault and risk having him sent to jail. Judge Rideout ruled that he could not hear the petition of a gay man regarding a homosexual relationship, because the domestic relations law is inapplicable to homosexuals. See Lou Chibbaro, Jr., "Attorney General Says Virginia Law Excludes Same-sex Couples," *The Washington Blade*, August 4, 1995.

4. Virginia's General Assembly enacted a Hate Crimes law in 1995. However, legislators struck language in the bill that would have included crimes motivated by hatred for a person's sex or sexual orientation. Only crimes motivated by hatred of a person's race, religion, or ethnicity count as hate crimes in this state. The absurdity of this situation was made clear on February 25, 1996, when in the course of one night several synagogues, predominantly African-American churches, and the Metropolitan Community Church were all vandalized, apparently by the same group of people. The vandalism of the synagogues and Black churches count as hate crimes, but the vandalism of the MCC does not.

5. John D'Emilio, "The Homosexual Menace: The Politics of Sexuality in Cold War America," in *Passion and Power: Sexuality in History*, ed. Kathy Peiss and Christina Simmons (Philadelphia: Triangle Press, 1989), 229.

6. Ibid., 230.

7. John D'Emilio, "Capitalism and Gay Identity," in *Making Trouble: Essays on Gay History, Politics, and the University* (New York: Routledge, 1992), 10–11.

8. Both of these articles are widely anthologized and frequently quoted. And, if the Internet's Foucault List is any indication, both are still (as of 1997) frequently read and taken very seriously. See Michael Walzer, "The Politics of Michel Foucault," *Dissent*, Vol. 30 (Fall, 1983): 481–90; reprinted in *Foucault: A Critical Reader*, ed. David Couzens Hoy (London: Blackwell, 1986), 51–68. Further references to this work will be taken from Hoy. See also Nancy Fraser,

"Michel Foucault: A 'Young Conservative'?" *Ethics*, Vol. 96 (Oct., 1985): 165–84. Further references to this work will occur as Fraser, 1985, and page number.

9. Walzer, 61.

10. Ibid., 62.

11. Ibid., 62.

12. Ibid., 65.

13. Friedrich Nietzsche, *On the Genealogy of Morals and Ecce Homo*, trans. Walter Kaufmann (New York: Vintage, 1967), 85.

14. Walzer, 63.

15. Ibid., 63.

16. Ibid., 67.

17. Fraser, 1985, 182.

18. Nancy Fraser, "Foucault on Modern Power: Empirical Insights and Normative Confusions," *Praxis International*, Vol. 1 (Oct., 1981): 279. Further references to this work will occur as Fraser, 1981, and page number.

19. Fraser, 1981, 279.

20. Ladelle McWhorter, "Natural Bodies, Unnatural Pleasures: Foucault and the Politics of Corporeal Intensification," *Symplokē*, Vol. 3, No. 2 (Summer, 1995): 201–10.

21. My colleague Ellen Armour (personal communication, 1997) insists that there is a sense in which Foucault does start with humanism. A major aspect of his work for more than two decades was an attempt to undermine and displace humanism, precisely because it is such a stumbling block for many of us both philosophically and politically. I think Foucault begins with humanism in much the same way that I began with sexual identity. I was fully within an arrangement of practices and institutions that made sexual identities real and gave me no other way to think. Yet I was suspicious of them and made every effort to undercut them. Foucault is clearly suspicious of "man," of humanism, and actively opposes it. In a sense he works from within, since there is hardly anyplace else to be, but his suspicion always means he resists humanism, and his resistance is his point of departure.

22. Linda Alcoff, "Feminist Politics and Foucault: The Limits to a Collaboration," in *Crises in Continental Philosophy*, ed. Arleen B. Dallery and Charles E. Scott with P. Holley Roberts (Albany: SUNY Press, 1992), 69.

23. Ibid., 69.

24. Ibid., 70.

25. Alcoff is certainly not the only critic to have made this charge. For similar claims, see Nancy Hartsock, "Foucault on Power: A Theory for Women?" in *Feminism and Postmodernism*, ed. Linda Nicholson (New York: Routledge, 1989), 167; Axel Honneth, *The Critique of Power: Reflective Stages in Critical Social Theory* (London: MIT, 1991), 189; and Christopher Norris, *The Truth about Postmodernism* (Oxford: Blackwell, 1993), 33.

26. Ibid., 75.

27. Ibid. 73.

28. Cited in ibid., 72.

29. Ibid., 73.

30. Althusser may well be an exception, but given the monolithic nature of his structuralism genealogy undermines it as well. My thanks to Todd May for pointing out this exception.

31. Alcoff, 72.

32. Ladelle McWhorter, "Foucault's Analytics of Power," in *Crises in Continental Philosophy*, 119–26, nn. 265–66.

33. I take it that this is also Bernard Flynn's understanding of Foucault's claims about power, which is why he argues that Foucault's work is really a form of metaphysics. See *Political Philosophy at the Closure of Metaphysics* (Atlantic Highlands, N.J.: Humanities Press, 1992), chapter 3, especially p. 92.

34. Alcoff, 72.

35. Diana Fuss, *Essentially Speaking* (New York: Routledge, 1989), 2. For another attempt at both clarification and definition, see Edward Stein, *Forms of Desire: Sexual Orientation and the Social Constructionist Controversy* (New York: Garland, 1990), chapter 12. Stein's definition of essentialism differs from Fuss's. He claims that an essentialist (regarding sexual orientation) is someone who looks for "culture-independent, objective and intrinsic properties—what might be called 'deep' properties—that are involved in sexual orientation" (338). These properties then function as the criteria for when we rightly apply a given word, such as *homosexual*. I've chosen to use Fuss's definition rather than Stein's here because (although his is much better known and more widely accepted than Fuss's in gay philosophical circles) Stein is really only saying essentialism amounts to having stable definitions of our words. If we define the word *homosexual* as "a man with a hypothalmus 20% smaller than average," we certainly might find homosexuals in every human society. But so what? The interesting issue would still be who gets to decide what the definition of the word is in the first place, who gets to set what John Locke would call the *nominal essence* (as opposed to the *real essence*) of homosexuality. And that, surely, is a political and historical issue. Fuss holds that essentialism amounts to believing that, if there is some invariant property that can serve as a criterion for application of a word like *homosexual*, then there is some kind of timeless essence that grounds the appearance of that property. The property itself is not an essence, by definition, since properties are predicates and an essence is that-which-is-predicated-of-but-cannot-itself-be-a-predicate. Locke was just such an essentialist (though not with regard to sexual orientations, since he didn't have that concept). He believed that nominal essences indicate real essences, but he also believed that we can never encounter or know real essences themselves; belief in them is a form of reasonable faith.

36. Fuss, 2.

37. Shane Phelan, *Identity Politics: Lesbian Feminism and the Limits of Community* (Philadelphia: Temple University Press, 1989), 59.

38. All of this may be complicated by the fact that the word *identity*, at least according to Steven Epstein, did not figure into discussions of sexual orientation at all until the 1970s, long after there were very active gay and lesbian communities. See Steven Epstein, "Gay Politics, Ethnic Identity: The Limits of Social Constructionism," in Stein, esp. pp. 265–74.

39. I think it would be possible to hold, however, that many people develop that identity slowly, so that there may be a time in a given person's life when others claim to know that he or she is gay while he or she still doesn't fully know that. Self-awareness is not an absolute cognitive state.

40. Fuss, 102.

41. Again, Stein disagrees. But he wants to equate *essence* with *nominal essence*; in other words, he wants to say there is an essence whenever it turns out that that term can be applied transhistorically and cross-culturally without violating the term's definition.

42. It is also important to distinguish between an essence and a cause of homosexuality. As Fuss points out, the essence of a thing is not the cause of that type of thing, although it may be the cause of the appearance(s) of individual

instances of that type of thing. If we accept the idea that there is an essence of homosexuality, that there is some one thing that is what homosexuality truly is, then we could say that the essence of homosexuality is what causes homosexual behavior or a homosexual physical appearance in an individual. But we would still not have an answer for the question: What causes homosexuality? Why do some people have a homosexual essence? Most researchers want an answer for the latter question. Dean Hamer's work in genetics is interesting in this regard. Hamer does not want to know what causes homosexual *behavior*. He wants to know what causes *homosexuals*. He defines *homosexual* as a person who experiences a desire for sexual union with a person of the same anatomical sex, whether that person acts on that desire or is even consciously aware of it or not, and he claims to have found the cause of the homosexual (not of homosexual behavior directly) in the genes. See Hamer, *The Science of Desire*.

43. Fuss, 102.

44. Minnie Bruce Pratt, a fellow Alabamian, writes of her ignorance of Jews in her community when she was growing up, an ignorance I shared. See Minnie Bruce Pratt, "Identity: Skin, Blood, Heart," in *Yours in Struggle: Three Feminist Perspectives on Anti-Semitism and Racism* (Brooklyn: Long Haul Press, 1984), esp. pp. 17–18. While it's true that there are many Southerners who are Jewish, it is also true that their identity is almost erased by the prevailing culture. And it isn't just Southerners who fail to notice the existence of Southern Jews; few people from other parts of the country expect to encounter Jews who consider Alabama or Georgia or Mississippi their home. The movie *Driving Miss Daisy* may have been one of the first popular cultural depictions of native Southerners who were Jews. The presence of Middle Eastern-born Moslems is more pronounced in the Deep South since the mid-1970s, but only now are Moslems in fairly large numbers settling into permanent membership in Southern communities. No doubt their participation will have interesting and significant effects. In addition, the growing strength of the Nation of Islam will have a significant impact on religious identities across the South over the next few decades.

45. For some interesting discussion of the tensions between Christian identity and homosexual identity, see James T. Sears' sociological study *Growing Up Gay in the South: Race, Gender, and Journeys of the Spirit* (New York: Harrington Park Press, 1991).

46. Some Christians, especially Catholics, might contend that we are essentially sinners and must recognize ourselves as such. I think most, though, would see the identity "sinner" as pervasive and definitive but inessential, something we rightly strive to change about ourselves through acceptance of the significance of the crucifixion. Even if we are born sinners, we pray for our sins to be washed away.

47. An argument can be made that in order to be recognized as a legitimate part of the modern state it is necessary to have some sort of identity. Chauncey Colwell, following Gilles Deleuze and Gorgio Agamben, writes, "States require communities with identities, communities that thus exclude other possible identities, in order to discipline, in order to ration out resources, in order to control. Ultimately, the state can recognize any community as long as it presents an identity that can be categorized and it will refuse to recognize, if not attack, any community that abjures identity." He goes on to talk specifically about gay and lesbian communities and politics. See "Deleuze and the Prepersonal," *Philosophy Today*, Vol. 41, No. 1 (Spring, 1997): 21b. Of course this is a practical, not a metaphysical, consideration.

48. It is important to note that I have not disproven the existence of essences (on Fuss's definition). I have just rendered them irrelevant to this discussion. I also have rendered Stein's "essences," his "invariant properties" irrelevant; for, even if we could locate some cross-culturally invariant properties that would allow us to recognize and label people "homosexual" or "heterosexual," the important issue both politically and philosophically is who gets to do that locating and labeling and for what purpose? How does the nominal essence get constructed?

49. My informal observations match those of Steven Epstein in his article, "Gay Politics, Ethnic Identity: The Limits of Social Constructionism," in *The Socialist Review*, Vol. 17, Nos. 3/4 (May/August, 1987): esp. pp. 9–12.

50. For an historical perspective on the diversity of lesbian communities in America, see Lillian Faderman, *Odd Girls and Twilight Lovers: A History of Lesbian Life in Twentieth-Century America* (New York: Penguin, 1991).

51. Urvashi Vaid, public lecture at the Valentine Museum, Richmond, Virginia, June 27, 1996.

52. See Beth Marschak, "Humphrey-Calder Field taken away from Women's Softball: Help us fight this!" *Richmond Lesbian-Feminists Flyer*, Vol. 22, No. 4 (April, 1996), p. 1, cols. 2–3.

53. Beth Marschak, "Small victory over women's softball field," *Richmond Lesbian-Feminists Flyer*, Vol. 22, No. 7 (July, 1996), p. 1, col. 1.

54. In fact, they would have to argue that they had been denied the field on the basis of *perceived* sexual orientation, since not all the members of all the teams are lesbian even if they all look like it when they sweat.

55. John D'Emilio, *Making Trouble*, xl.

56. John D'Emilio, "Dreams Deferred: The Birth and Betrayal of America's First Gay Liberation Movement," in *Making Trouble*, 17–56, but see especially pp. 22–24.

57. Much of my information about the early history of Virginians for Justice comes from conversations with former Board chair and current Executive Director Shirley Lesser, especially a conversation we had in the VJ office in Richmond on July 20, 1996.

58. In the 1996 session, there were seven co-sponsors for a bill that would have repealed those sections of the Crimes Against Nature law that make oral and anal sex a felony; in 1997 that number had increased to ten co-sponsors. In 1996 there were nineteen co-sponsors for a bill that would have added "perceived sexual orientation and perceived gender" to the law that now stiffens penalties for those who commit crimes motivated by hatred of the victim's race, religion, or ethnicity; in 1997 that number had grown to twenty-one. (In the 1995 session similar bills had drawn significantly fewer co-sponsors.) In 1997 there were also bills introduced that would have made discrimination on the basis of sexual orientation in employment and housing illegal and that would have provided benefits for the domestic partners of state workers. All failed.

4. DISORIENTATION

1. It is interesting to note that Social Security came into existence around the same time that heterosexual identity became current in the U.S. At about the same time that people began to think of themselves as identified by their sex-desire rather than their familial relationships, they also began to realize that it was not necessary to participate in a traditional family structure in order to provide for themselves in old age. In other words, it became simultaneously

conceptually and materially possible for sexual identity to replace familial identity.

2. If you don't think wifery could be a recognized occupation and the basis for an identity, that is because you are not thinking of it in the context of a vastly different, basically preindustrial society. Consider, then, the phenomenon of the county fair. County fairs are events at which men, women, and even children all compete for recognition of the quality of their work in food and textile production, food preservation, and animal husbandry—work that was once absolutely essential to continued existence of both families and communities and that was not necessarily sex-typed. To be a good wife once meant, in great part, to be good at such work and to be recognized and rewarded within a community for being good at it.

3. What people say they believe and how they live and expect others to live are two very different things, a fact analytic epistemologists should pay more attention to.

4. Isaiah may not be part of my genetic lineage, but he sure is a part of my cultural lineage, and I was taught to claim him just as I was taught to claim Abraham, Isaac, and Jacob—just as I was taught to claim Adam and Eve. The passage to be quoted comes from the Revised Standard Version of the Bible.

5. Friedrich Nietzsche, *Beyond Good and Evil*, trans. Walter Kaufmann (New York: Vintage, 1966), section 41: "Not to remain stuck to a person—not even the most loved—every person is a prison, also a nook. Not to remain stuck to a fatherland—not even if it suffers most and needs help most—it is less difficult to sever one's heart from a victorious fatherland. Not to remain stuck to some pity—not even for higher men into whose rare torture and helplessness some accident allowed us to look. Not to remain stuck to a science—even if it should lure us with the most precious finds that seem to have been saved up precisely for us. Not to remain stuck to one's own detachment, to that voluptuous remoteness and strangeness of the bird who flees ever higher to see ever more below him—the danger of the flier. Not to remain stuck to our own virtues and become as a whole the victim of some detail in us, such as our hospitality, which is the danger of dangers for superior and rich souls who spend themselves lavishly, almost indifferently, and exaggerate the virtue of generosity into a vice. One must know how *to conserve oneself*: the hardest test of independence." The German reads as follows: "Nicht an einer Person hängenbleiben: und sei sie die geliebteste, —jede Person ist ein Gefängnis, auch ein Winkel. Nicht an einem Vaterlande hängenbleiben: und sei es das leidendste und hilfsbedürftigste, —es ist schon weniger schwer, sein Herz von einem siegreichen Vaterlande loszubinden. Nicht an einem Mitleiden hängenbleiben: und gälte es höheren Menschen, in deren seltne Marter und Hilflosigkeit uns ein Zufall hat blicken lassen. Nicht an einer Wissenschaft hängenbleiben: und locke sie einen mit den kostbarsten, anscheinend gerade *uns* aufgesparten Funden. Nicht an seiner eignen Loslösung hängenbleiben, an jener wollüstigen Ferne und Fremde des Vogels, der immer weiter in die Höhe flieht, um immer mehr unter sich zu sehn: —die Gefahr des Fliegenden. Nicht an unsern eignen Tugenden hängenbleiben und als Ganzes das Opfer irgendeiner Einzelheit an uns werden, zum Beispiel unsrer 'Gastfreundschaft': wie es die Gefahr der Gefahren bei hochgearteten und reichen Seelen ist, welche verschwenderisch, fast gleichgultig mit sich selbst umgehn und die Tugend der Liberalität bis zum Laster treiben. Man muß wissen, *sich zu bewahren*: stärkste Probe der Unabhängigkeit."

6. See for example Judith Butler, *Gender Trouble: Feminism and the Subversion of Identity* (New York: Routledge, 1990), 93–11. For a response to Butler, see

Ladelle McWhorter, "Foucaults Herculine Barbin en de strategie van verdubbelte deviance," *Krisis*, No., 57 (December, 1994): 10–25.

7. Elizabeth Grosz, *Volatile Bodies: Toward a Corporeal Feminism* (Bloomington: Indiana University Press, 1994), 155–56.

8. I was not the only one disappointed. David R. Shumway, who spends only three pages total on the two volumes in his commentary on Foucault's *oeuvre*, declares them "not particularly satisfying" to most readers. See Shumway, *Michel Foucault* (Charlottesville: University of Virginia Press, 1988), 153. However, Shumway and I were only disappointed, whereas Martha Nussbaum was deeply saddened—as she declared in her article in *The New York Times Book Review*, where she asserted that *The Use of Pleasure* "is not only disappointing, but also a retreat from the principles that defined [Foucault's] career." (See "Affections of the Greeks," Nov. 10, 1985, p. 13, col. 1.) I will have a great deal more to say about this issue in chapter 7.

9. If you want more than the anecdotal evidence I have gathered through private empirical research, authoritative documentation of the fact that straight people have homosex is available in John Money, *Gay, Straight, and In-Between: The Sexology of Erotic Orientation* (New York: Oxford University Press—now take note here, this is OXFORD UNIVERSITY PRESS—1988), especially p. 12.

10. Some have contended that Foucault's historical research in these two volumes lacks depth and that he himself lacked the credentials to undertake serious study of the period in the first place. Martha Nussbaum, for example, has called his last work "mediocre" (see "Affections of the Greeks," p. 13, col. 2). She asks, "Can such a study be written . . . by someone who lacks all the usual scholarly tools, including knowledge of Greek and Latin? Foucault hopes that, with due 'care, patience, modesty, and attention,' it can. The result makes us doubt this" ("Affections," p. 14, col. 1). (It should be noted that Foucault did in fact read Latin and Greek. He studied both languages throughout his formal schooling and excelled at both. See David Macey, *The Lives of Michel Foucault* (New York: Pantheon, 1993), especially pp. 10 and 17.) Nussbaum also asserts that Foucault's ignorance of "Greek political and social history and of the problems of scholarship surrounding the texts he uses" (14) renders him unable to put any of the texts he uses in their proper context. It is not clear which "context" Nussbaum considers the proper one, nor is it clear that his apparent failure to do so renders his claims untrue. In contradistinction to Nussbaum, a number of classical scholars find Foucault's work very valuable. Walter Stevenson, for example, refers to Foucault, along with Peter Brown, as "probably the two most important historians of sexuality writing on the Greco-Roman period." See Stevenson, "The Rise of Eunuchs in Greco-Roman Antiquity," *The Journal of the History of Sexuality*, Vol. 5, No. 4 (April, 1995): 510. David Halperin uses Foucault's work extensively in his study of sexuality in ancient Greece. See for example "Is There a History of Sexuality?" *History and Theory*, 28 (Oct., 1989): 257–74. While Simon Goldhill criticizes many of Foucault's points (mainly in *The Care of the Self*), he views Foucault as a serious scholar and devotes an entire book to dialogue with him. See *Foucault's Virginity: Ancient Erotic Fiction and the History of Sexuality* (Cambridge: Cambridge University Press, 1995). Goldhill's main point is that Foucault's interpretation of the Hellenistic novel merely follows conventional readings and misses many important nuances. However, Goldhill seems to miss an important point in Foucault's genealogy: He reads Foucault's work as a history of the articulation of the desiring subject rather than as a genealogy of the desiring subject and so does not problematize his own concept of desire. By translating the word *eros* as

desire throughout his book, he does not come to grips with Foucault's attempt to see the ancient world as a time just prior to the emergence of the subject of desire.

11. In addition to HS2, especially pp. 44–45, see also OGE, 234.

12. Nussbaum faults him for failing to include women's sexual experience in his study. See Nussbaum, "Affections," 14. But Foucault was not examining sexual experience; he was examining ethical practices.

13. Perhaps the clearest statement of this view can be found in Epictetus' injunction in *Enchiridion*, No. 14: "If you wish your children and your wife and your friends to live forever, you are foolish, for you wish things to be in your power which are not so, and what belongs to others to be your own. So likewise, if you wish your servant to be without fault, you are foolish, for you wish vice not to be vice but something else. But if you wish not to be disappointed in your desires, that is in your own power. Exercise, therefore, what is in your power. A man's master is he who is able to confer or remove whatever that man seeks or shuns. Whoever then would be free, let him wish nothing, let him decline nothing, which depends upon others; else he must surely be a slave." This passage comes from the Thomas W. Higginson translation, pp. 21–22.

14. He mentions the existence of this latter text in OGE, 231.

15. Some of those studies include: Michel Foucault, "Technologies of the Self," in *Technologies of the Self: A Seminar with Michel Foucault*, ed. Luther H. Martin, Huck Gutman, and Patrick H. Hutton (Amherst: University of Massachusetts Press, 1988), 16–49, and "The Battle for Chastity," in *Michel Foucault: Politics, Philosophy, Culture: Interviews and Other Writings, 1977–1984*, ed. Lawrence D. Kritzman (New York: Routledge, 1988), 227–41. This essay was originally published as "Le combat de la chasteté," *Communications*, No. 35 (May, 1982): 15–25. It is reprinted in *Dits et Écrits*, Vol. 4, ed. Daniel Defert and François Ewald (Paris: Gallimard, 1994), 295–308. (Hereafter this volume will be referred to as DE 4.) Interviews containing interesting comments on this subject include: "The Return of Morality" and "The Concern for Truth," both in Kritzman, 242–54 and 255–67 respectively. The first of these was originally published as "Le retour de la morale" in *Les Nouvelles* (June 28, 1984), 36–41, and is reprinted in DE 4, 696–707. The second was originally published as "Le souci de la vérité," *Magazine Littéraire*, No. 207 (May, 1984): 18–23, and is reprinted in DE 4, 668–78. See also OGE.

16. He makes this point twice in OGE. On p. 234 he claims that in our day everyone "explains that what is important is desire, and pleasure is nothing at all. . . ." Then on p. 243 he says, "I could say that the modern 'formula' is desire, which is theoretically underlined and practically accepted, since you have to liberate your own desire. Acts are not very important, and pleasure—nobody know [sic] what it is!" In *The Use of Pleasure*, he points to an "'elision' of pleasure (a moral devaluation through the injunction given in the preaching of the Christian clergy against the pursuit of sensual pleasure as a goal of sexual practice; a theoretical devaluation shown by the extreme difficulty of finding a place for pleasure in the conception of sexuality) . . ." (HS2, 42; UP, 51–52).

17. Augustine believes that lust (the body's disobedience to the soul) is part of the punishment Adam, Eve, and their offspring receive for disobedience to God. There are many kinds of lust, Augustine notes, but the most difficult to control is lust for carnal intercourse. In fact, when it comes to carnal intercourse, it seems that the soul's will has little if any power. Lust rather than will has become the only means of inciting the organs of procreation to do their work. But, just as the soul is able to move or halt so many of the other organs of the

body, Augustine asks, "May we not similarly believe that those organs of procreation could, like the others, have served mankind by obedience to the decision of the will for the generation of children even if there had been no lust inflicted as punishment for the sin of disobedience?" See the Loeb Classical Library translation (Cambridge: Harvard University Press), trans. Philip Levine, Vol. 4, p. 381. Further, on p. 387, Augustine begins section 24 with this heading: "That if human beings had remained innocent and had earned the right to stay in paradise by their obedience, they would have used their genital organs for the procreation of offspring in the same way as they used the rest, that is, at the discretion of their will."

18. For some discussion of the Council of Trent, see Foucault, CF, 200.

19. For a thorough discussion of the conception and role of the body in early Christianity, see Peter Brown, *The Body and Society: Men, Women and Sexual Renunciation in Early Christianity* (New York: Columbia University Press, 1988). For a look at slightly later Christian doctrines and practices, see Caroline Walker Bynum, *Fragmentation and Redemption: Essays on Gender and the Human Body in Medieval Religion* (New York: Zone Books, 1991).

20. Foucault, CF, 211: "We have had sexuality since the eighteenth century, and sex since the nineteenth. What we had before that was no doubt the flesh."

21. Foucault, TS, 49.

22. For these dates, see Foucault, P&S, especially p. 115, and CF, especially pp. 217 and 221. The word *perversion* was first introduced into psychiatric discourse in 1842, according to Teresa de Lauretis in *The Practice of Love: Lesbian Sexuality and Perverse Desire* (Bloomington: Indiana University Press, 1994), 16.

23. The way I have formulated this claim is probably anachronistic. Ian Hacking claims that seventeenth-century thinkers, including Descartes, lacked our concept of evidence. See Hacking, *The Emergence of Probability* (Cambridge: Cambridge University Press, 1975), chapter 4.

24. Immanuel Kant's critical philosophy could be read as an attempt to work through and stabilize the relationship between the subject of knowledge and the subject of desire.

25. It is interesting that on this point feminist philosopher Marilyn Frye's work agrees with Foucault's. Frye contends that the word *sex* does not name lesbian practices or pleasures and that the word is used mainly as a way to produce a certain set of social and gender arrangements despite the fact that there is nothing particularly natural or inevitable about them. See Marilyn Frye, "On Seeing and Being Seen: The Politics of Reality," in *The Politics of Reality: Essays in Feminist Theory* (Trumansburg, New York: The Crossing Press, 1983), esp. pp. 156–60.

26. That is why Foucault says all current discourses of sexuality orient themselves, one way or another, in relation to psychoanalysis. See CF, 219.

27. For several years now psychologists have been saying that extremely homophobic people, in particular violent gay-bashers, are really homosexual themselves. *The Advocate* cites a study published in *The Journal of Abnormal Psychology* in which homophobic and non-homophobic heterosexual men were shown two videos, one with heterosexual and the other with homosexual content. During the screenings, the men's penises were measured to determine their levels of arousal—which many people would equate with desire. Both groups of men got much more aroused by the heterosexual video than by the homosexual video, but arousal did occur in both groups during the homosexual video. The difference between the two groups was that the homophobic men got more aroused by the homosexual video than the non-homophobic men got, although they didn't get as aroused by it as they got during the hetero-

sexual video. Are we to conclude that men who have sex with women, get married, call themselves straight, enjoy all the privileges of being straight, never participate in gay activities of any sort, have no gay friends, and only interact with gay people by beating them up are sufficiently like us to be considered ones of us? That's apparently what *The Advocate* concluded, since their article begins with these words: "It has long been held that, deep down, homophobes are really self-hating homosexuals. Now comes evidence to support that notion." See "A Thin Line Between Love and Hate," *The Advocate*, No. 728 (March 4, 1997): 17. I think such a conclusion is dangerous, since it adds support to the notion that gay people are mentally defective in some way and since it gets heterosexuals off the hook by allowing them to disclaim any responsibility for the oppression and violence that gay people suffer.

28. As U.S. federal law states (since 1996), marriage is a legal bond between one man and one woman, a husband and a wife. In many states' codes of law, responsibilities and benefits conferred on partners by a marriage contract differ depending on whether one is the husband or the wife. The most glaring example of inequality becomes evident in states' legal blindness to the phenomenon of "marital rape." In many states a husband has right of access to his wife's genitals whenever he likes. He does not need her consent for sex, so it is not possible for him to be guilty of raping her. A wife has no corresponding right of access to her husband's genitals. In a same-sex union, inequalities like this would be impossible to maintain, since it would be unclear which of the partners was the husband and which the wife.

29. This declaration by The Army of God was announced on a noontime broadcast of "The 700 Club" on FOX television network on February 25, 1997.

30. The National Coalition of Anti-Violence Projects reports that hate crimes against people based on their sexual orientation rose six percent in 1996, while violent crimes in general fell nationwide. Since to a great extent the purpose of these anti-gay hate crimes is to intimidate and punish all queer people, they can be classified as acts of terrorism.

31. The most prominent of these, which I will discuss below, is detailed in Dean Hamer and Peter Copeland, *The Science of Desire: The Search for the Gay Gene and The Biology of Behavior* (New York: Simon and Schuster, 1994). Another well-known study that attempts to link physiology and homosexuality is Simon LeVay, "A Difference in Hypothalamic Structure Between Heterosexual and Homosexual Men," *Science,* Vol. 253 (Aug. 30, 1991): 1034–37. See also LeVay's *The Sexual Brain* (Cambridge: MIT Press, 1993) and *Queer Science: The Use and Abuse of Research into Homosexuality* (Cambridge: MIT Press, 1996).

32. Hamer, 1994, 20.

33. Dean Hamer, "Searching for that perfect pair of genes," *The Advocate* (Oct. 14, 1997): 65.

34. Hamer, 1994, 211.

35. For more discussion of the likely political impact of Hamer's and others' work in the science of sexual orientation and for a thorough treatment of the ethics of such science, see Timothy F. Murphy, *Gay Science: The Ethics of Sexual Orientation Research* (New York: Columbia, 1997), esp. Chapters 6 and 7.

36. How many of us fit that description?

37. Dean Hamer, Stella Hu, Victoria L. Magnuson, Nan Hu, and Angela M. L. Pattatucci, "A Linkage Between DNA Markers on the X Chromosome and Male Sexual Orientation," Appendix A in *The Science of Desire*.

38. And if we get to count all the openly gay people AND all the openly homophobic people, surely we could get a figure at least that high!

39. Hamer, 1994, 115.

40. Hamer, 1994, 78. Chandler Burr disputes this claim and asserts that most of the scientists who embrace it publicly don't really believe it. Burr himself believes the trait probably is simple rather than complex. But because that information would lend fuel to the fires burning over the question of aborting gay fetuses and so on, Burr speculates that scientists are afraid to avow it publicly. See Chandler Burr, *A Separate Creation: The Search for the Biological Origins of Sexual Orientation* (New York: Hyperion, 1996).

41. See Eric Lander and Leonid Kruglyak, "Genetic Dissection of Complex Traits: Guidelines for Interpreting and Reporting Linkage Results," *Nature Genetics,* Vol. 11 (Nov., 1995): 241–47. Note that Lander and Kruglyak propose four standards, which they label as follows: "suggestive linkage" with a LOD score of 2.2; "significant linkage" with a LOD score of 3.6; "highly significant linkage" with a LOD score of 5.4; and "confirmed linkage," which can only be established by a combination of studies by independent researchers all of which yield significant linkages. They offer complex mathematical arguments for these standards. But, note further, none of their levels of linkage involves causal explanation. "Confirmed linkage" only means that the DNA strip and the complex trait in question occur together much more frequently than makes sense if their coexistence is coincidental; it does not mean that the DNA caused the trait, only that the trait and DNA are associated somehow. It is a long way from protein synthesis to Valentine cards.

42. Hamer, 1994, 107.

43. Ibid., 1994, 218.

44. Hamer's hypothesis assumes that women control their own sexuality, which is an extremely questionable assumption in the present day and is demonstrably false through much of recorded history.

45. This latter theory is seriously compromised by Hamer's own evidence that presence of the DNA strip he suspects is the cause of homosexuality does not correlate at all with effeminacy. See the subsection of chapter 10 entitled "The 'Sissy Gene,'" especially p. 167.

5. NATURAL BODIES

1. Probably the best-known discussions of feminine bodily regimes in the secondary literature on Foucault's work are by Sandra Bartky and Susan Bordo. See Sandra Lee Bartky's essay, "Foucault, Femininity, and the Modernization of Patriarchal Power," in *Feminism and Foucault: Reflections on Resistance*, ed. Irene Diamond and Lee Quinby (Boston: Northeastern University Press, 1988), 61–86. In the same volume, see Susan Bordo, "Anorexia Nervosa: Psychopathology as the Crystallization of Culture," 87–117. See also Bordo's "The Body and the Reproduction of Femininity: A Feminist Appropriation of Foucault," in *Gender/Body/Knowledge: Feminist Reconstructions of Being and Knowing*, ed. Alison M. Jaggar and Susan Bordo (New Brunswick, N.J.: Rutgers University Press, 1989), 13–33.

2. It was a woman, Descartes' young friend Princess Elizabeth of Bohemia, who first challenged the philosopher's dualistic account of body and mind.

3. The use of this term in Foucault scholarship can be traced to Foucault's comments on *problematiques* in OGE, 231. What interests Foucault, he claims there, are the ways in which cultures take up problems rather than the ways in which they solve those problems.

4. And thus to produce great Russian literature.

5. In Virginia bodies are even transferable by bequest; in other words, I can will my body to someone just as I can will someone my house. Many gay people take advantage of this law to prevent their families of origin from dictating funeral arrangements. I can will my body to my lover who can then bury me in our contiguous burial plots or keep my ashes in her home, and there is nothing my parents or siblings can do about that. If I don't will my body to her, of course, my family members would inherit me and possibly take me back to Alabama for a funeral and burial there.

6. We ought to remember that Locke's contemporaries accused him of stealing almost everything in his philosophy from Descartes. In 1690 Locke's close friend James Tyrell wrote to him that people in Oxford thought Locke "had taken all that was good in it [the *Essay Concerning Human Understanding*, Locke's major work] from Des Cartes or divers new late moderne French Authors, not only as to the notions but the manner of connexion of them." (Quoted in H.A.S. Schankula, "Locke, Descartes, and the Science of Nature," *Journal of the History of Ideas* (July, 1980): 459. Locke's correspondent Edward Stillingfleet, Bishop of Worcester, also intimated on more than one occasion that the *Essay* lacked originality and had an undue dependence on the work of Descartes. All this annoyed Locke, who denied Cartesian influence graciously in his letter to Stillingfleet, but in a letter to Edward Clarke he claimed not to be a Cartesian and never to have read any books on the subject of human understanding before writing Book 4 of his essay. (See Schankula, 465.) Schankula argues that Locke is to some extent a Cartesian, as does P. A. Schouls in "The Cartesian Method of Locke's *Essay concerning Human Understanding*," *The Canadian Journal of Philosophy*, Vol. 4, No. 4 (June, 1975): 579–601. At the very least, Locke seems to have been very well acquainted with Descartes' work and to have made a careful study of it long before he wrote any of his political treatises. There is no indication that he disagreed with Descartes' conception of the mind as distinct from the body, except insofar as he held that minds are inactive during sound sleep.

7. For a lengthy account of a teenager's three-year confinement to mental institutions, see Daphne Scholinski (with Jane Meredith Adams), *The Last Time I Wore a Dress* (New York: Riverhead, 1997).

8. Foucault is most explicit on this point in ECS, 292.

9. Boethius, *The Consolation of Philosophy*, trans. Richard Green (Indianapolis: Bobbs-Merrill, 1962). Boethius was a fifth-century nobleman who was persecuted for his version of Christianity. He wrote his book while in prison.

10. Lloyd is best known for her 1984 work *The Man of Reason: "Male" and "Female" in Western Philosophy* (Minneapolis: University of Minnesota Press). For her earliest work on this topic, see "The Man of Reason," *Metaphilosophy*, 10: 1 (1979): 18–37.

11. Carol Pateman, *The Sexual Contract* (Stanford: Stanford University Press, 1988).

12. David Michael Levin, "The Body Politics: The Embodiment of Praxis in Foucault and Habermas," *Praxis International*, Vol. 9, Nos. 1/2 (Apr./July, 1989): 114–15.

13. Or of its main tool, statistics, which developed during this same period.

14. This is why when Judith Butler accuses Foucault of returning to some concept of the natural body in *Herculine Barbin*, she is both right and wrong. She is right in that Foucault does hold to a concept of the natural body as an operative entity in the nineteenth century, especially in discourses of sexuality. She is wrong in that she fails to see that Foucault's "natural body" is not an

ahistorical body; she fails to understand that Foucault's natural body is an historically emerging functional component of discourses of normalization. For her reading of Foucault's allegedly ahistorical turn to the natural, see *Gender Trouble: Feminism and the Subversion of Identity* (New York: Routledge, 1990), especially pp. 94–106, and "Foucault and the Paradox of Bodily Inscriptions," *The Journal of Philosophy*, Vol. 81, No. 11 (Nov., 1989): 601–7. Butler is not the only scholar to have drawn such an erroneous conclusion about Foucault's *Herculine Barbin*. Rudi Visker offers a similar reading in his "From Heidegger to Foucault: A One Way Ticket?" *Research in Phenomenology*, Vol. 21 (1991): 122. Historian Jeffrey Weeks may hold a similar misconception. See "Uses and Abuses of Michel Foucault," in *Against Nature: Essays on History, Sexuality and Identity* (London: Rivers Oram Press, 1991), 164.

15. I believe this was in a short-lived but excellent publication called *Garbage*.

16. One year I had a bean plant just a little too close to a trench. The effects on the morphology of the plant were remarkable. Though it lived, it remained small, stunted, and actually shriveled. Its leaves looked like spinach, and the few bean pods it produced were short and irregularly ridged.

17. Roy Donahue, John C. Schickluna, and Lynn S. Robertson, "Functions of Soil," in *Soils* (Brooklyn: Brooklyn Botanic Garden, Inc., 1990), 7.

18. See John Paul Bowles, "The Physical Properties of Soil," in *Soils*, 9.

19. Carol Anderson, photocopied dance instruction sheet, 1996. Used with permission.

6. SELF-OVERCOMING THROUGH ASCETIC PLEASURES

1. An exception is Paul Rabinow, a sociologist by training but a philosophical commentator, who has made some remarks about Foucault's work on pleasure in his introduction to volume one of *Ethics, Subjectivity, and Truth* (New York: New Press, 1997), especially p. xxxvii.

2. See for example Elaine Scarry, *The Body in Pain: The Making and Unmaking of the World* (New York: Oxford University Press, 1985). Scarry's analysis of the effort to externalize the experience of pain in various cultural practices is especially interesting in this regard. One wonders whether such an analysis could be made of pleasure; no one has done so as yet.

3. I have made this same point in "Natural Bodies/Unnatural Pleasures: Foucault and the Politics of Corporeal Intensification," *Symplokē*, Vol. 3, No. 2 (1995): 201–10.

4. Although he doesn't develop this idea very much, Morris Kaplan points to this same possibility at the end of his book *Sexual Justice: Democratic Citizenship and the Politics of Desire* (New York: Routledge, 1997), especially pp. 236–38, where he describes the ways in which sex clubs and bathhouses in San Francisco have developed and imposed a kind of normalizing discipline (i.e., safer sex practices in commercial venues). These disciplines are not simply a compromise measure to enable clubs to stay open despite the AIDS epidemic; they are laboratories for the development of sexual pleasures that involve the use of safety-enhancing tools and products.

5. Samois, *Coming to Power: Writings and Graphics on Lesbian S/M* (Boston: Alyson, 1987). Mark Thompson, ed., *Leatherfolk: Radical Sex, People, Politics, and Practice* (Boston: Alyson, 1991).

6. See for example Robin Ruth Linden, Darlene R. Pagano, Diana E. H. Russell, and Susan Leigh Starr, eds., *Against Sadomasochism: A Radical Feminist Analysis* (San Francisco: Frog in the Well Press, 1982). I've rarely heard members of the religious right condemn either violence or cruelty, so I assume their reasons for condemnation have to do with the fact that most sadomasochistic practitioners are not married to one another and don't usually conceive white, non-Semitic children during the course of sexual gratification.

7. Mark Blasius echoes this view when he writes that "such erotic practices are a 'school' for *agency*. While undertaken 'in private,' they can have significant political implications: through them, we learn about how we can be subjected within power relationships; at the same time, we learn how we are agents who can submit to power or, refusing, change power relationships." He maintains that this is a self-transformative and self-forming *askesis*. See Mark Blasius, *Gay and Lesbian Politics: Sexuality and the Emergence of a New Ethic* (Philadelphia: Temple University Press, 1994), 88.

8. Georges Canguilhem, "On *Histoire de la folie* as an Event," in *Foucault and His Interlocutors*, ed. Arnold I. Davidson (Chicago: University of Chicago Press, 1997), 28.

9. Ibid., 32.

7. COUNTERATTACK

1. For another account of "style" for differently situated individuals—in this case school teachers—see Frank Pignatelli, "What Can I Do? Foucault on Freedom and the Question of Teacher Agency," *Educational Theory*, Vol. 43, No. 4 (Fall, 1993): 411–32. Pignatelli discusses three elements of a politics of "care or well-being of the self and others"; he says such a politics would be "reactive, nonprogrammatic, and aesthetically informed." See especially pp. 424ff.

2. According to J. P. Hattingh, Foucault's project suffers from the same defects as the projects he condemns. It is ultimately both metaphysical and nihilistic, Hattingh asserts, because it participates in a history of aestheticism that really is no more than an effort to overcome the fragmentary and unknowable through the establishment of an artistic totality that posits order where order does not exist. He goes on to argue that Foucault's project is also objectionable because of its "insular self-referentiality which changes little or nothing in the world. In Foucault's aestheticist choice for a beautiful life, an attitude of narcissistic self-absorption is favoured in which there is little or no discernable trace of human solidarity, mutuality, or fellow-feeling. In fact, in Foucault's aesthetic life, the central focus is on the self rather than world and its inhabitants." See "Living One's Life as a Work of Art," *The South African Journal of Philosophy*, Vol. 15, No. 2 (May, 1996): 69. As I will show in this chapter, in particular in the section on governmentality, this interpretation of Foucault's project is extremely misguided.

3. The book is not even indexed in Alan Sheridan's classic "guidebook" (as he calls it on page one) to the work of Michel Foucault, *Michel Foucault: The Will to Truth* (London: Tavistock, 1980).

4. One reason she wanted this change of legal status was that the only way she could secure the right to marry Sara was by becoming a man. But there was another reason: Should anyone have realized that she was using her apparent femaleness as a means of access to Sara's bed, Barbin could have been arrested and prosecuted; hiding her condition from the authorities constituted an act of

fraud. Basically, then, there were only two alternatives: either Barbin could submit to the judgment of medical authorities who would determine her true sex and assign her to that sex through legal means, or she could be made to submit as both a sexual outlaw and a common criminal. This was something anyone as well-read as Alexina would have known, especially since she read everything she could find about sexual metamorphosis. (For information about such metamorphoses and the legal status of those who underwent them, see Thomas Laqueur, *Making Sex: Body and Gender from the Greeks to Freud* [Cambridge: Harvard University Press, 1990], especially pp. 136–42.) Had it been possible in 1860 for two people legally defined as female to live together in sexual intimacy without legal, religious, or economic reprisal, Herculine Barbin's story might have ended quite differently. But of course that was not possible. Barbin, therefore, chose not to live his/her life as a criminal. He/she submitted him/herself to the authorities for judgment.

5. It is important to note here that Foucault's conception of "governmentality" changes a great deal over the course of his use of that term. The conception I am elaborating in this chapter is a relatively late one. Earlier Foucault used the term very restrictively to apply to a certain way of thinking about the role of governmental institutions and political management of populations. For that more restricted use of the term, see for example his essay "Governmentality," in *The Foucault Effect: Studies in Governmentality*, ed. Graham Burchell, Colin Gordon, and Peter Miller (Chicago: University of Chicago Press, 1991), 102–3. This essay was composed in 1978.

6. Sodomy laws exist but are probably not enforceable in three of those states, Massachusetts, Michigan, and Texas. The other seventeen states in which sodomy laws are enforceable and sometimes enforced are: Alabama, Arizona, Arkansas, Delaware, Florida, Idaho, Louisiana, Maryland, Minnesota, Mississippi, Missouri, North Carolina, Oklahoma, South Carolina, Virginia, and West Virginia. Montana's sodomy law was struck down in 1997, following the judicial demise of Tennessee's law in 1996. For a discussion of all this, see Lisa Keen, "Court Strikes Down Montana's Sodomy Law," *The Washington Blade*, July 18, 1997, p. 23. Rhode Island's law was repealed in June of 1998. See Rhonda Smith, "Rhode Island Law Nears Repeal," *The Washington Blade*, June 5, 1998, pp. 1, 22. Georgia's sodomy law was struck down in 1998.

7. What my father actually said was: "It's always more honorable to go down swinging." I sanitized it for middle class readers of the nineties, in other words, for people who think it's fine to swear but wrong to hit anyone. Hey, I'm cross-culturally adaptable.

8. In fact, just for the record I should say that while neither of my representatives supported reform of the crimes against nature law, both have subsequently supported inclusion of sexual orientation in existing hate crimes law and job protection. Neither my delegate nor my state senator are exactly what you think of when you think of Virginia good old boy politicos. Both are from predominately black districts and, as black men themselves, have a pretty good idea what oppression is all about. Would that they were more typical of Virginia legislators.

9. Monique Deveaux argues that: "Foucault's analysis allows little room for an account of the processes involved in developing personal and collective capacities for political activism; empowerment is not about actions upon agents in a relationship of power and so cannot be understood within the confines of this analysis." See "Feminism and Empowerment: A Critical Read-

ing of Foucault," in *Feminist Interpretations of Foucault*, ed. Susan Hekman (University Park: The Pennsylvania State University Press, 1996), 232. I have described here precisely what Deveaux says Foucault's analysis does not accommodate, a process of empowerment, of becoming a subject capable of exercising certain kinds of power, and I believe my description is nothing more than an elaboration on Foucault's work. *Ergo*, I take Deveaux to be wrong.

10. The thought of this makes me laugh out loud, but at the same time I believe it is true and I take it very seriously; and then *that* makes me laugh all the more.

INCONCLUSION

1. Michel Foucault, "Preface to *The History of Sexuality* Volume Two," trans. William Smock, in *The Essential Works of Foucault, 1954–1984: Volume 1: Ethics, Subjectivity and Truth*, ed. Paul Rabinow (New York: New Press, 1997), 205.

INDEX

LADELLE McWHORTER is Professor of Philosophy and Women's Studies and Chair of the Department of Philosophy at the University of Richmond. Her previous publications include an edited volume entitled *Heidegger and the Earth: Essays in Environmental Philosophy* and numerous articles on Foucault, Bataille, and feminist and queer theory.

...mation can be obtained at www.ICGtesting.com

0BV00002B/3/A

CPSIA i
2619